THERAPEUTIC APPROACHES TO THE CARE OF THE MENTALLY ILL

EDITION 2

D0061313

THERAPEUTIC APPROACHES TO THE CARE OF THE MENTALLY ILL

EDITION 2

DAVID S. BAILEY, Ed.D.

Director, Division of Behavioral Medicine, Northeast Georgia Medical Center, Gainesville, Georgia; and Consultant, Department of Human Resources, State of Georgia

SHARON O. COOPER, R.N., M.S.N.

Nurse Clinician; Formerly Assistant Professor, Department of Social Sciences, Brenau College; and Assistant Director, Hall School of Nursing, Gainesville, Georgia

DEBORAH R. BAILEY, R.N., B.S., B.S.N.

Coordinator, Primary Nursing, Northeast Georgia Medical Center, Gainesville, Georgia

F. A. Davis Company　　Philadelphia

Printed in the United States of America

Library of Congress Cataloging in Publication Data

Bailey, David S.
   Therapeutic approaches to the care of the mentally ill.

   Bibliography: p.
   Includes index.
   1. Psychotherapy. 2. Mentally ill—Care and treatment. I. Cooper, Sharon O., joint author. II. Bailey,
Deborah R., joint author. III. Title. [DNLM: 1. Mental disorders—Therapy. 2. Mental disorders—Prevention
and control. WM400 B154t]
RC480.5B27   616.8'914   84-71007
ISBN 0-8036-0551-X

Dedication

This book is dedicated to Donny Bailey. The VietNam war left him physically scarred and mentally tormented. That torment caused him first to try to make the real world fit his unrealistic perception of it and, failing that, he sought to escape through agents which numbed his senses and dulled his pain. His life ended tragically on the eve of his twenty-fifth birthday. His pain is gone, but those of us who remember him also remember his pain and hope that we can help diminish such pain in others.

Listen

When I ask you to listen to me
  and you start giving advice
  you have not done what I asked.

When I ask you to listen to me
  and you begin to tell me why I shouldn't feel that way,
  you are trampling on my *feelings*.

When I ask you to listen to me
  and you feel you have to *do* something to solve my problem,
  you have failed me, strange as that may seem.

Listen! All I asked, was that you listen.
  not talk or do—just hear me.
Advice is cheap: 10 cents will get you both Dear Abby and
  Billy Graham in the same newspaper.
And I can do for myself; I'm not helpless.
  Maybe discouraged and faltering, but not helpless.

When you do something for me *that I can and need to do
  for myself*, you contribute to my fear and weakness.

But, when you accept as a simple fact that I do feel what I feel,
  no matter how irrational, then I can quit trying to convince
  you and can get about the business of understanding what's
  behind this irrational feeling.
  And when that's clear, the answers are obvious and I
  don't need advice.
Irrational feelings make sense when we understand what's
  behind them.

Perhaps that's why prayer works, sometimes, for some people
  because God is mute, and he doesn't give advice or
  try to fix things. "They" just listen and let you
  work it out for yourself.

So, please listen and just hear me. And, if you want to
  talk, wait a minute for your turn; and I'll listen to you.

Anonymous

Preface to the Second Edition

Seven summers ago, the first ediction of this book was born amid the national crisis of a President falling in disgrace, a world that seemed forever on the brink of war, and an American psyche girding itself to battle cancer, drug abuse, violent crime, and the possibility of nuclear war. Our book, thanks to all of you, has enjoyed considerable success. Three printings, a book of the month selection by a national bookclub, and many, many thousands of copies sold for use in various mental health curricula are among the elements of that success.

We now present a revision of that work which includes recognition of changes in diagnostic practices offered by the DSM III, recent changes in mental health law, a new chapter on crisis intervention and the addition of learning objectives for each chapter. We wish especially to thank Patricia Westbrook Fields, R.N., who did a tremendous amount of research to find articles of excellence for the annotated bibliographies. They were carefully chosen to augment the material presented in this book. The changes and the new material significantly increase its usefulness.

We decided to do this revision because the need for it persists. Unfortunately, most of the maladies present those several summers ago are still with us . . . and there are new ones. The Vietnam experience has been replaced by the personal hardships found in Iran, Nicaragua, and a dozen other places in the world. Russian fighter planes shot down a civilian plane carrying 269 human beings. And, amid thousands of more private tragedies, the nation and the world consider the reality of a nuclear war which seems to grow more possible year by year.

And yet we must somehow cope—with all of these world conditions—

every day. However brief or inconsequential our lives might seem in the macrocosm of time, our life is all we have. Is it so unworthy a goal to try to make our own time as meaningful and fulfilling as possible? We think not. Meaningfulness and fulfillment in one's life seem to make coping easier and lead to healthier functioning. And, if your life is made more meaningful by trying to help those whose coping efforts have failed, then you are indeed a special person.

It is for those special persons that this second edition is written. Human misery abounds, and caring enough to alleviate it often means exposing oneself to a human closeness that sometimes exacts a high price and demands a commitment that taxes even the strong.

Let us hope that when seven more summers have passed, we will all still be going strong, that tragedy will spare us, and that our efforts to help others will be enhanced by the growth and wisdom the additional years bring to us.

DAVID S. BAILEY
SHARON O. COOPER
DEBORAH R. BAILEY

Preface to the First Edition

This book is intended to provide the mental health worker with basic information about current concepts, techniques, and procedures used in the prevention, treatment, and rehabilitation of the mentally ill.

In addition to regular classroom use, this book is designed to be used either individually or as part of an educational or inservice program. Many patient situations which you are likely to encounter are identified and described, and various self-testing techniques which facilitate understanding and retention of materials are provided.

Concepts of communication are stressed and particular emphasis is placed on dealing with inappropriate patient behaviors. In many cases the actions and behavior of the worker will have a significant effect on the outcome of prescribed treatment. Mental health is a field where one's personality becomes a vital link in the healing process and where one has an opportunity to utilize fully one's intelligence, understanding, and resourcefulness. The impact that a single mental health worker can have in helping another human being is profound.

As a member of a mental health team, the development of an ability to form positive interpersonal relationships with patients and the ability to reinforce healthy aspects of a patient's personality are of primary importance. When these two factors are combined with compassion and a genuine respect for the rights and dignity of the patient as a person, an atmosphere is created in which the patient feels comfortable, cared for, and secure.

Finally, let us encourage you to enjoy your work. As you see patients come and go and realize that you have played an important part in their recovery, you may take pride in the realization of a uniquely human experience, that of giving back to someone the essence of life—the ability to live it.

DAVID S. BAILEY
SHARON O. DREYER

Contents

Part 1

GENERAL THEORETIC CONSIDERATIONS

1

Introduction to Working with the Mentally Ill

OBJECTIVES: Student will be able to:
1. Evaluate own feelings and attitudes about mental illness.
2. Compare own personal views with those commonly held by practitioners in the mental health field.
3. Understand the importance of the relationship between the mental health worker and client.
4. Increase the awareness of own anxieties related to caring for the mentally ill.

ATTITUDE INVENTORY EXERCISE*

Before you begin to use this book, take a few minutes to examine *your own feelings and attitudes* about mental illness. React to the following statements and decide whether *you* believe them to be true or false. Let your feelings be your guide. Circle your choice—true or false.

T F 1. People who enjoy working with mentally ill patients are somewhat mentally unstable themselves.

T F 2. Most people who are emotionally disturbed are overly active.

T F 3. Mental illness may develop suddenly.

T F 4. Mentally ill people are also mentally deficient.

T F 5. People who have been mentally ill may recover from their illness and live a normal life again.

T F 6. People who have mental illness should not marry or have children.

T F 7. Heavy consumption of alcohol may be a symptom of mental illness.

T F 8. People who work with mentally ill patients soon realize that their own emotional problems are insignificant.

T F 9. Most mentally ill patients are dangerous and may kill others.

T F 10. People who are wealthy rarely become mentally ill.

---

*Slightly modified from Dreyer, S., Bailey, D. and Doucet, W.: *A Guide to Nursing Management of Psychiatric Patients*. C. V. Mosby, St. Louis, 1975, with permission.

T F 11. Most people doubt their own sanity at one time or another.

T F 12. Most people who are mentally ill have a certain look that identifies them as being disturbed.

T F 13. The largest number of mentally ill people come from underprivileged families.

T F 14. The actions and speech of most mental patients are revolting and disgusting to others.

T F 15. The main reason that people are committed for psychiatric treatment is to protect the community.

T F 16. It is usually necessary to put emotionally ill patients in seclusion rooms.

T F 17. Hereditary factors will determine whether or not a person becomes mentally ill.

T F 18. Physical disease may influence emotional balance.

T F 19. People who are mentally ill are often very sensitive to the happenings in their environment.

T F 20. Working with mentally ill patients may often cause one to become mentally ill.

T F 21. Learning about mental disease, psychiatry, and the functions of one's mind is harmful to well adjusted, normal people.

T F 22. Unfortunately, not much can be done for mental patients aside from administering to their physical needs and hoping that they will get well.

T F 23. Mentally ill patients have no sense of humor.

T F 24. To convince a patient that he should behave in a socially acceptable manner, it is necessary to use punishment.

T F 25. Mentally ill patients often have feelings and emotions similar to normal people.

T F 26. People who are mentally ill can be dangerous to themselves.

T F 27. Working long hours causes mental illness.

T F 28. Withdrawal from normal activities may be a sign of mental illness.

T F 29. A person may handle anxiety by becoming mentally ill.

T F 30. Mentally ill persons develop strong sexual urges and are unable to control their behavior.

T F 31. Mentally ill patients who are doing well and seem capable of assuming responsibility for their behavior should not be allowed to do so because they may suddenly become ill again.

T F 32. It is easy to identify the needs of the mentally ill.

T F 33. Symptoms of mental illness may be very deeply hidden within a person.

T F 34. Children should be protected from all frustrating situations.

T F 35. Experiencing feelings of inferiority is a sign of mental illness.

T F 36. Early recognition and treatment does not affect the course of mental illness.

T F 37. Today mentally ill people have no problem being accepted by other members of society.

T F 38. People readily admit that they need help for emotional disturbances.

T F 39. Members of the medical and nursing profession accept and have an understanding attitude toward mental illness just as they do about other types of illness.

T F 40. People whose behavior is deeply disturbed are best treated on the back wards of state hospitals.

T F 41. Attitudes and feelings about mental illness learned previously may affect one's ability to deal effectively with mentally disturbed patients.

GENERAL DISCUSSION

Using the Mental Health Attitude Inventory which you have just completed, compare your views with those commonly held by practitioners in the mental health field (answers are given in the Appendix). If your responses differ significantly from the views held by mental health practitioners, you should not feel too uncomfortable. Even in this day of heart transplants, moon walks, and laser beams, a large part of our population still attaches a great deal of fear and shame to mental illness.

While it is true that some unhealthy attitudes toward mental illness still exist, during the last hundred years or so considerable gains have been made in treating persons afflicted with mental disorders. We no longer consider them to be under spells or curses, or to be possessed by demons. For the most part, mental illness is now viewed as a sickness which may be caused by a wide variety of factors.

Although it is difficult to pinpoint a specific reason for a person becoming mentally ill at a particular time, we do know that factors such as physical illness, one's work, family crises, broken love relationships, repeated disappointments, prolonged frustration, and so forth, are frequently associated with a person's loss of ability to cope with the demands of day-to-day living. Many authorities believe that while a person cannot inherit a specific mental illness, one may inherit a predisposition to certain types of mental problems. Whether or not one develops the illness to which one is predisposed depends largely upon personal life experiences and the environment in which one lives. The question of why a particular person becomes mentally ill under certain conditions while another person exposed to the same conditions manages to continue to function is a puzzling one.

Probably the most reasonable explanation lies in the fact that different personal experiences cause a difference in what a person perceives as stressful and how much stress a person can tolerate. Some people are afraid of all snakes, some are only afraid of poisonous snakes, and some do not fear snakes at all. Some people fear heights, some do not. It is the way an individual views a situation that determines his response. The mentally ill patient often has learned many inappropriate behaviors that must be unlearned or replaced with more acceptable behaviors. Such relearning frequently takes a great deal of time, and hospitalization or prolonged outpatient treatment may be required.

Thanks to recent medical advancements leading to the development of more effective drugs and improved treatment methods, many psychiatric patients are able to return home to their families in a matter of weeks following hospitalization. Others may never have to be hospitalized but are treated as outpatients or in day care programs. Some continue to perform their jobs and receive therapy in evening programs. No longer is it necessary to send thousands of mentally ill patients to large institutions many miles from their homes and families in order to receive treatment.

With treatment, many patients are able to make a complete recovery and some are even better adjusted than they were before their symptoms appeared. Others are helped to function more effectively but may have to remain on medication for the rest of their lives and avoid certain stressful situations that might cause their symptoms to reappear.

Most people, however, are still extremely concerned about what their friends, relatives, boss, and neighbors would think if they were hospitalized for mental illness. Because of these fears, many people who need help will not seek it and those who are hospitalized are extremely concerned about confidentiality of information. Until they develop a trusting relationship with staff members, they may be very reluctant to disclose any information about themselves. Trusting relationships are not built quickly. Mentally ill patients are very sensitive to how other people feel and react toward them. Perhaps this acute sensitivity is one of the reasons why they have become ill, for in our society it is extremely important to be accepted, well liked, and a member of the group.

Since mental illness affects all races, ages, and socioeconomic groups, any of us, if subjected to enough stress, may suffer an emotional crisis. In fact, new workers in the mental health field often worry about their own "wellness" since they see many similarities between their patients and themselves. At one time or another, everyone has minor mood swings, gets depressed, or feels anger, anxiety, or fear. We all occasionally mistrust others. How many of us have said at one time or another, "I'm going to go crazy" or have said to a friend, "Are you off your rocker?" *The difference between being mentally healthy and mentally ill lies in the frequency and intensity of inappropriate behavior and often in the public's tolerance of such behavior.*

New mental health workers often experience considerable anxiety because they feel that they don't know what to do for their patients. Physical health team members work in a more structured environment. They have tests to run, medicines to give, patients to be bathed, diagnostic and treatment procedures to do, and patients who are generally cooperative. Of course, they too must listen to their patients but mental health workers must realize that often their primary contribution to a patient may be simply that they are there and are available to listen if the patient wishes to talk. In their book, *Psychiatric Nursing in the Hospital and the Community* (Prentice-Hall, 1973), Burgess and Lazare state, "It takes some time to realize that listening to that which aches in the heart of the patient may touch him more profoundly than a back rub."

This brief overview of selected general factors related to the mental health field was intended to provide the mental health worker with a framework from which to view mental illness as it is seen by people currently active in this field. It may be helpful to keep these points in mind as you study the other chapters in this book.

ANNOTATED BIBLIOGRAPHY

Hoeffer, B., and Murphy, S.: *The unfinished task: Development of nursing theory for psychiatric and mental health nursing practice.* Journal of Psychosocial Nursing and Mental Health Services, 20(12):8–14, 1982.

> *Describes current psychiatric nursing theory and discusses areas in which theoretical basis still needs to be developed.*

Johnson, R.M., Richardson, J., VonEndt, K., and Lindgren, K.: *The professional support group: A model for psychiatric clinical nurse specialists.* Journal of Psychosocial Nursing and Mental Health Services, 20(2):9–13, 1982.

> *Describes a model for a support group for psychiatric nurse practitioners that was established to provide the following: 1) sharing of experiences; 2) practical help; 3) stimulation of ideas; 4) information giving.*

Karshmer, J.F.: *Rules of thumb: Hints for the psychiatric nursing student.* Journal of Psychosocial Nursing and Mental Health Services, 20(3):25–28, 1982.

> *Provides eight basic guidelines for the beginning student to aid in dealing with psychiatric patients. Includes examples of therapeutic communication with the use of these rules.*

Mark, B.: *From "lunatic" to "client": 300 years of psychiatric patienthood.* Journal of Psychosocial Nursing and Mental Health Services, 18(3):32–36, 1980.

Recounts historical perspectives of attitudes toward the mentally ill.

Mitsunga, B.K.: *Designing psychiatric/mental health nursing for the future: Problems and prospects.* Journal of Psychosocial Nursing and Mental Health Services, 20(12):15–21, 1982.

Discusses the future prospects and future needs in psychiatric nursing.

Peplau, H.E.; *Some reflections on earlier days in psychiatric nursing.* Journal of Psychosocial Nursing and Mental Health Services, 20(8):17–24, 1982.

Perspectives of psychiatric nursing history by an outstanding nursing educator.

Prepare for major shifts in psychiatry. Roundtable discussion. Patient Care, January 15, 1982, 167–223.

Roundtable discussion forcasts the relationships, laboratory tests, and diagnoses in the future of psychiatry.

Williams, J.B., and Wilson, H.S.: *A psychiatric nursing perspective on DSM-III.* Journal of Psychosocial Nursing and Mental Health Services, 20(4):14–20, 1982.

Thorough and basic guide for understanding DSM-III. Includes relevance for nursing intervention, teaching-learning, and nursing perspectives.

POST-TEST

Chapter 1

Introduction to Working with the Mentally Ill

True or False. Circle your choice.

T F 1. One may inherit a predisposition to certain types of mental illness.

T F 2. Mentally ill patients are usually very sensitive to how other people feel toward them.

T F 3. The treatment of mental illness is usually a very clear-cut process.

T F 4. Any person, if subjected to enough stress, may have a "mental breakdown."

T F 5. Minor mood swings are signs of mental illness.

T F 6. People do not inherit mental disorders but may inherit a predisposition to certain types of mental problems.

T F 7. Trusting relationships are easily established with the mentally ill.

T F 8. If you feel you have said the wrong thing to a patient and feel it has caused him harm, continue to apologize until the apology is accepted.

T F 9. It is not normal for a mental health worker to be disappointed or angry with a patient.

T F 10. It is usually quite simple to pinpoint specific reasons for a person becoming mentally ill at a particular time.

Fill in the Blanks. From the group of terms listed on the right, select the letter of the most appropriate term(s) to complete the following sentences.

1. The difference between being mentally healthy and mentally ill lies in the _____ and _____ of inappropriate behavior.

A. decrease
B. increased
C. response
D. intensity
E. sensitive
F. frequency

2. Mentally ill patients are very

    _____ to how people feel and react toward them.
3. It is the way a person views a situation that determines his

    _____.
4. New drugs have helped to

    _____ the length of hospitalization of the mentally ill.
5. Mental health workers must realize that often their primary contribution to a patient may be simply that they

    are _____.

G. available to listen
H. insensitive
I. confused
J. aware of the problem

Multiple Choice. Circle the letter you think represents the best answer.
1. As a member of one's community, the mental health worker can help reduce the loss to society that often occurs when someone becomes mentally ill by:
    1. Increasing the public's knowledge of the mental health services available in one's community.
    2. Remembering that the mentally ill are permanently disabled.
    3. Having a personal attitude of acceptance in regard to mentally ill persons.
    4. Alerting the public to the early signs of mental illness through education.
        A. 1 and 3.
        B. 2 and 4.
        C. 1, 3, and 4.
        D. All of the above.
2. To be an effective mental health worker, it is important that an individual:
    1. Understand the basic dynamics of human behavior.
    2. Be willing to explore his own feelings and reactions.
    3. Be able to give patients sound advice.
    4. Be able to work effectively with other members of the psychiatric team.
        A. 1 and 3.
        B. 1, 2, and 4.
        C. 1, 3, and 4.
        D. All of the above.
3. Which of the following statements are true about community mental health centers, day care programs, and halfway houses?

1. Offers care to the patient without removing him from his community or family for long periods of time.
2. Prevents regression and dependency of the patient which often occurs due to long-term hospitalization.
3. Are rapidly growing approaches to care of the mentally ill.
4. Will probably help the patient learn to cope with the environment in which he became ill.
   A. 1 and 2.
   B. 2 and 4.
   C. 1, 2, and 3.
   D. All of the above.
4. In working with emotionally or mentally disturbed patients, effective measures include:
   1. Acceptance of the patient as a unique and worthwhile individual.
   2. Support and understanding of the patient's feelings.
   3. Recognition and reinforcement of the patient's strengths.
   4. Prevention of regression on the part of the patient.
      A. 1 and 4.
      B. 2 and 3.
      C. 1, 2, and 3.
      D. All of the above.
5. The aim of psychiatric treatment is to:
   1. Release the patient of symptoms.
   2. Return the patient to his home and family.
   3. Help the patient become a better adjusted individual.
   4. Prevent the patient from becoming psychotic.
      A. 1.
      B. 2.
      C. 3.
      D. 4.

2

Personality Development

OBJECTIVES: Student will be able to:
1. Recognize the stages of personality development.
2. Identify the developmental tasks related to the stages of development.
3. Define id, ego, and superego.

Before discussing various reasons for abnormal behavior, it is essential for one to have a basic understanding of how a human being learns to behave in a normal (socially acceptable) manner. Since an individual's personality and perception of self are key factors in determining the type behavior the individual exhibits, this chapter presents a basic overview of personality development.

Although events occurring throughout life may affect emotional adjustment, most experts in the field of mental health believe that the experiences which occur during the first 20 years have the most significant impact on the development of the personality. Some even say that the first six years of life are the most crucial. Regardless of which opinion is correct, all agree that the early life experiences of an individual directly influence mental health.

For the sake of discussion, the stages of personality development are usually divided in the following manner: infancy (birth to age $1\frac{1}{2}$), toddler period (ages $1\frac{1}{2}$ to 3), preschool period (ages 3 to 6), school age (ages 6 to puberty, which usually occurs between ages 11 and 13), adolescence (end of puberty to age 18 or 20), and adulthood (from age 18 or 20 on). Each developmental stage serves as a building block in the foundation of personality. If a stage is completed successfully, the foundation remains firm; but if there are serious problems during any of the stages, the personality structure has been weakened.

One should remember that individuals develop at their own rate and that no two human beings are exactly alike; however, each of the stages listed above has certain tasks which most people will accomplish during that stage. For example, one of the developmental tasks of the toddler is to learn to walk and most children will learn the basics of walking between the ages of 1 and 3. On the other hand, most of those same children will still be refining their ability to walk after they have entered the preschool stage and are busy conquering the tasks of that period.

INFANCY

Most authorities believe that normal newborns possess all the basic ingredients (genetic inheritance) to become biologically functioning human beings; however, the ability to utilize inherited potential will depend on life experiences. For example, if a child has the genetic potential to become a great pianist, but is born into a poor family, never hears a piano, and never has a chance to take piano lessons, this great genetic potential will likely go unrecognized and unused. On the other hand, a child may have the finest music lessons and the best piano that money can buy, but have no genetic potential for musical talent. That child will develop at best, into an average piano player.

Just as a new computer is mechanically ready to function and solve all sorts of complicated problems, it cannot begin to function until it is fed, by a human being, a massive dose of raw information and facts. A human infant functions in much the same manner. A 5- or 6-year-old child will have great difficulty learning to read unless someone, usually the child's parents, spends five or so years programming the child's "computer" (the brain). They do this by saying over and over that a chair is a chair, a cow is a cow—not a moo, that a stove burner is hot, and by providing the child with a large variety of learning experiences such as trips to the zoo, the store, the fire department, and so forth.

Newborn children also have no concept of morality. They are gradually taught right from wrong over the first few years of life according to what their parents consider right and wrong. Sigmund Freud considered the newborn to be a "bundle of id." Simply stated, *id* was Freud's term for that part of one's personality which is unconscious and contains all of the "wants" of an individual (e.g., to eat, to sleep, to be comfortable, to have fun and to do pleasurable things). In other words, infants want their basic needs (food, diapers changed, sleep, attention) met at the exact moment they want them, regardless of whom it inconveniences (usually mom and dad at 2:00 A.M.). Gradually throughout the first year of life infants learn that there are others in the world and that despite their mother's best efforts, it takes a few minutes to warm a bottle or change a diaper.

If one observes 3- or 4-month-old infants demanding a feeding, one can see that most will cry, indicating their hunger need, but will become quiet when their mother takes the bottle out of the refrigerator and begins to warm it. The child has begun to trust the mother to follow through in meeting his needs, and thus begins to develop the feeling that the world is a good place in which to live and grow. On the other hand, if the infant is allowed to cry for hours before being fed or is constantly abused and neglected, the child begins to mistrust people and to feel that the world is not a very likable place. If deprivation and neglect are severe enough, an infant or young child will withdraw from the world of reality into a world of fantasy which feels less threatening. Therefore, in the first year of life, infants need as little frustration as possible in order to learn to trust their environment and to feel good about themselves and the world in which they live.

An unfortunate characteristic of children is that they tend to blame themselves for failures of their parents and thus develop feelings of inadequacy which may affect them all of their lives. For example, when parents divorce, young children often feel that they are to blame and will plead with the parents to stay together, promising never to be bad again. This sense of being able to make all sorts of things happen is apparently a carryover from early infancy, when young infants, being unable to see well enough to distinguish themselves from others, feel that they themselves meet their own needs. Of course, by the time they are 4 to 6 months old, infants can recognize their mother and see her as the source of relief for all their tension; therefore, they transfer their feeling of omnipotence to their mother and expect her to cure all ills. For example, you have probably heard a young child ask his mother to make the rain go away or to make an injured finger stop hurting.

Although not omnipotent, a mother's role (or mother substitute) is an extremely important one in the life of an infant. Infants need the psychologic satisfaction that comes from being held close to another human while being caressed and talked to in a gentle, caring way. The mother figure is the first love object for all mankind. An infant is completely dependent on her and thus the mother-child relationship is perhaps more intense than any other relationship in one's life. In the more serious psychologic illnesses, one frequently finds a flaw in the mother-child relationship along with the other causative factors. Often to their dismay, young children soon realize that neither they nor their mothers are omnipotent. Hopefully, this realization will occur gradually as children begin to master more of the skills of daily living which will allow them to feel more in control of their environment and thus less insecure and dependent.

TODDLER PERIOD

Between the ages of 1 and $2\frac{1}{2}$, children begin to develop a sense of autonomy. In other words, they begin to view themselves as individuals in their own right, apart from their parents although still dependent on them. The child now has a mind of his own and wants to try to deal with reality in his own way. Parents tend to remember this stage of development well, for it seems that all of a sudden the quiet, cuddly, agreeable, helpless, dependent, clinging little infant has become a tyrant who states over and over, "no, no, no" while refusing all offers of help and scurrying around as if in training for the Olympics.

Unfortunately, many parents fail to recognize and accept this stage for what is is—the child's first attempts at establishing independence and self-reliance. They become threatened. A ridiculous battle may ensue, especially since one of the warring parties is 2 years old and the other is an adult. An insecure parent may be heard yelling, "No two year old is going to say no to me." What parents may fail to realize is that the world is a very frustrating place for toddlers. They are quite interested in their world and want to do a great many things; however, they are too short to see much of what is going on, can't walk or climb well enough to get where they want to go, can't dress themselves and, most of all, are constantly being told what to do by someone three times their size.

The world is also frustrating for adults who have children. This is especially true when parents are faced with the delicate task of toilet training. It is hard for most adults to believe that they once thought that freedom constituted being able to mess in their pants whenever they wanted to do so, or that they once felt that fecal material was something special they had created. This, however, is apparently the way many toddlers view it. Toddlers are unable to look ahead and realize that when they are toilet trained mom and dad will take them more places. They must also be taught by their parents that their feces are not artistic creations, that they smell bad and that they belong in only one place— the toilet.

In other areas of muscle and motor development, this conflict of interest does not exist because the child and the parents are in agreement concerning their goals. Parents are delighted when their children learn to walk, and encourage and reward them for doing so. In regard to being toilet trained, children want to please their mothers and fathers and at the same time want to retain their freedom. Having both positive and negative feelings about the situation, the child experiences conflict. However, in the end, the child's desire to please his mother usually wins out and her attitude about fecal material is adopted.

This stage of development would progress much more smoothly if parents would not attempt to begin toilet training until the child is physically and psychologically receptive to the idea. Voluntary control of the anal sphincter muscle does not develop until a child is 18 to 24 months of age, and by that time the child is usually beginning to show signs of disgust at having "accidents." Serious psychologic problems may

16

occur if a mother tries to toilet train a child too early, if a mother is excessively preoccupied with neatness or cleanliness, or if a mother is overpermissive and enjoys rearing a child with no shame, guilt, or need to conform to the norms of the society in which they live. Man does not live in isolation and, therefore, must conform to some extent to societal norms. This socialization process takes place in childhood, and when parents fail to assume their responsibility for making sure that socialization does indeed occur, the individual usually has a great deal of difficulty adjusting as an adult. For example, people who are considered antisocial or sociopathic because they function as a "bundle of id," wanting what they want, when they want it, regardless of whom it inconveniences or hurts, frequently had overly permissive parents. Society does not tolerate such behavior well and sociopaths often spend their lives on the fringes of society or in and out of jail or mental institutions.

PRESCHOOL PERIOD

By the end of the toddler or muscle training period, children have greatly increased motor and intellectual skills. Three year olds have fairly good vocabularies which enable them to tell about their experiences, they can ride tricycles, run with only a few falls, dress themselves if the buttons are big and in the front, and can generally stay dry through the night. These accomplishments boost self-esteem and help children feel good about themselves. They are then ready to learn more about the world outside their families. It is during this period (ages 3 to 6) that the ego and superego begin to function. The *superego* is that part of the personality which is called our conscience. It is composed of all the "controls," the shoulds and should nots we learn from our parents, churches, schools, teachers, and so forth. Its structure will depend largely on the type and quality of discipline.

Parents frequently do not realize how critical they are and how little room they allow for mistakes. If a child mispronounces a word, they may ridicule and try to force the child to say the word correctly. Later they wonder why the child is so quiet and seldom talks. Parents tend to forget the words they mispronounce or the times they stutter. If Johnny spills a glass of milk, he may be called clumsy and be punished. His parents react to the inconvenience of cleaning up without realizing that they caused the problem by not understanding that a 2-year-old child's hand will not reach around a large milk glass. Events such as these chip away at the feeling of self-worth, especially when parents add injury to insult by telling the child over and over that he is bad or should be ashamed of himself.

By the time children are 5 to 6 years of age, parents no longer have to be physically present to enforce discipline. The children have incorporated their parents' scolding into their own minds, and before starting to do something they hear that still, small voice (the superego or conscience) saying, "You better watch out. You know how clumsy you are and if you break that toy you're going to be a bad boy."

Of course children need to be disciplined, but discipline needs to be given consistently, in small doses, and only when absolutely needed. Proper environmental structure tends to reduce the need for excessive discipline because the child knows what is expected of him. A child needs to learn to respond to reasonable limits. If there is no discipline, children fail to develop a sense of right or wrong and will lack respect for other people and their belongings. On the other hand, if discipline is too severe, the child becomes afraid to try anything new or different, experiences extreme guilt and shame, and, in effect, becomes a maladapted person who is afraid of the world. Individuals need a well balanced personality. They need a conscience (superego) that allows them to make changes and mistakes and to be successful in give and take situations with other people. Yet they must be able to accept blame when they are wrong and change their behavior when it needs changing without becoming so guilt-ridden that continued functioning is impossible. This is where the ego plays its major role.

The *ego* is conscious and functions as the "manager" of the personality. It deals with reality and must manage the impulses or demands of the unconscious id and superego and help find acceptable ways to meet those demands in the conscious world of reality. Of course, the ego must have help in its managerial role. It gets that help from the psychologic defense mechanisms which will be discussed in the next chapter.

The preschool period has been called the family triangle period by some authorities and is the first time that boys and girls encounter different conflicts and achievements. By age 3 the baby no longer exists and the child either looks like a little boy or little girl. Each sex is acutely aware of their own bodies and the physical changes that are occurring. The genital area is now the body region of emotional significance and both boys and girls seek a sexual type of pleasure through manipulation of their external genitals. This occurs in nearly all normal children and is even seen in infants, though more at random and less purposeful.

Unfortunately, many parents react negatively when they find their child masturbating and may resort to various threats and punishments in order to stop the behavior. Some parents verbally instruct the child to stop, stating that masturbation is not nice or may be harmful. Other parents resort to threats of cutting off the child's penis or retaliation from supernatural beings since they feel masturbation is a sin. Most children usually stop masturbating or continue it with less frequency and greater discrimination either due to fear or to a desire to please their

18

parents. In either case, a great deal of guilt is produced and must be handled by the child. The guilt is often handled by *repression*—an unconscious forgetting of threatening events. Unfortunately, the individual does not really forget the event, but it becomes part of the individual's unconscious where, although not remembered, it may motivate future behavior.

SCHOOL AGE

Psychologically, the early school years are quiet and peaceful ones for the child. Some authorities have even gone so far as to describe the span of time between ages 6 and 10 as the "Golden Era of Childhood." At this point in a child's development, sexual frustrations and problems of the family period have usually been at least partially resolved. Most children have given up masturbation in return for parental approval and are actively attempting to become more like the parent of the same sex, instead of trying to possess the parent of the opposite sex. The child, therefore, has greater energy to devote to other areas of interest and thus great social and intellectual strides are made in this period. During this stage, the child is extremely interested in learning, and sexual curiosity has been replaced by intellectual curiosity. Instead of daydreaming about sexual achievement, the child seeks success in real life social interactions.

The school age child identifies with the parent of the same sex and also begins to identify with other children of the same sex. Boys greatly prefer the company of other boys, and girls enjoy being with other girls. Individual friendships are extremely important, but the school age child begins to become interested in group activities and membership as well.

ADOLESCENCE

The onset of puberty (10 to 14 years of age) is actually the beginning of adolescence. Sexual development once again becomes of prime importance. Masturbation is usually resumed or increased if it was never discontinued. Girls begin their menstrual periods and boys experience nocturnal emissions (wet dreams). Both sexes begin to have romantic fantasies involving sexual contacts with members of the opposite sex. Instead of the parent of the opposite sex, who captured their interest during the family triangle period, their partners in these sexual fantasies are often classmates, older friends, movie stars, or other idolized individuals.

During puberty it is of prime importance that the parent-child relationship be a good one. Ideally, all children would be given adequate sex information before the onset of puberty. As new and drastic body changes begin to occur, children need to be able to discuss their feelings with their parents. They have questions that need to be answered and fears that need to be expressed and understood.

Since actions often speak louder than words, the way parents relate to each other and their acceptance of their own gender greatly influences adolescents' acceptance of their own developing sexuality. For example, the way a young girl accepts the onset of her menstrual period is largely influenced by the way that her mother has accepted her own sexual and reproductive functions. Fears, inhibitions, and tension related to menstruation are often passed on to daughters and surface in physical complaints such as severe cramps and headaches, moodiness, and incapacitation during a portion of the menstrual period.

Adolescence is a stormy period for both teenagers and their parents since both have ambivalent feelings about the changes that are taking place. Parents are not sure that they want to give up control of the adolescent and allow development of a sense of independence. On the other hand, the adolescent is not always sure that he wants to assume that responsibility. There is a great deal of security in having parents make decisions and be responsible for one's care. Such dependency/independency conflicts probably account for much of the adolescent's often irate and erratic behavior. One moment he is the most responsible, mature acting creature one could ask for and the next moment, childish and irresponsible.

Although most adolescents are not emotionally capable of engaging in a mature and responsible sexual relationship, they are capable of developing emotionally satisfying relationships which provide companionship and the opportunity of experiences and affection with members of the opposite sex.

Since an adolescent is still deeply involved in trying to establish his own feelings of self-worth and is working through feelings of inadequacies and dependence at a time when he longs to be independent and self sufficient, "love" relationships are likely to be based on what the "loved" person does to strengthen the adolescent's own self-esteem. You have probably heard a young man brag to his fraternity brothers about his date with one of the college cheerleaders, or a 16-year-old high school sophomore bragging to her friend about the guy she's dating who just happens to drive a shiny Corvette.

Peer approval is extremely important to the adolescent. A girl often wants to be asked out on lots of dates in order to appear popular since this increases her status in the eyes of her girlfriends. A boy accomplishes the same thing by bragging about his sexual accomplishments to his male friends.

"Falling in love" usually begins to occur around age 16 and is likely to happen a number of times before young adults experience the type of relationship in which their wish to receive is overcome by their wish to give. These fleeting relationships, however, are important since they help adolescents develop their ability to form close relationships based on give and take situations which ultimately lead to the establishment of a lasting relationship.

When the point of establishing mature relationships is reached, the individual at long last has conquered the possessive feelings of early childhood and has changed the love object from a parent to a person of one's own peer group. With this final act, the individual prepares for the transition from adolescence to adulthood and goes out to face the world carrying with him all that he has learned to be, a small fear of being alone, and a hope for the future.

ANNOTATED BIBLIOGRAPHY

Brink, R.E.: *The gifted preschool child*. Pediatric Nursing, 8(5):299–303, 1982.

Relates the behaviors, frustrations, and unique psychosocial needs of gifted preschoolers.

Clore, E.R., and Newberry Y.S.G.: *Nurse practitioner guidance for the adoptive family from birth to adolescence*. Pediatric Nursing, 7(6):16–25, 1981.

Excellent and detailed guide relates the developmental changes of the child from infancy to adolescence. Relates the specific needs of the newborn, infant, early childhood stage, school-age stage, and adolescent. Also discusses child-adopted parent bonding. This was written as a guide for the adoptive parent, but it is broad and complete enough for any general application.

Fox, K.: *Adolescent ambivalence: A therapeutic issue*. Journal of Psychosocial Nursing and Mental Health Services, 18(9):29–33, 1980.

Ambivalence is a distinguishing feature of adolescent development. This article addresses ambivalence in three main areas; dependency, body image, and sexual identity.

Hayes, J.S.; *The McCarthy Scales of Children's Abilities: Their usefulness in developmental assessment*. Pediatric Nursing, 7(4):35–37, 1981.

Describes the use of the MSCA as a tool in the developmental assessment of children aged $2^1/_2$–$8^1/_2$.

Mellencamp, A.: *Adolescent depression: A review of the literature with implications for nursing care*. Journal of Psychosocial Nursing and Mental Health Services, 19(9):15-20, 1981.

Covers the losses of adolescence which contribute to depression such as separation from parents, loss of self-esteem, and loss of sexual innocence. Differ-

21

entiates between adolescent and adult depression and lists important points of nursing intervention.

Pontious, S.L.: *Practical Piaget: Helping children understand.* American Journal of Nursing, 82(1):114–117, 1982.

Describes the differences in the perceptions of a child who is in Piaget's pre-operational stage (ages 2–7), and the child who is in the concrete operational stage (ages 7–12). Offers insights for dealing with the child in each stage.

When the child is learning disabled. Patient Care, March 30, 1982, 17–57.

Discusses the effect of a learning disability on the socialization and personality development of the child. Includes a section on developmental testing and recommended reading list on learning disabilities.

POST-TEST

Chapter 2

Personality Development

Fill in the blanks. From the group of terms listed on the right, select the letter of the most appropriate term(s) to complete the following sentences.

1. Some experts say that the first _____ years of life are the most crucial.
2. One's ability to utilize all of one's inherited potential depends on _____.
3. If neglect is severe enough, an infant or young child will withdraw from reality into a world of fantasy which feels _____.
4. The _____ relationship is perhaps more intense than any other relationship is one's life.
5. Between the ages of _____, a child's superego develops rapidly.

A. life experiences
B. six
C. mother-child
D. less threatening
E. three to six
F. six to ten
G. sibling
H. husband-wife

True or False. Circle your choice.

T F 1. All human beings develop in the exact same pattern and almost at the same rate.

T F 2. The mother figure is the first love object for all mankind.

T F 3. If there is no discipline, children fail to develop a sense of right and wrong.

T F 4. Adolescence appears to be an easy developmental stage for teenagers and their parents.

T F 5. Peer approval is of little importance to the adolescent.

Multiple Choice. Circle the letter you think represents the best answer.

1. What is the outstanding characteristic of growth and development?
   A. It occurs at a uniform rate.
   B. Each individual follows a unique pattern.
   C. It is a simple process.
   D. It rarely influences behavior.

2. What is the most important factor in the home environment of a child?
   A. Assurance of proper nutrition.
   B. Provision for play space.
   C. Atmosphere that lets the child feel secure.
   D. Protection from overstimulation.

3. A basic factor contributing to the security of a child is:
   A. The knowledge that he is an individual.
   B. The setting of realistic boundaries and limits.
   C. Allowing for dependence on his mother for his needs.
   D. Allowing him to have what he wants.

4. Growth and development of children are influenced by their:
   1. Heredity.
   2. Cultural heritage.
   3. Environment.
   4. The way their parents treat them.
      A. 1 only.
      B. 1 and 3.
      C. 2, 3, and 4.
      D. All of the above.

5. The fact that boys fight and generally display greater aggressiveness than girls is probably best explained on the basis of difference in:
   A. Social expectation.
   B. Endocrine balance.
   C. Inherited predisposition.
   D. Hereditary factors.

6. The Freudian theory of personality development divides the "mind" into three basic parts. Of the terms listed below which one is *not* a basic part?
   A. Ego.
   B. Libido.
   C. Id.
   D. Superego.

7. The ego is that part of the "mind" that:
   A. Helps the individual deal with reality.
   B. Constantly attempts to satisfy its own demands.
   C. Is concerned with morals, values, precepts and standards.
   D. Represses painful thoughts from the conscious.

8. A 2-year-old child is frequently negativistic and resistant to adult demands. This behavior is usually regarded as an indication of:
   A. Inconsistent techniques on the part of the parents.
   B. Overindulgence on the part of the parents.
   C. Too great strictness on the part of the parents.
   D. A growing awareness of self on the part of the child.
9. Independent behavior is learned from a mother who:
   A. Is permissive and allows the child to do as he desires.
   B. Is fearful of injury or of the child getting dirty.
   C. Permits exploration and experimentation but sets limits.
   D. Rewards accomplishments and avoids restrictions.
10. The best advice to give parents on the subject of toilet training is:
    A. To wait until the child indicates that he is ready via behavioral clues.
    B. To begin bladder training around 15 months of age.
    C. Tell parents it is up to their discretion.
    D. To place the child on the potty for 15 minutes at the same time each day.
11. The best way to manage the aggressive behavior of a 2-year-old boy is:
    A. Tell him he is a bad boy and that you won't love him if the behavior continues.
    B. To rechannel his activity into a more acceptable area.
    C. Let him vent his aggressive feelings however he wishes.
    D. Provide punishment for any aggressive behavior.
12. Questions of a preschool child may become annoying. Adults should understand that:
    1. This is a period of rapid vocabulary growth.
    2. The child's "computer" is being programmed.
    3. Answers provide the child with a concept of adult attitudes and feelings.
    4. The child should always be given an answer.
       A. 1 and 3.
       B. 2, 3, and 4.
       C. 1, 2, and 4.
       D. 1 and 4.
       E. All of the above.
13. The typical characteristic of a girl during the preschool stage of development is:
    A. Little curiosity about sex difference.
    B. Strong interest in and attraction to her father.
    C. Intense admiration of her peers.
    D. Interest in "gangs" with girls her age.
14. The so-called "golden years" of childhood are:
    A. 1 to 3.

B. 3 to 6.

C. 6 to 10.

D. 10 through puberty.

E. 14 to 20.

15. Family relations for the school child are characterized by:

1. Identification with parent of the same sex.

2. Increasing independence.

3. Individual friendships become important.

4. Resentment of rigid rules.

   A. 1 and 4.

   B. 2 and 3.

   C. 1, 2, and 3.

   D. 2 and 4.

   E. All of the above.

16. A teacher finds a group of first graders involved in dramatizing a funeral. Which idea in regard to their play is likely to be most justified?

A. Realistic play of this nature is unusual in children of this age.

B. This play behavior is likely to be unrelated to the actual experience.

C. The children should be gently guided to other types of play.

D. Such play is an attempt to explore the reality of death.

17. The attitudes of a young girl toward menstruation usually reflect those of:

A. Her best friend.

B. The person who tells her about it.

C. Her mother.

D. Her family.

18. The major adjustments the adolescence has to make are:

1. Physical adjustment to body changes.

2. Social adjustment with peers.

3. Sexual adjustment in boy-girl relationships.

4. Moral adjustment so he will have a moral code to live by in the future.

   A. 1 only.

   B. 3 only.

   C. 2 and 3.

   D. All of the above.

19. Usually the strictest behavioral control over the adolescent is exerted by:

A. Parents.

B. Church.

C. Peers.

D. School.

3

Basic Concepts
of the Mind

OBJECTIVES: Student will be able to:
1. Define psychopathology.
2. List three specific behaviors used to evaluate one's overall mental health.
3. Define the term defense mechanism; give two examples.
4. Define neurosis and psychosis.

THE MENTAL HEALTH CONTINUUM

If one successfully accomplishes the developmental tasks discussed in the preceding chapter, one can approach adulthood with the skills necessary to function as a mentally healthy, mature adult. Maturity and mental health are not dependent on the number of years lived but rather on an individual's problem solving skills, ability to cope with life stresses and ability to make good choices.

The emotionally healthy person is accepting of himself and others and has developed the ability to give as well as receive. Such persons have an appropriate amount of self-confidence because they have realistically evaluated their own assets as well as liabilities and have found that they have the ability to cope with the challenges of life. They make decisions based on sound judgment and then accept responsibility for their actions.

Of course, one needs to remember that even the most emotionally competent and responsible individual sometimes acts in an immature or childish manner. It is only when one's behavior is frequently irresponsible or is significantly at odds with society's expectations that one begins to experience the maladjustments referred to as psychopathology.

Psychopathology is a term used to indicate that a person is emotionally unable to deal with the stress and strain of everyday life. Such a condition usually comes about when a person's defense mechanisms are no longer able to defend him against the anxiety created by stress and strain, when he has not been able to develop defense mechanisms against such forces, or when he uses defense mechanisms so excessively that he does not accurately perceive reality. If a person's defenses work adequately and he seems to be able to get along reasonably well in everyday life, he is said to be "adjusted." If he is not able to get along well and people see him as being strange or peculiar, or if his behavior is obviously inappropriate, he is said to be manifesting a significant degree of psychopathology.

In order to understand the difference between mental health and mental illness, it is helpful to think in terms of specific behaviors. For example, let's take the rather simple behavior of laughing. If one never laughs, we say that he is depressed and that he does not have the capability of enjoying himself. If one laughs all the time, we suspect that something is wrong with him, particularly if he laughs at inappropriate times. The point is, of course, that somewhere in between never laughing and laughing constantly there is a range in which the behavior of laughing is both acceptable and expected. This then demonstrates the idea of the mental health continuum. By looking at behaviors in terms of a mental health continuum, it is easy to see that any given behavior has a socially acceptable range of occurrence while either the absolute absence or the constant presence of that behavior might be seen as abnormal. The drawing below demonstrates this idea.

```
———+————————+———————————————+—————————+———
 no laughter    appropriate laughter    constant laughter
```

With the idea then that most behaviors have an appropriate range, which is both acceptable and expected, let's look at some of the specific things which may be used to judge one's overall mental health.

1. Thinking well of oneself; being fairly free of feelings of inadequacy and inferiority; being able to express or to communicate one's emotions.
2. The ability to trust oneself to make decisions and to act on those decisions after careful consideration of the consequences of one's actions.
3. A genuine feeling of well being and a realistic degree of optimism (expectation that things will turn out well).
4. Accepting one's real limitations while developing one's assets.
5. Evaluating one's mistakes, determining their causes, and learning not to repeat the same behavior.
6. Being able to delay immediate gratification for future satisfaction. (For example, putting off getting married until one's career preparation is finished).
7. The ability to form close and lasting relationships with persons of both sexes; being relatively satisfied with one's own sex and having the ability to enjoy an active and satisfactory sex life.
8. An appropriate conscience that prevents the individual from get-

28

ting into trouble by resisting behavior that is destructive either to the individual or to others; a conscience that also produces guilt when one behaves in an antisocial fashion.

9. The ability to accept authority (obey traffic laws, follow the rules of the organization for which one works, and so forth) but in appropriate situations, not to be afraid of authority and to contest authority if necessary.
10. The ability to meet one's needs in a socially acceptable manner while taking into consideration the needs of others.
11. The absence of petty jealousies and the need to exploit and manipulate others.
12. An ability to maintain a reasonably accurate perception of reality and of one's social and interpersonal interactions.
13. The ability to work alone and to work effectively with others; compromising and sharing when appropriate while being able to compete and be aggressive when necessary; being organized and systematic in order to get things done; possessing an acceptable amount of cleanliness, promptness, orderliness, and neatness.
14. The ability to function in both dependent and independent roles; to follow or to lead; to take care or to be taken care of, depending on the circumstances.
15. Acceptance of the fact that stress and change are part of everyday life; being flexible enough to adapt to these continual changes without a great deal of psychologic discomfort.
16. A sense of humor; the ability to laugh at self and others when life situations are absurd.
17. The ability to maintain a balanced or integrated personality so that one can respond adaptively to life experiences.

It is difficult to define these factors accurately, to measure them, and to decide just how much of a behavior is acceptable and how much is not acceptable. Psychologists and psychiatrists attempt to make these decisions and often are asked to do so in court cases and competency hearings. Value judgments relative to these points should be avoided. For example, some societies reward their young men for stealing, and some subculture groups in our country reward the young members of their gangs for stealing, running away from home, and going to reformatory schools. Very often the fact of having been in a reformatory school gives a young man a special status in his group and he is looked up to by the other members.

It seems that, in the final analysis, the degree to which a particular behavior is acceptable by individuals in our society is determined by how much of that particular behavior a society is willing to accept. Of course, what is acceptable to society changes from time to time. In 1950, it would probably have been quite upsetting to most people to have naked persons running around town; however, in the streaking fad of 1974, a great many young people were running around town wearing nothing but tennis shoes and a smile and were frequently applauded for their efforts. This particular fad even made its way to Hollywood where perhaps the ultimate was reached when a very daring young man streaked the televised 1974 Academy Awards Presentation.

Had these behaviors occurred in 1950, it is likely that the streakers would have been jailed and there would have been considerable public outrage; however, the permissiveness of the late '60s and early '70s has made this behavior merely amusing to a great many Americans. Most of the court cases involving streakers were either dismissed or the streakers were given minimal fines; however, even with the permissive attitudes prevalent in 1974, a "dirty old man" in the park wearing nothing but a raincoat and exposing himself to young girls as they passed by would not have met with a similar fate in court. He probably would have received a substantial sentence for indecent public exposure and, at least, been committed for psychiatric treatment.

One further point should be made. Even though a person is seen as being well adjusted by most of his friends and peers, it is unlikely that he is totally adjusted. In fact, it has been said that the only totally adjusted person is a dead one. Every person who is active and who participates in his environment is continually subjected to conflicts which he must resolve. The young lady who meets a handsome young man and wants to go out with him but who also has a big exam the following day must confront the conflict and decide whether to go out with the young man or to study for the exam. A healthy response would be to decide to do one or the other. A less healthy response would be to permit the conflict to remain unresolved and not do either.

Return then to the question of what happens when an individual becomes unable to manage his anxieties and conflicts, and thus becomes unable to function in a "well adjusted" fashion. By and large, there are two major classifications for such maladjustments, the *neurotic maladjustment* and the *psychotic maladjustment*. Before these are discussed, however, it is necessary to know something about the psychologic defense mechanisms which help us to function when we encounter highly stressful situations. The following section provides an overview of the defense mechanisms, how they work, and how they may be abused.

DEFENSE MECHANISMS

Each of us has a basic image of ourselves (self-image) which is important to our general psychologic well being. Basically, the self-image is the collection of ideas we have about what kind of person we are.

30

Sometimes persons who have poor self-images will try just as hard to maintain that poor self-image as other persons try to maintain a good self-image. Since we frequently react to other people the way we react to ourselves, it is easy to see that the way we view ourselves is quite an important factor in our relationships with other people.

It is in this area of the self-image that the defense mechanisms work. In our efforts to maintain a constant way of viewing ourselves, we sometimes face situations which are threats to our worth or adequacy or to our cherished way of viewing ourselves. Such situations are stressful because they pressure us to change our ways of seeing ourselves and thus upset our feelings of "constancy."

The defense mechanisms are sometimes called adjustment or coping mechanisms. They are usually unconscious although we sometimes become aware of their presence. At times, we may even use them consciously. These mechanisms are used daily by almost everyone. They are neither good nor bad. Whether they are healthy or unhealthy is probably best determined by whether they serve to help or hurt the individual using them. If they help him to meet his personal and social goals in acceptable ways, they are healthy. If they cause him to distort reality unrealistically and to deceive himself, they are unhealthy. For example, if one always explains his failures by blaming someone else or always rationalizes away his inadequacies, he may never consider that he might be more successful if he learned to look for the real reasons for his failures. A classic example which demonstrates this point occurs when a student fails an examination and blames the teacher for not giving a "fair" exam, for making the exam too difficult, or for not asking what she said she would ask on the exam. The student may be ignoring the fact that he only studied an hour when he needed to have studied four or five hours.

To summarize, defense mechanisms are used by almost everyone. They are frequently used without one's conscious awareness and they are used to help the individual maintain his cherished beliefs about himself and the world. The rest of this section lists specific mechanisms with a brief example to show how they are used and how they might be abused.

Repression

Repression is considered by many authorities to be the most common defense mechanism. An individual is using repression when he "forgets" or excludes from conscious thought those things which he finds too painful or anxiety-provoking to remember. The repression of anxiety-producing situations is often incomplete, frequently resulting in vague feelings of worthlessness and insecurity. Sometimes people feel guilty almost constantly and are unable to discover why they have such feelings.

Perhaps one of the more classic and usual cases associated with repression occurs with sexual matters. A young female patient seen by one of the authors complained of not being able to "let go" sexually with her husband. She admitted that she wanted to like intercourse because she knew that it would please her husband; yet each time they started to have intercourse, she could feel herself "tighten up." The patient even "tightened up" talking about it to the therapist and became quite anxious. After several visits, the patient started to say something about an incident she dimly remembered but could not quite bring herself to talk about it. At the next therapy session, she began talking about an incident in which she and her brother, ages 7 and 9, had been playing together and had become interested in how they were different from each other. Her mother discovered them while they were undressed and were marveling at their differences. When the screaming, yelling, and whippings were over, the patient was confused, upset, and unaware of what she had done wrong. She was visibly uncomfortable talking about the incident but following her recollection and further discussion and supportive therapy, she began to respond to her husband sexually and, at last contact, was feeling much like a woman who had been, in her words, "set free." Of course, not all episodes of repression are so dramatic or have such an impact on one's behavior. Lesser incidents of repression occur daily. A young child "forgets" to bring his report card home to be signed—he had an F on it. A husband "forgets" his wife's birthday following a big fight. A businessman "forgets" the name of a customer whom he really does not like.

In any case, although it may help reduce anxiety temporarily, repression uses up valuable psychologic energy and may block one's efforts toward leading a "comfortable" existence. It is usually better to deal with the repressed material since doing so will help one to a more healthy adjustment.

Rationalization

This defense mechanism is a favorite for many people. It allows us to do what we want to do when we know that we shouldn't, and it helps us to accept ourselves when we don't live up to our goals or the expectations we and others have for us. It involves thinking up reasons for our behavior which are more acceptable than the "real" reason. A good rationalization may contain some elements of truth and this, of course, makes it seem even more plausible. For example, a woman was about to be jailed for having written bad checks amounting to more than nine thousand dollars. When asked why she had written the worthless checks, she stated that her husband deserved to have some of the finer things in life and that all of his hard work had not gotten him anything.

Other examples of rationalization include statements such as "If I were only taller, the girls would like me better" or "If I just had some new clothes, I would really knock them dead." How about "Yeah! If I were captain of the football team, I'd have ten girlfriends too" or "If I had his brains, I could make A's too". One final example, "Everyone else cheats so I have to; if I don't, I won't pass." The most serious consequence of rationalization is self-deception. Although it may be painful at times, one is probably better off to accept the truth about the motives for his behavior. In doing so, he is more likely to benefit from his experiences.

Denial of Reality

Denial of reality occurs when one simply refuses to see what is obvious to everyone else around him. The husband who refuses to recognize that his wife is "running around on him" when everyone else knows that she is represents the case in point. This mechanism is also frequently found among persons who have physical disabilities or who have lost limbs due to amputation. One young man was injured in an automobile accident and was paralyzed from the waist down. He was extremely attractive and bright. When asked what effect he thought the physical disability would have on his social life, he insisted that there would be little, if any, effect. He was denying the facts that he could not walk, that he had to be picked up and moved from a wheelchair to a car, or from a wheelchair to a bed, and that he had no control over his bowel and bladder functions.

A more common example of the use of denial as a defense mechanism is demonstrated by the insistence of a lady who wears a size 16 dress that she can wear a size 14 or 12 dress and, in fact, she buys the smaller dress. Someone who is ashamed of his very large feet may wear a pair of shoes one or two sizes too small for him and suffer the pain rather than admit that he has large feet. The old addage that "love is blind" also demonstrates a popular usage of the denial mechanism.

Of course, the major problem with denial is that if one is unable to recognize a legitimate problem, he is unlikely to react in a way which would lead to more adequate personality development and to a higher level of maturity.

Conversion Reactions

In conversion reactions, the individual's emotional stress is converted into physical complaints. The individual attempts to blame physical factors for his condition. An extreme example is demonstrated by a young patient who attempted to get out of bed one morning and discovered that he couldn't walk. After several days of physical examinations, roentgenography, and neurologic examinations, no evidence of a physical abnormality was found. The patient was referred for psychiatric treatment. In the course of treatment, it was discovered that the patient had a sister who died from a muscular disease which rendered her progressively less able to care for herself. The young man had been ignored during her illness when the parents took care of her. The patient came to resent his sister and when she died, he felt guilty. The patient apparently repressed most of his guilt feelings and seemed well for a while before becoming "paralyzed." Within a matter of six weeks, using behavior modification techniques, the patient was able to walk. There have been no recurrences of his paralysis.

A more common example of this particular defense mechanism occurs when we get "uptight," have a hard day, and subsequently develop a headache. Persons who have peptic ulcers also demonstrate the conversion mechanism.

Perhaps the greatest advantage of conversion is that it permits a great many people to blame their tiredness, headaches, and so forth on physical ailments. The disadvantage is that once such a satisfactory explanation is discovered, the individual may not try to discern the cause of his stresses and to do something to make his life more acceptable and more livable.

Compensation

Compensation is a mechanism whereby one tries to cover up an area of weakness by showing a great deal of strength or excellence in another area. An example of this defense mechanism is the young man who is too frail or too small to play football but becomes an excellent student. A more direct example of compensation occurs in instances where an individual loses the use of an arm and then uses the remaining arm to equal or surpass the performance that would have been possible using the lost arm.

Although the mechanism of compensation frequently produces desirable results, it may also produce undesirable results. For example, the young man from the "wrong side of the tracks" who feels that he is socially unacceptable and undertakes to become the meanest fighter on his block. Numerous television programs are built around the compensation theme where a brilliant scientist is offended by his company or his country and subsequently develops weapons of tremendous capability for a competing power simply to "show" the people who rebuffed him.

Positive examples of the use of this defense mechanism occur when an individual has a poor figure but compensates by dressing in a particularly flattering manner, or when an overweight person develops an especially winning personality.

Compensation mechanisms frequently help persons to excel in some particular area when otherwise they might not have excelled in anything.

34

The negative side of compensation may show up when the chosen areas of compensation are antisocial or detrimental to the individual. Perhaps Evel Knievel is an outstanding example of this latter point.

Projection

Projection is a defense mechanism which enables one to justify his own behavior and feelings by accusing others of having these same feelings, and by permitting one to blame shortcomings on other people or objects. One of the easiest ways to spot this mechanism is to recognize the "blaming" theme which is usually present. An example of this mechanism occurred in a state hospital. A court service worker who sometimes referred patients to the hospital always wrote letters describing the behavior of the referred patients. He never failed to mention the homosexual tendencies of the patients. As a matter of fact, he always found something to indicate the presence of homosexuality. In reality, very few of the patients referred had homosexual tendencies. The worker's fear of his own homosexual impulses and characteristics were being projected onto other people. Another example of this mechanism is demonstrated by a tennis player who, after completely missing the ball, looks at his tennis racket as if it had a hole in it. In effect he is saying, "There must be something wrong with this racket. Surely I couldn't have missed the whole dang ball." Frequently one will blame many of his troubles on bad luck and the "fickle finger of fate."

The advantage obtained by the individual who uses projection is that he successfully avoids accepting the responsibility for his own behaviors and is able to avoid some of the feelings of rejection which might come from having socially unacceptable thoughts and feelings. The major disadvantage is that such individuals may become constant "fault-finders" and do little or nothing to straighten out the internal problems which make the use of projection necessary.

Fantasy

Fantasy is a defense mechanism which practically everyone employs. In reasonable amounts, daydreaming can be fun and even productive. At one time or another most people have daydreams about being a hero. In his daydreams, an adolescent boy may rescue the girl of his dreams from some terrible situation and thus become her hero and lover. A young girl imagines herself in a dazzling evening gown which causes the teacher upon whom she has a crush to be taken by surprise when he suddenly recognizes how mature and beautiful she really is. Other typical fantasy activity involves a small, skinny child who imagines himself beating up the school bully and thus becoming a hero, or a young man from a poor family seeing himself as becoming rich and powerful.

Perhaps the greatest benefit derived from fantasy is that it can permit temporary escape from painful environmental situations or it can help to achieve solutions to problems which might not otherwise be solved. On the other hand, fantasy can be overdone to the point that one begins to "live in his head" and thus lose touch with reality. When one begins to respond to fantasies as if they were real, one is in psychologic trouble. It is probably not too harmful for a young man to imagine himself as quite rich and important. It is something else, however, when he starts writing checks on his imaginary bank account.

Introjection

Introjection is a defense mechanism whereby an individual incorporates into his own personality structure the attributes of persons or institutions in his environment. A good example of introjection occurs when a person is taken as a political prisoner and a year or two later the individual is released and appears to have been "brainwashed" by his captors. That is, he appears to have accepted their ideals and ideas. The expression "If you can't beat them, join them" is a popular concept which expresses the use of this defense mechanism. A young man who is beaten up by a bully may subsequently become friends with him. The idea of peer group pressure is also an expression of this defense mechanism.

The basic idea in introjection is to protect oneself from threatening circumstances by attuning oneself to the ideas and characteristics of the environment so as to lessen the threat.

The advantage in using this mechanism is that it allows one to survive in some situations which might otherwise be destructive. Perhaps the greatest disadvantage is that if one is suddenly thrown into another culture or a different environment, those traits and behaviors which have been introjected may no longer be appropriate and may create adjustment problems.

Reaction Formation

Reaction formation is a defense mechanism whereby one denies unacceptable feelings and impulses by adopting conscious behaviors which, at least on the surface, appear to be contradictory to the thoughts, feelings, and impulses. A reformed alcoholic may become a teetotaler and spend a great deal of time and effort preaching against the ills of alcohol. The sexually promiscuous husband may spend hours lecturing his teenage daughter against the evils of sex. The "good Christian person" may be a malicious gossiper, and the businessman who always has a lecture ready about the poor morals of other businessmen may be found to short-change customers in one way or another. It is interesting to note that there is some evidence to indicate that public censors who protect us from the evils of sex and violence in movies, magazines and television have a hard time not enjoying their jobs. The Shakespearean quote from *Macbeth* aptly summarizes this defense mechanism, "Methinks the lady doth protest too much." It is one thing to be genuinely concerned about a particular issue. It is something else to be obsessed with it.

It is undoubtedly true that persons with reaction formations control some of their more unacceptable impulses. It is quite likely, however, that they would be much more comfortable with themselves and much more tolerant of other people if they could resolve the internal conflicts which make the use of reaction formation necessary.

Regression

Regression is a defense against anxiety or threatening situations which permits the individual to go backward in development to a time when one felt more at ease and more capable of handling the environment. This, of course, permits escape from the painful situations in the present and allows enjoyment of the relative peace and quiet of the stage of regression. Perhaps the most obvious case of regression is one in which an adult begins to behave in a childlike manner.

One of the more common examples occurs when a 3- or 4-year-old who has been toilet trained begins to wet himself and to talk baby talk when a newborn baby is brought into the home. Other examples of this at a more advanced age occur when people become highly dependent and demanding when they are threatened. Regression frequently occurs when patients are hospitalized.

Another form of regression is seen when individuals have grown up and gotten into the business world. They subsequently decide to "get out of the rat race" and go back to a more simple form of living. Frequently they go to rural areas and become farmers or, in some cases, choose to live in communes. The idea of "getting back to nature" expresses the desire to go back to a simpler time and to escape the complexities of a highly technologic world.

Sublimation

Sublimation is a defense mechanism which allows an individual to divert unacceptable impulses and motives into socially acceptable channels. Rather than becoming a peeping Tom or a simple voyeur, an individual may become an artist and draw nudes, a physician, or a photographer for *Playboy* magazine. As a matter of fact, *Playboy* magazine, at least in some circles, is a socially acceptable form of voyeurism. The popularity of X-rated videocassettes would seem to suggest that satisfaction of voyeuristic impulses is substantial. They are said to account for greater than 70 percent of all videocassette sales.

Other examples of sublimation occur when individuals with very strong aggressive impulses become football players or hockey players, or participate in other physically violent activities which are sanctioned by society.

The advantages of sublimation are obvious in that they allow expression of questionable desires and impulses in socially acceptable ways. The disadvantage might come when the drives are so strong that even the sublimation is not sufficient to control the impulses.

Restitution

The defense mechanism of restitution permits one to atone for things that he has done which he may feel are unacceptable. For example, the individual who gets his wealth by highly questionable means may become the greatest benefactor of an orphanage or otherwise contribute great sums of money to charity. This defense mechanism is sometimes referred to as "undoing" and its aim is to reduce the guilt and anxiety experienced by the individual for having engaged in behaviors which he now views as unacceptable.

Displacement

Displacement is a defense mechanism in which the individual transfers his hostile and aggressive feelings from one object to another object or person. A classic example of this mechanism occurs when a man comes home from work after having been chewed out by his boss and spies Fido lying in front of the door. Poor Fido gets a swift kick, gets yelled at, and slinks away wondering what in the world he did to deserve such treatment. Other examples, of course, include the wife and kids being yelled at as a result of some frustration the husband or father experienced in his work, or the husband getting yelled at because of a very frustrating day his wife had.

The advantage of displacement, of course, is that one can stay on good terms with the offending person thus avoiding the possibilities of being fired or otherwise facing the wrath of the offending person. On the other hand, if displacement becomes a way of life, alienation of friends or family members is probable.

The great effort at improving communications between people in business and other areas attests to the fact that it is important to learn to communicate feelings with the people involved in the interaction. It is discomforting to be yelled at and not know why.

NEUROSIS AND PSYCHOSIS

Now that we have covered the major defense mechanisms, the next step is to try to discover how these defense mechanisms are related to psychopathology. For all psychologic disorders which are functional in nature (that is, not related to physical or organic causes), we must presume that stressful situations are responsible for maladaptive behavior. Most authorities have suggested that the concepts of threat, anxiety, and malfunctioning defense systems are very much related to development of abnormal behavior. Therefore, when an individual tries to use his defense mechanisms to ward off feelings of anxiety or threat but cannot do so either because his defense mechanisms are not strong enough or they are generally inadequate, there is an increase in both anxiety and the inappropriate use of defense mechanisms. If the individual is unable to deal with the anxiety-provoking problem through his defense systems, he is likely to develop more and more inappropriate and maladaptive behavior which will result in the collapse of his biologic, psychologic, and sociologic functioning. It is at this point that "symptom formation" begins to occur.

Depending upon how well the defense system is able to handle threat and anxiety which generate stress on the defense system protecting the individual's psychological structure, the individual may simply experience a mildly disruptive interpersonal relationship problem or he may experience severe personality decompensation to the point of losing contact with reality.

The difference between experiencing mild personality decompensation and severe personality decompensation is generally described by the terms neurosis and psychosis. In a *neurosis,* the individual experiences mild interference with his social relationships, his occupational pursuits and his sexual adjustment. He is rarely dangerous to himself or to society. The neurotic patient usually maintains contact with reality although there is often some distortion in the concept of reality. The neurotic patient usually realizes that he has some emotional problems and may have some insight into the nature of his problems. He is usually well oriented in time, person, place, and so forth, and does not have delusions or hallucinations. He does often show various symptoms such as obsessions, compulsions, phobias, and hysteric paralyses. Except in severe cases, neurotic patients do not require hospitalization and many neurotic patients go through life without obtaining any help for their problems.

On the other hand, in *psychosis,* the patient frequently experiences a severe personality decompensation which interferes with vocational pursuits, interpersonal relationships, and, of course, contact with reality is poor. In fact, in most cases of psychosis, there is a definite split between the reality of the world and reality for the patient. The psychotic patient frequently loses track of time, place and person. Psychotic patients usually require hospitalization and their behavior is sometimes injurious to themselves and other people. Psychotic patients rarely have any insight whatsoever into the nature of their behavior and, in fact, frequently insist that there is nothing wrong with them and that they should be released. Table 1 summarizes the different characteristics of neurotic and psychotic patients.

This chapter has presented the concepts necessary for the formation of a framework from which to view the different types of mental illness. The following chapter will discuss specific diagnostic categories and some of the problems inherent in the diagnostic process.

TABLE 1. Characteristics of Neurosis and Psychosis

Factor	Neurosis	Psychosis
1. Description	A neurosis usually causes a loss of personal efficiency and a decrease in activity. Some personality disorganization may be present. Neurotics frequently have some insight into the fact that they have emotional problems.	A psychosis is characterized by serious personality disorganization. Impaired memory, perception and judgment are often apparent. Patient may have difficulty recognizing that they are emotionally ill.
2. Symptoms	Various complaints about nervousness, emotional upset, physical illnesses (with little organic basis), poor self-esteem, and feelings of worthlessness. Hallucinations do not occur.	Reality testing is impaired. Hallucinations, delusions, and bizarre bodily sensations occur frequently. A lack of reality contact is apparent.
3. Social Elements	Social relationships are likely to show some deterioration but are not likely to be completely disrupted. Patient's behavior is not likely to be injurious to self or others.	Social relationships are likely to be significantly impaired and in some cases totally disrupted. Patients may show behaviors injurious to self or others.
4. Orientation	Patients usually oriented to time, place, and person. Patient's behavior will probably not seem especially peculiar.	Patients frequently disoriented as to time, place, and person. Patient's behavior may appear to be quite odd or peculiar.
5. Therapeutic Measures	Usually treated in outpatient facilities, and many neurotic people receive no treatment at all. Only the most severe cases require hospitalization.	Frequently requires hospitalization but may be maintained in outpatient facilities.

ANNOTATED BIBLIOGRAPHY

Elliott, S.M.: *Denial as an effective mechanism to allay anxiety following a stressful event.* Journal of Psychosocial Nursing and Mental Health Services, 18(10):11–15, 1980.

Deals with the positive aspects of the use of denial as a coping mechanism. Describes the differences between beneficial denial and detrimental denial.

Hagerty, B.K.: *Denial isn't all bad.* Nursing '80, 10(10):58–60, 1980.

Guidelines for aiding a patient working through denial. Describes the constructive use of denial in protecting the individual against an overpowering threat.

Peterson, M.H.: *Understanding Defense Mechanisms.* American Journal of Nursing, 72:1651–74, 1972.

Programmed instruction on defense mechanisms that allows reader to actively respond to material presented.

Smitherman, C.: *Dealing with the patient's denial—What should you do?* Nursing '81, 11(12):70–71, 1981.

Techniques to deal with the patient utilizing the defense mechanism of denial.

Tatro, S.E., and Marshall, J.N.: *Regression: A defense mechanism for the dying older adult.* Journal of Gerontological Nursing, 8(1):20-22, 1982.

Differentiates between senile dementia and the defense mechanism of regression in the older adult who is unable to face impending death.

Witt, J.: *Transference and countertransference in group therapy settings.* Journal of Psychosocial Nursing and Mental Health Services, 20(2):31–34, 1982.

Defines and provides examples of these two defense mechanisms in group therapy situations.

Woosley, D.G.: *A working concept of intellectualization.* Journal of Psychosocial Nursing and Mental Health Services, 18(1):36–39, 1980.

Describes the defense mechanism of intellectualization and provides nursing implications.

41

POST-TEST

Chapter 3

Basic Concepts of the Mind

Matching. Match the defense mechanism listed in Column B with the appropriate statement listed in Column A. There is only one defense mechanism for each descriptive statement.

Column A

_____ 1. Denies unacceptable feelings and impulses by adopting conscious behaviors which are contradictory to the thoughts, feelings and impulses.

_____ 2. Blames others for personal inadequacies or guilt feelings.

_____ 3. Refuses to see what is obvious to everyone else.

_____ 4. "Forgets" or excludes from conscious thought things too painful or anxiety provoking to remember.

_____ 5. Unacceptable impulses diverted into socially acceptable channels.

_____ 6. "Undoing."

_____ 7. Transference of hostile and aggressive feelings from one object to another object or person.

_____ 8. Going backwards in one's development.

Column B

A. Repression
B. Displacement
C. Projection
D. Restitution
E. Denial
F. Regression
G. Reaction formation
H. Introjection
I. Sublimation
J. Fantasy
K. Supression
L. Identification
M. Conversion

True or False. Circle your choice.

T   F   1. The emotionally healthy person is accepting of himself and others.

T F 2. The inability to accept authority or make decisions for oneself is a sign of good mental health.
T F 3. Our self-image is basically the ideas we have about what kind of person we are.
T F 4. Defense mechanisms are always healthy.
T F 5. To be effective, defense mechanisms must be consciously used.
T F 6. Psychotic patients rarely have insight into the nature of their behavior.

Fill in the Blanks. From the group of terms listed on the right, select the letter of the most appropriate term to complete the following sentences.

1. _____ is a term used to indicate that a person is no longer emotionally able to deal with the stress and strain of everyday life.
2. If a person's defenses work adequately and he seems to get along reasonably well in everyday life, he is said to be _____.
3. There are two major classifications of maladjustments: _____ and _____ maladjustment.
4. Defense mechanisms are sometimes called _____ mechanisms.
5. _____ is sometimes called the granddaddy of all the defense mechanisms.

A. adjusted
B. neurotic
C. psychopathology
D. denial
E. coping
F. psychotic
G. repression
H. insane
I. normal

Multiple Choice. Circle the letter you think represents the best answer.
1. The mentally healthy individual has the capacity to:
   1. Accept his strengths and weaknesses.
   2. Love others.
   3. Have effective conscience.
   4. Tolerate stress and frustration.
      A. 1 and 2.
      B. 1 and 3.
      C. 1, 2, and 3.
      D. All of the above.
2. When observing behavior, the nurse should remember that behavioral symptoms:

1. Have meaning.
2. Are purposeful.
3. Are multidetermined.
4. Can easily be understood.
   A. 2 only.
   B. 1 and 3.
   C. 1, 2, and 3.
   D. All of the above.

Situation: Mrs. White is in the hospital for diagnostic tests. She says to you, "Yesterday my doctor told me he was referring me to a psychiatrist. There's nothing wrong with me that any psychiatrist can cure. I'm here to find out why I've been getting these backaches and that's all."

3. Mrs. White may be using the defense mechanisms(s) of:
   A. Denial.
   B. Conversion reaction.
   C. Regression.
   D. A and B.
   E. B and C.

4. Your most therapeutic response to Mrs. White would be:
   A. "I can see why this would be upsetting, but don't worry. Everything will turn out all right."
   B. "I'm sure he had a good reason for suggesting this, so try not to be upset about it."
   C. "I have some time now. Could you tell me some of your feelings about seeing a psychiatrist?"
   D. "The x-rays of your back show nothing is wrong there."

5. Being referred to a psychiatrist may be perceived by Mrs. White as a threat to her:
   A. Self-esteem.
   B. Security.
   C. Identity.
   D. Independence.

6. Many people experience compulsions in everyday life. In the following examples, which actions would be fairly normal (not neurotic)?
   1. Habitually emptying ashtrays in the living room before retiring.
   2. Carrying soap and towel around and washing one's hand to the extent that no other activity is possible.
   3. Picking up every piece of paper one sees all day.
   4. Having a morning routine in order to get to work on time.
      A. 1 only.
      B. 2 and 3.
      C. 1 and 4.
      D. All of these.

7. Mental processes and behavior that serve to protect our self-esteem by defending us against excessive anxiety are:
   A. General adaptation syndrome.
   B. Psychological adaptation process.
   C. Defense mechanism.
   D. Stressor reactors.
   E. Flight and fight response.

8. Which of the following are true of defense mechanisms?
   1. To resolve intrapsychic conflicts.
   2. Minimize or eliminate anxiety.
   3. May operate unconsciously.
   4. May operate consciously.
   5. Are the same as mental mechanisms.
      A. 1, 3, 4, and 5.
      B. 1, 2, 3, and 4.
      C. 2, 3, 4, and 5.
      D. 1, 2, 3, and 5.
      E. 1, 2, 3, 4, and 5.

9. A patient has been told by her doctor that she needs to have surgery. This thought is very upsetting to her. She leaves the doctor's office and says to herself, "I won't think about it now. I'll do some shopping instead." She is utilizing which defense mechanism?
   A. Repression.
   B. Identification.
   C. Sublimation.
   D. Regression.
   E. Suppression.

10. A man is reprimanded by his boss. He comes home and proceeds to kick the family dog. This is an example of:
    A. Identification.
    B. Repression.
    C. Introjection.
    D. Suppression.
    E. Displacement.

11. Jane has done poorly on an examination. When asked about it, she replied, "I couldn't help it. I had planned to study all day Sunday and then my relatives came and stayed all day so I couldn't study." She is using the defense mechanism of:
    A. Compensation.
    B. Fantasy.
    C. Rationalization.
    D. Reaction formation.

12. Johnny was the shortest boy in the class and could never do well in

athletics. However, he worked very hard at his studies and achieved the honor roll. The defense mechanism here is:
A. Substitution.
B. Fixation.
C. Displacement.
D. Compensation.

13. Mrs. Green is a patient who is scheduled for shock treatment. Miss Jaynes, a new staff member, becomes very anxious and is unable to help with the treatment. She is using:
A. Identification.
B. Denial.
C. Regression.
D. Suppression.

14. A patient is angry because he was hit by a car and injured for several weeks. His wife is working and taking care of their three small children at home. He directs his angry energy into pounding designs into leather wallets. He then sends the small amount of money home, thus making him feel better. This is an example of:
A. Displacement.
B. Identification.
C. Sublimation.
D. Regression.
E. Suppression.

15. A person who consciously acts ill to avoid an unpleasant experience is referred to as a:
A. Neurotic.
B. Hypochondriac.
C. Malingerer.
D. Procrastinator.

16. Which of the following is true of neurosis?
1. Profound withdrawal from people.
2. Impared but not prevented occupational efficiency.
3. Fragmentation of thought processes.
4. Severe distortion in memory.
5. May cause short-term memory problems.
   A. 1, 2, 3, and 5.
   B. 2 and 5.
   C. 2, 3, and 4.
   D. 3, 4, and 5.
   E. 2 only.

17. Which of the following are true of psychosis?
1. Possible illusions and hallucinations.
2. No impairment in judgment.

3. Awareness of personality disorder.
4. Withdrawal from reality.
5. Distorted affect.
    A. All of the above.
    B. 2, 4, and 5.
    C. 1, 3, and 5.
    D. 1, 4, and 5.
    E. None of the above.
18. Psychotic patterns of response are:
    A. Not as severe as neurotic disturbance.
    B. Involve minor defects in reality testing.
    C. Characterized only by hallucinating behavior.
    D. Disturbances in total personality functioning.

4

Understanding the Patient's Diagnosis

OBJECTIVES: Student will be able to:
1. Define and describe the DSM III.
2. Define generalized anxiety disorder, conversion disorder, dissociative disorder, phobic disorders, obsessive-compulsive disorder, dysthmic disorder, organic and functional psychoses, schizophrenia, paranoia, and antisocial personality disorder.
3. List five sexual behavior patterns that are considered deviant.

A diagnosis is used primarily by members of a treatment team as a shorthand method of describing a group of behaviors which might be expected from a particular person.

When one describes a patient as depressed, one simply uses that diagnosis to pass along the information that the patient is having trouble sleeping, has lost interest in life, has a poor appetite, may cry a great deal, is generally unhappy, chooses to be alone much of the time, and perhaps has undergone a recent loss.

Frequently, a diagnosis is necessary so that the insurance company can classify the particular disorder that the patient has so that reimbursement can be made to the treatment personnel and to the hospital or clinic. The advent of Diagnostic Related Groups (DRGs) as a basis for third-party reimbursement has also affected the need for accurate diagnosis and assessment. All categories of mental illness fall within one of nine Diagnostic Related Groups. A fixed amount of money is paid for each illness depending upon its DRG classification.

There is a considerable movement in the mental health field to do away with assigning diagnoses to patients. They are criticized as being inaccurate, misleading and potentially damaging. Of course, in many cases, these criticisms are valid. There are incidents of patients treated over a period of years having as many as five or six diagnoses. Of course, it is possible that the diagnostic changes may have been warranted. However, the reason for different diagnoses is frequently that different professionals tend to have favorite diagnostic categories that they prefer for certain classes of behavior. Sometimes the professional doing the diagnosing simply pays special attention to a different set of factors or behavioral characteristics than did the other persons who diagnosed the same patient. Except for some rather specific diagnoses, the reliability of diagnostic categories from one professional to another may be low. This is largely due to the inexact nature of the diagnostic process.

The *Diagnostic and Statistical Manual III* of the American Psychiatric Association attempts to reduce subjectivity in assigning diagnoses. Specific patient behaviors are given significant weight, while psychodynamic formulations are de-emphasized. Hopefully, this will lead to more reliability in assigning diagnoses. However, the success of the DSM-III in improving the diagnostic process has been questioned by some. For the sake of consistency, the terminology used in this chapter to describe complexes of behavior is that suggested by the DSM-III.

NEUROTIC DIAGNOSTIC CATEGORIES

The differences between the neurotic disorders and the psychotic disorders have been discussed in Chapter 3. They are pertinent to the following discussion of the specific diagnostic categories within the broad category of the neurotic disorders. As with almost any behavior, neurotic conditions have their basis in past events and past learning situations. Symptom formation provides neurotic persons with a means of escaping the anxiety which they feel and, in many cases, provides secondary gain, such as sympathy, sick leave, or financial benefits in the form of disability income or workmen's compensation.

It is unlikely that all symptoms exhibited by a patient will fall into any one diagnostic category nor is it particularly unusual for symptoms to change over time from one category to another and different symptoms may be dominant at different times.

Anxiety Disorders

A person suffering from an anxiety neurosis is usually tense, anxious, and worried, but is unable to say exactly why he feels that way. Such patients frequently have a history of having been faced with childhood situations and other life situations which did not provide clear-cut approval or disapproval of their behavior. In addition, they have frequently found themselves in situations in which they were uncertain of what was expected of them.

When an individual is kept in a state of uncertainty, a general fear of one's environment often develops, accompanied by a low frustration level and a tendency to view the world as a hostile, cruel place. These feelings frequently cause the anxious neurotic patient to be uncertain of himself, even in minor stress situations, and to have difficulty concentrating. The anxiety may affect practically all aspects of life. Frequently, in order to avoid anxiety producing situations, the neurotically anxious individual will restrict daily activities so severely that he has a very limited life. The individual is usually unaware of his reasons for restricting his activities; he only knows that he feels more comfortable in highly structured and familiar surroundings. In the process of reducing his anxiety, however, he gives up many of the satisfactions that life has to offer through relationships with other people and with the environment in general.

As the individual tries to restrict his life, he may experience strong anxiety reactions or anxiety attacks which include sweating, difficulty getting his breath, and increased heart rate. Many anxious individuals become dizzy, experience dry mouths, and feel that they are dying. Frequently such patients come to the Emergency Room complaining of heart attacks. In such cases, hospital admission and treatment usually ensues.

A good understanding of the neurotic anxiety reaction is important for two reasons: 1) anxiety reactions constitute probably 30 to 40 per cent of all neurotic disorders, and 2) many elements of the anxiety reaction are seen in patients with other types of neurotic disorders.

Conversion Disorder (Hysterical Neurosis, Conversion Type)

At one point in our country's history, many people believe that being "struck" blind, dumb, speechless, or with a paralysis of some sort was due to the wrath of God or to demonic possession. However, as our society has become more educated, such explanations for the sudden onset of blindness, paralysis, or mutism have given way to more sophisticated explanations. Most people no longer believe that babies are "marked" at birth because the mother was frightened by a bear or was scared by a "devil" or because she had evil thoughts during her pregnancy. Perhaps, because of our increased educational level, such explanations for behavioral characteristics in people have changed although we still see many patients who suffer conversion disorders.

A conversion disorder is an attempt by the individual to defend himself from some anxiety-provoking situation by developing symptoms of a physical disorder which has no underlying organic or physical basis. The symptoms are then said to be *psychogenic* in origin even though they are quite real to the patient. The basic characteristics of this disorder are that the patient loses the ability to perform some physical function which he could perform before the onset of the disorder. The lost function is usually symbolically related to some situation which produces stress or

51

anxiety for the individual. The patient may lose sensitivity in some area of his body, be unable to hear or talk, have unusual sensations such as tingling or burning, or lose the ability to perform some motor function such as walking or the movement of an arm or a hand. Frequently, these behaviors gain sympathy from the family or friends of the individual and thus are reinforced. Such persons are usually first seen by a physician who can find no physical basis for the symptoms. They are then often referred to a neurologist whose tests are also negative. As a last resort, the patient is then referred to a psychologist or a psychiatrist.

A young woman had suddenly become paralyzed from the waist down and was unable to walk. The patient was 18 years old and had already been seen by her family physician and by a neurologist, neither of whom could discover any physical basis for the paralysis. In reviewing the patient's history, the psychologic factors leading to the paralysis were fairly clear-cut. The patient had a younger sister who contracted polio at age 2 and was disabled by the disease. She died at age 15. Due to her disability, most of the family's efforts and attentions were focused on this child and the older girl receivied little attention. Consequently, she developed some rather strong hostile feelings toward her sister. Of course, her hostility could not be expressed directly, and the patient suffered severe guilt feelings for the hostility which she felt.

A few months after her sister died, the patient was involved in an accident in which she was hit by a falling tree limb. The patient did not suffer any significant injury as a result of the accident and no medical follow-up was required. However, several months later, the patient developed the paralysis. The patient's family, being afraid that another tragedy was about to befall one of their children, became quite concerned and showed a great deal of sympathy and attention to the patient.

Several weeks of treatment were required for both the patient and her family before she was able to walk again.

Conversion disorders are not common. They constitute less than 5 per cent of all neurotic reactions and unless one works in a hospital or clinic setting, one may never see a patient in this diagnostic category. Of course, a great many people have headaches, stomach aches, and minor aches and pains which may be related to emotionally stressful situations. It is only when they become severely debilitating that they really affect a person's life.

Perhaps the most important aspect of conversion disorders is that they are caused by situations which an individual perceives as highly stressful and by the person's need to escape from the anxiety and stress created by that situation. The pain or the paralysis which may develop is real to the individual and the fact that it is psychogenic in origin does not diminish the effect of the condition.

Because there is no apparent organic dysfunction, people frequently assume that the patient is faking or that the paralysis or the pain is not real. However, the particular conversion reaction has meaning to the patient and whether or not members of the treatment team understand it, the patient will not be helped by derogatory comments about his illness or by telling him that the illness is "all in his head."

Dissociative Disorders (Hysterical Neurosis, Dissociative Type)

Dissociative disorders form an interesting diagnostic group even though they, too, account for less than 5 per cent of all neurotic reactions. The dissociative disorders are like the conversion disorders in that they frequently occur in the same personality type and both disorders serve to protect the individual from an especially stressful situation. Amnesia, fugue, and multiple personality are the major categories of dissociative reactions along with somnambulism or sleepwalking.

Amnesia is temporarily forgetting information about one's life or environment. The patient usually forgets specific information for a specified but undetermined length of time. For example, a patient may forget his name or a particular period of time in his life, such as a stressful operation or an unhappy family situation. The patient does not, however, forget his basic habits and his basic lifestyle.

In *fugue,* the patient not only has amnesia but combines the amnesia with flight, leaving the area wherein the stressful situation lies. The patient attempts to remove himself both mentally and physically from the stressful situation as a means of reducing his anxiety and fear. The removal, however, is unconscious rather than conscious in that the patient is usually unaware of where he is going or where he has been.

Multiple personalities are perhaps the most famous of all dissociative disorders if you consider the number of television shows, movies, and novels which have been written about people who suffer from this disorder. In reality, there are very few actual cases of true multiple personalities. One of the most famous documented cases of multiple personality is that described in *The Three Faces of Eve* (C. Thigpen and H. M. Cleckly, Regent House). In such cases, an individual usually shows evidence of having different patterns or ways of responding to the environment. Because these ways of responding to the environment are usually quite different, the term *split personality* has been used to refer to the multiple personality disorder. Many people confuse the term split personality with schizophrenia (discussed later in this chapter) but the two disorders are very different.

Usually each individual "personality" within the patient is a complete personality system of its own and the patient responds to the particular personality which is conscious at any given time by allowing that personality system to dominate his behavior or his reactions to his environment. Again, we point out that this is a very rare disorder and regardless of how many such cases one may see on television, it is unlikely that one will encounter a case of multiple personality in one's entire mental health career.

Phobic Disorders (Phobic Neuroses)

Phobias frequently occur in persons who have other personality problems. Phobias are usually described as a persistent and irrational fear of some object, place or condition. Some of the more common phobias are related to high places, thunderstorms, closed places, being alone, crowds, darkness, and syphilis. The particular object of an individual's phobia is usually not actually related to that object but represents a displacement of anxiety from the original cause to the phobic object. The phobia helps the individual by allowing him to avoid the anxiety-provoking situation. For this reason, the phobia usually has symbolic significance to the individual. For example, a young man who is fearful of his hostile impulses which involve fantasies about shooting his father may develop a phobia of guns. He is not actually afraid of guns but displaces his fear of killing his father to guns. By avoiding all guns he tries to avoid the anxiety associated with thoughts of killing his father. If untreated, a phobic person's fears may generalize to other related areas and may lead to increased isolation from relationships.

In all phobias, the basic elements involved are a persistent, strong, and irrational fear of some object or situation. Because of the tendency for a phobia to generalize or to become associated with objects other than the original phobic object, it sometimes is difficult to discover the symbolic significance of a particular phobic reaction. From a therapeutic standpoint, it should be recognized that phobias often generate feelings of dependency and helplessness in individuals and they are likely to need support and encouragement from the treatment team. It is also important to remember that phobias protect the individual from anxiety and that the individual does not understand the phobia any better than anybody else, and probably not as well as members of the treatment team. Except under controlled treatment procedures, exposure to the phobia is not helpful to the patient. Reassurance, support, and acceptance of the patient as well as psychotherapeutic efforts on the part of the staff are necessary for a return to adequate functioning by the patient.

Obsessive-Compulsive Disorders (Obsessive-Compulsive Neuroses)

Patients experiencing an obsessive-compulsive disorder are unable to prevent thoughts or ideas which they do not wish to think about, or to keep from engaging in some repetitive behavioral act. The patients usually recognize the fact that the thought or behaviors are irrational but are unable to prevent them.

As with most other disorders, there are specific behavioral characteristics associated with obsessive-compulsive patients. They tend to be neat, perfectionistic, usually rather rigid, and sometimes obstinate. They very often have difficulty making up their minds and thus are unable to make decisions effectively. These patients may tend to blurt out particular statements or words and seem unable to control themselves. They may also show a strong need for structure or for doing things in a specific way, at a certain time, or in a certain position. Although obsessive thoughts include a wide range of subjects, the most common concerns are about bodily functions, right and wrong, religion, and suicidal thoughts.

In patients experiencing compulsive disorder, there is a strong desire to repeat some particular behavior or action or to repeat a series of behaviors. Frequently the patients believe something drastic will happen to them if they do not carry out their rituals. One patient had a particular series of behaviors which he felt he had to complete before going to bed each night. If he did not complete his routine, he believed that something terrible would happen to him and his anxiety level became so high that he could not sleep. His ritual included crossing his left leg over his right leg twice, lacing his left shoe lace inside his shoe, and placing the left shoe string across the laces of the shoe. He would also face the door and bow three times as well as recite a short poem that he had learned. Eventually, with therapy, he was able to relinquish most of his ritual but he maintained some of the behaviors and added others from time to time.

Of course, many of us engage in minor obsessive-compulsive behavior patterns when we are under stress or when we wish to accomplish a certain goal. As long as the obsessive-compulsive behavior patterns are relatively temporary and help us obtain our goal, there is probably no cause for great concern. However, when they begin to unduly restrict one's behavior, treatment is indicated.

In dealing with the obsessive-compulsive patients in a treatment center, it is important to recognize that they are highly sensitive to stressful or threatening situations. One can expect these patients to try to rearrange their environment in an attempt to impose structure and rigidity so that they can control what happens. If they believe they can control their environment, they feel safer. The rituals and the behaviors of obsessive-compulsive individuals are designed to help them make adjustments to the dangers and threats which they perceive as being all about them. Kindness, reassurance and tolerance are necessary staff behaviors when treating these patients.

Dysthymic Disorders (Depressive Neurosis)

In dysthymic disorders, there is an increase in the intensity of normal grief reactions. Grief is a normal reaction to a loss suffered by an individual, but it is usually relatively brief and the individual learns to establish new ways of behaving and forms new relationships which help to gradually lessen the pain the individual felt over the initial loss. Some researchers have suggested that persons who are prone to have dysthymic disorders are unable to bounce back from disturbing or discouraging events, and that these individuals tend to overreact to stressful situations, losses, or discouraging events. Personality traits such as a tendency to be self-degrading, a poor self-concept, and exaggerated dependency needs are characteristic of patients who suffer from depressive reactions. A final factor frequently associated with persons who suffer depressive reactions is a tendency to feel guilty about almost anything, and to turn these guilt feelings against themselves in such a way that they become very self-punitive.

The possibility of suicide must be considered when working with depressed patients since the tendency for guilt feelings to overwhelm these patients may lead them to try to take their life either as a means of escaping the anxiety caused by the guilt or as a means of atoning for their supposed transgressions.

PSYCHOTIC DIAGNOSTIC CATEGORIES

The psychoses are generally divided into two categories, the *organic psychoses* and the *functional psychoses*. Organic psychoses are those caused by some disorder of the brain for which physical pathology can be demonstrated. The functional psychoses are psychotic disorders which are caused by psychologic stress. That is, they occur in response to psychologic stresses and in the absence of demonstrated neurologic pathology. In both categories, patients exhibit bizarre behavior and are obviously ill. One is much more likely to notice the strangeness of a psychotic person's behavior than to notice a patient with a neurosis. This is largely due to the fact that the psychotic patient's behavior differs a great deal from the so-called "normal" behavior of human beings. A third category of psychotic reactions is sometimes used when mental health teams wish to separate psychotic reactions caused by toxic substances. These are called *toxic psychoses* and are generally caused by the ingestion of drugs or poisons of some type.

In psychotic reactions, as opposed to neurotic reactions, it is important to realize that the patient is not dealing with reality. The reality which the individual experiences is unique to him and is not the same reality that a healthy person experiences. To the psychotic patient, the spiders he sees on his arm are real and the person to whom he is talking, but who is unseen by others, is also real. The voices that psychotic patients hear are real to them, and they are sincerely convinced that they are Jesus Christ or Napoleon or a prophet or an F.B.I. agent. Arguing with the patients or trying to logically demonstrate that their perception of reality is in error is of very little benefit. This is primarily true because "logical" arguments by staff members appeal to a reality which does not exist for the patient. He just does not see the world in the same way that staff members do.

Since the difference's between neuroses and psychoses have been discussed previously in Chapter 3, what follows is a description of the different psychotic reactions. They are presented in order that one may develop some familiarity with the major diagnostic classifications of psychotic disorders.

Schizophrenic Disorders

Schizophrenia is the largest single diagnostic group of psychotic patients. Approximately 1 per cent of the people in the U.S. suffer from schizophrenia, and schizophrenia accounts for approximately 25 per cent of all first admissions to mental hospitals. There are many different classifications. In *schizotypal personality disorder,* the patient shows a marked loss of interest in the environment and is shy and withdrawn. There is a noticeable lack of emotional contact with other people. The *paranoid schizophrenic* often shows much hostility and suspiciousness and may show a great deal of overt aggression. The glaring intenseness of many of these patients has often led people to refer to the "paranoid stare" as a characteristic of the paranoid schizophrenic. In *disorganized schizophrenia,* patients may appear manic and have bizarre mannerisms. They often laugh and giggle inappropriately and are preoccupied with trivial things. They represent one of the most severely disorganized personality structures in the schizophrenic group. The *catatonic schizophrenic* is quite striking because of the extreme nature of the person's withdrawal. Catatonic patients may refuse to eat and may remain motionless for hours or days. The two phases of catatonia are the *stuporous phase* wherein the patient is motionless and *catatonic excitement* wherein the patient is overactive, shouts, talks, paces, and appears quite manic. Patients may alternate between these phases but most seem to show a preference for one or the other. In *schizoaffective schizophrenia,* a significant thought disorder is apparent along with a significant mood variation. These patients may at first appear to be merely depressed or manic but further inquiry reveals a basic personality disorganization. In *undifferentiated schizophrenia,* there are prominent delusions or hallucinations, incoherence, or other evidence of grossly disorganized behavior that does not meet the criteria for other types of schizophrenia or meets the criteria for more than one.

The general symptoms exhibited by schizophrenic patients include an inability to deal with reality (sometimes called withdrawal from reality), the presence of delusions and/or hallucinations, inappropriate affect, autism, and various other unusual behaviors such as giggling inappropriately, making meaningless signs, and engaging in meaningless speech or verbal garbage. There is usually a noticeable inability on the part of the patient to organize his thoughts. In fact, difficulty with thought processes is one of the cardinal signs of schizophrenia.

Schizophrenic reactions may occur suddenly, in which case they are referred to as being *acute* schizophrenic reactions. They may also be of long duration and may develop slowly over a rather lengthy period of time. In this latter case, they are called *chronic* schizophrenic reactions.

Contrary to what many people in the general population believe, a very large percentage of patients admitted to hospitals with a psychotic disorder recover and are able to once again function effectively. After a sufficient period of recovery, many patients suffering from acute schizophrenic disorders are able to resume their lives and to make a fairly good adjustment subsequent to hospitalization.

In general, most authorities are uncertain about why people develop schizophrenia. Hereditary factors have been linked to schizophrenia and research suggests that individuals may be predisposed to develop schizophrenia under stressful environmental conditions. Factors such as family behavioral patterns and other sociologic and cultural differences have been designated as causative factors of schizophrenia. It seems more likely, however, that schizophrenia is the result of a complex relationship between biologic, psychologic, and sociologic factors.

Paranoid Disorders

Paranoid patients are frequently disliked by staff members, other patients, their family, and everyone in general because they are so very difficult to get along with and are frequently quite hostile. They are resentful and usually mistrust the motives of almost everyone. Frequently they are overly concerned with religious issues and with issues of right and wrong. Paranoid patients may also show signs of grandiosity and persecution. Delusions of reference, in which the patient believes that whatever happens is related to him, are also common. For example, a patient may believe that two staff members talking at the nurse's station are talking about him, or that if a horn blows, someone is blowing for him to come outside.

A major difference between paranoid patients and paranoid schizophrenics is that the paranoid patient usually has better intellectual control and is able to make more appropriate intellectual and social responses. Compared with paranoid schizophrenics, paranoid patients are usually more reality-oriented. Except in the area of their delusions, their intellectual capacities are much better organized and they are able to present their feelings in a much more effective manner.

One of the most important things for a mental health worker to recognize is that paranoid patients have tremendous difficulty recognizing their own hostilities and anger, and that they tend to project their anger onto others. The defense mechanism of projection is used heavily by the paranoid patient, helping to prevent him from having to recognize his own anger and hostility. The paranoid patient will frequently do something deliberately to anger a staff member or a fellow patient in order to confirm his delusion that other people do not like him or are angry at him. If the staff member or fellow patient responds in an angry fashion, the paranoid patient feels that his original belief was correct and justified.

In general, paranoid patients are rather difficult to deal with. However, they represent a very small percentage of psychiatric patients and probably account for less than 1 per cent of all psychiatric admissions.

Affective Disorders

The affective disorders are so named because they represent a change in the affect (mood) of the individual. The affective disorders in DSM-III are divided into three major groups: 1) *major affective disorders*, in which there is a full affective syndrome, 2) *other specific affective disorders*, in which there is only a partial affective syndrome that has lasted for at least two years, and 3) *atypical affective disorders*, for mood disturbances not classified in the first two categories.

Under *major affective disorders*, the DSM-III lists two classes, *bipolar disorders* and *major depression*, based on whether or not there has ever been a manic episode. *Bipolar disorders* are further divided into *bipolar mixed*, *bipolar manic*, and *bipolar depressed*. *Major depression* is further classified as *single episode* or *recurrent*.

In the bipolar disorders, there is a cycling of manic and depressive phases. In the *manic phase*, the patient is usually extremely elated, agitated, or talkative, and very active physically and verbally. Behavior frequently shows elements of grandiosity. In the *depressive phase*, the patient sits alone, talks very little, looks sad, and refuses to eat.

Under other specific affective disorders are *cyclothymic disorder* and *dysthymic disorder*. Symptoms are not of sufficient severity or duration to be classified as major affective disorders but do reflect symptoms characteristic of both manic and depressive syndromes.

SELECTED PERSONALITY DISORDERS

This category includes patterns of behavior which are neither psychotic nor neurotic but which are nonetheless maladaptive. This group of disorders includes the antisocial reactions, the sexual deviations, and the abuse of alcohol and other drugs. Personality disturbances in this group are usually long standing and frequently are apparent from early adolescence. Since the alcohol and other drug abuses will be presented in a later chapter, only the antisocial reactions and sexual deviations are considered here.

Antisocial (Sociopathic) Personality Disorder

This personality type is characterized primarily by a lack of what most people call a conscience. Such individuals fail to develop a concern for the welfare of others and use relationships to get what they want. There is little or no concern for what effect their behavior might have on others and they seldom feel remorse or guilt.

They are frequently friendly, outgoing, likable, intelligent people who can be quite charming. Their relationships with others, however, tend to be quite superficial because they lack the capacity for deep emotional responses. Sexual activity is usually for the sake of sex and is not used as a means of expressing affection or intimacy. Sexual activity is carried out with many different people and usually with little regard for the partner's satisfaction.

Sociopaths have great difficulty learning or profiting from experience and they are often at odds with authority figures, especially the police. They have difficulty holding jobs because of conflicts with supervisors. They are unreliable, untruthful, undependable, and insincere. Because the sociopath does not feel "responsible," he is often impulsive and seeks immediate gratification of his wants. There is little or no concept of the need to delay or put off anything even though it might be beneficial in the long run to do so.

A large number of people in our society have sociopathic traits which, as with most other personality characteristics, vary in number and severity. Sociopaths are found in all professions although many manage to contain their acting out behaviors because they are intelligent enough to be aware of the external controls placed on them by society. They avoid acting out not because of internal values or controls but because they do not wish to be punished. It is also true that the more intelligent a sociopath is, the better he is able to find socially acceptable ways to meet his needs and wants.

Sociopaths have a very low frustration tolerance and find it difficult to work at any task for a prolonged period. They are easily bored and continually seek excitement. When they are unable to manipulate their environment to meet their wishes, they may threaten suicide. Many

60

sociopaths die by accident as a result of a manipulative suicidal gesture. Such a case occurred when a young girl broke up with her boyfriend. He tried to get her to come back to him and when she refused, he impulsively told her he was going to kill himself. He jumped in his car and in full view of the girl headed straight for a high bank at the edge of a large lake. Although he tried to swerve away before he got to the edge, the car turned over and rolled over the bank into the water. He was trapped inside the car and drowned before he could be rescued.

The sociopath usually comes to treatment as a result of having been "caught" in some fashion. He may have committed either a minor or major crime, in which case he will be sent for evaluation by the court, he may have attempted suicide, or he may have been required to seek treatment by an employer or family member. He can be expected to continue his manipulative ways with the clinic or hospital staff and to show very little positive change. Sociopathic behavior patterns are difficult to alter and show poor response to therapeutic intervention. External controls are necessary to control the sociopath's acting out behavior and often represent the only means of effectively controlling the sociopath. The lack of a social conscience prevents the normal use of guilt and the desire for approval from being effective controlling mechanisms.

Although many factors are important in determining one's personality structure, the sociopathic person usually has a history of not being required to live within defined limits and of not having to face the consequences of his behavior. There is usually a history of a distant parent-child relationship which lacked warmth, intimacy, and genuine emotion. Severe conflicts between parents may also lead to the development of sociopathic behavior since such conflicts leave the growing child with no choice but to learn to manipulate in order to avoid being rejected by one or both parents.

In summary, the sociopathic patient is often well liked by staff members. He is usually helpful and friendly and provides the staff a lot of verbal reinforcement. He learns to speak the language of psychology and can often report his personality dynamics as thoroughly as his therapist. He can make great promises and build great dreams but when the time comes to face reality, he can usually be found going merrily on his charming way, never giving a thought to the lies he told, the hearts he broke, or the misery he caused.

Psychosexual Disorders

The diagnosis of sexual deviation is reserved for those persons who fail to develop what society deems as appropriate patterns of sexual behavior. What is appropriate is determined by the society in which one lives and there is usually some distinction between the relatively mild sexual

61

deviations, such as voyeurism, and the more serious sexual deviations, such as child molestation and rape. Many sexual behavior patterns which were considered deviant in the past are not considered deviant by most people in our present society. Masturbation, the manual or mechanical stimulation of one's gentials for the purpose of obtaining sexual pleasure, is one of the most notable examples of this change. Masturbation is not considered abnormal unless it is used to totally replace sexual activity with another person. Homosexuality, being sexually attracted to a person of the same sex, is another example.

Many people have the misconception that violent, unrestrained behavior is characteristic of sexual deviates. Actually, research indicates that most sexual deviates are rather reserved and timid, and have a great deal of difficulty interacting effectively with people of either sex. The more serious and the more persistent the sexual deviation, the more difficulty the individual is likely to experience in other areas of his life. A few of the major deviations are defined briefly below. If more in-depth information is desired, a good abnormal psychology text should be consulted.

Transvestism. Transvestism is a disorder in which sexual gratification is obtained by wearing the clothing of the opposite sex. Transsexualism is sometimes associated with transvestism. Transsexualism involves a more drastic form of changing one's sexual identity by actually changing the anatomical structure of the individual to that of the opposite sex.

Exhibitionism. This disorder involves the attainment of sexual gratification by exposing one's genitals to another person. Male exhibitionism involves the display of the male genitals primarily to women or children. There are few reported cases of female exhibitionism. However, females who are exhibitionists may find a socially appropriate outlet for exhibiting themselves, such as becoming a stripper.

Sadism. This sexual deviation occurs when one is able to obtain sexual gratification only through the mechanism of inflicting physical or mental pain on another individual. The most deviant example of this category is the person who can receive sexual pleasure only from drawing blood from the tortured individual or even causing the death of an individual. Sadism is usually practiced with a masochistic partner.

Masochism. This term refers to the attainment of sexual satisfaction by being physically or mentally abused. Inflicted pain becomes a source of pleasure and sexual excitement. Masochism may range from something as simple as needing a "cave man" approach to sexual activity to the necessity for severe punishment before sexual gratification is achieved. It is diagnosed only when such punishment is necessary for sexual fulfillment.

Voyeurism. Voyeurism is the term used when sexual gratification is obtained from observing the sexual organs of others or as a result of watching others in the act of sexual behavior or sexual intercourse. Many people enjoy viewing the nude bodies of members of the opposite sex and this is not voyeurism unless the voyeuristic desires exceed the individual's desire for intercourse.

Fetishism. This occurs when a material object, usually a part of the body, some article of clothing, or other object belonging to members of the opposite sex, or in some cases the same sex, produces sexual gratification and fulfillment for an individual.

Pedophilia. This deviation occurs when an adult, usually male, has some form of sexual relationship with a child. This sexual activity may be either heterosexual or homosexual and is said to occur frequently among persons who are unable to obtain sexual gratification with adults because of fears of inadequacy or impotence.

Incest. Incest is the act of engaging in sexual activity with a person who is considered to be a family member. The distance of the relationship that people may have with each other and still engage in socially acceptable sexual relationships is usually defined by the culture in which individuals live.

ANNOTATED BIBLIOGRAPHY

American Psychiatric Association: *Diagnostic and Statistical Manual of Mental Disorders*, ed. 3. APA, Washington, D.C., 1980.

Dixson, D.L.: *Manic depression: An overview.* Journal of Psychosocial Nursing and Mental Health Services, 1981, 19(6):28–31.

General discussion of the etiology, manifestations, and therapy of manic depression.

Hardin, S.B.: *Comparative analysis of nonverbal interpersonal communication of schizophrenics and normals.* Research in Nursing and Health, 1980, 3(2):57–68.

Research study that explores the differences in non-verbal communication in three groups: 1) Normal-normal interaction; 2) Normal-schizophrenic interaction; 3) Schizophrenic-schizophrenic interaction. In particular, engagement behaviors and defensiveness were examined.

Koontz, E.: *Schizophrenia: Current diagnostic concepts and implications for nursing care.* Journal of Psychosocial Nursing and Mental Health Services, 1982, 20(9):44–48.

Explores schizophrenia from the DSM-III multiaxial approach. Describes the various types of schizophrenia: disorganized, paranoid, catatonic, undifferentiated, and residual.

Lynn, L.M.: *Lisa and the 2:00 miracle.* Nursing '80, 1980, 10(5):68–70.

Case study about a 22 year old girl who experiences a sudden, severe psychotic break. Her treatment includes drug therapy, electroconvulsive therapy, and eventually talk therapy.

Schmidt, C.S.: *Withdrawal behavior of schizophrenics: Application of Roy's model.* Journal of Psychosocial Nursing and Mental Health Services, 1981, 19(11):26–33.

Research study that investigates the application of Roy's Adaptation Model in withdrawn schizophrenics. Includes case studies.

Segal, J.S.: *Sexuality normality: What is it?* Health Values, 1980, 4(6):256–261.

Research study that investigates the legal, moral, social, and phylogentic viewpoints of sexual "normalcy."

White, E.M., and Kahn, E.M.: *Use and modifications in group psychotherapy with chronic schizophrenic outpatients.* Journal of Psychosocial Nursing and Mental Health Services, 1982, 20(2):14–20.

Describes the function of group psychotherapy for schizophrenic outpatients. Includes a broad overview of group therapy, roles within the group, and the use of special techniques.

POST-TEST

Chapter 4

Understanding the Patient's Diagnosis

Matching. Match the diagnoses listed in Column B with the appropriate symptoms listed in Column A.

Column A

_____ 1. Person feels tense, anxious or worried but unable to pinpoint exactly why.

_____ 2. Engages in repetitive behavioral acts.

_____ 3. Abnormal continuous grief over a lost one.

_____ 4. General symptoms exhibited are inappropriate affect, autism, and inability to deal with reality.

_____ 5. Show signs of grandiosity and persecution.

_____ 6. Loss of hearing with no physical basis.

_____ 7. Sometimes called "split" personality by laymen.

Column B

A. Obsessive-compulsive

B. Paranoid disorder

C. Conversion disorder

D. Anxiety disorder

E. Dysthymic disorder

F. Schizphrenia

G. Dissociative disorder

True or False. Circle your answer.

T F 1. Diagnostic categories are helpful only for insurance purposes.

T F 2. Diagnosis is necessary because from that diagnosis the mental health worker is able to predict the exact behavior that will be exhibited by the patient.

T F 3. Anxiety disorders constitute approximately 30 to 40 per cent of all neurotic disorders.

T F 4. The obsessive-compulsive person feels that if he isn't allowed to carry out his rituals something drastic will happen to him.

T F 5. The patient with a diagnosis of organic psychosis usually will exhibit more bizarre behavior than the patient with a functional psychosis.

T F 6. Arguing with the psychotic patient in order to make him realize that his thinking is not logical is a major role of the mental health worker in caring for the psychotic patient.
T F 7. Schizophrenia basically means "split personality."
T F 8. Paranoid patients are usually disliked by everyone.
T F 9. Paranoid patients are usually the easiest of all the psychiatric patients to accept and manage.
T F 10. Some authorities feel that the manic phase of a bi-polar disorder is a defense against anxiety.

Short Answer. Answer the following questions as briefly and specifically as possible.

1. Phobias are usually described as _____

_____.

2. Give three of the basic behavioral characteristics associated with the obsessive-compulsive patient.

    1. _____

    2. _____

    3. _____

3. List three of the personal traits one would expect to see in a patient with a diagnosis of dysthymic disorder.

    1. _____

    2. _____

    3. _____

4. One of the most important things a mental health worker can do in caring for the patient with a diagnosis of dysthymic disorder is:

_____

5. What is the basic difference between an organic and functional psychosis?

_____

_____

Multiple Choice. Circle the letter you think represents the best answer.

1. The person diagnosed as paranoid schizophrenic will present all the following symptoms except:
    A. Waxy flexibility.
    B. Extreme suspiciousness.

C. Delusions of persecution.

D. Hallucinations.

2. The most common characteristics of schizophrenia are:

   A. Apathy and autistic thinking.

   B. Flat affect, autistic thinking, ambivalence, and associative looseness.

   C. Ambivalence, ideas of reference, autistic thinking, and associative looseness.

   D. Confabulation and intuition.

3. All of the following statements are generally true of schizotypical personality except:

   A. The patient is often eccentric.

   B. Delusions and hallucinations are rare.

   C. They often become vagrants, wandering from place to place picking up menial jobs.

   D. The onset is sudden.

4. All of the following are considered possible causes of schizophrenia except:

   A. A disturbed mother-infant relationship.

   B. A poorly adjusted family situation.

   C. The precipitating factor may be a situation calling for close interaction with another human being.

   d. Abnormalities in the way the brain is formed.

5. Fifty per cent of the resident population of long-term mental hospitals is comprised of patients with a diagnosis of:

   A. Senile brain disease and cerebral arteriosclerosis.

   B. Schizophrenia.

   C. Alcohol intoxication or addiction.

   D. Personality disorders.

   E. Psychoneurosis.

6. The antisocial individual usually:

   A. Profits from his mistakes.

   B. Assumes responsibility for his own conduct.

   C. Does not feel shame for his conduct.

   D. Is responding to hallucinations.

7. In relating to an antisocial patient, the mental health worker should anticipate that rapport will be established:

   A. Without difficulty, but within a few days.

   B. With difficulty over a long period of time.

   C. With difficulty but within a few days.

   D. Without difficulty within a few hours.

8. Mr. Green is a 24-year-old patient who has been diagnosed as an antisocial personality. Your primary responsibility for him will most likely be to:

A. Set firm and consistent limits on his behavior.

B. Help him to develop insight.

C. Encourage him to get involved in ward activities.

D. Arrange opportunities for him to develop stronger superego controls.

9. *Situation:* Mrs. M., a 23-year-old newlywed was admitted to a psychiatric hospital after a month of unusual behavior which included eating and sleeping very little, talking or singing constantly, charging hundreds of dollars worth of furniture to her father-in-law, and picking up dates on the street. In the hospital, Mrs. M. monopolized conversation, insisted upon unusual privileges, and frequently became demanding, bossy, and sarcastic. She had periods of great overactivity and sometimes became destructive. She frequently used vulgar and profane language. Mrs. M. had formerly been witty, gay, and the "life of the party." Her many friends say she was ladylike in spite of her fun-loving ways and was a kind, sympathetic person. The symptoms which Mrs. M. exhibited are suggestive of which of the following diagnostic entities:

A. Manic bipolar disorder.

B. Schizophrenic disorder.

C. Paranoid disorder.

D. Major depression.

10. Exaggerated mood swings from deep depression to wild excitement are seen in:

A. Anxiety disorders.

B. Schizophrenic disorders.

C. Mixed bipolar disorders.

D. Paranoid disorders.

11. Which of the following are characteristic of the obsessive-compulsive disorder:

1. Flexibility.

2. Enjoyment of people.

3. Excessive conformity to standards.

4. Easily relaxes.

5. Expresses self with difficulty.

A. 1, 3, and 5.

B. 3, 4, and 5.

C. 2 and 4.

D. 3 and 5.

E. None of the above.

12. One of the major personality characteristics of an obsessive-compulsive patient is:

A. Dependency.

B. Self-depreciativeness.

C. Impulsiveness.

D. Orderliness.

13. The symptom which characterizes paranoia in its true form is:
    A. Bizarre hallucinations.
    B. Inappropriate affect.
    C. Severe depression.
    D. Systematized delusions.

14. The major defense mechanism utilized in paranoid thinking is:
    A. Reaction formation.
    B. Rationalization.
    C. Compensation.
    D. Sublimation.
    E. Projection.

15. Malingering differs most significantly from a conversion disorder in that the malingerer:
    A. Unconsciously simulates illness to avoid an unpleasant situation.
    B. Converts anxiety arising from some conflictual situation into somatic symptoms.
    C. Seems unconcerned and shows no anxiety about his disabling symptoms.
    D. Simulates illness on a conscious level to avoid intolerable alternatives.

16. The term which best describes the reaction of an individual who makes an emotional response through an organic illness is:
    A. Neurotic reaction.
    B. Organic reaction.
    C. Psychosomatic reaction.
    D. Psychotic reaction.

17. Another problem from which neurotic patients suffer is:
    A. Memory loss.
    B. Indecision.
    C. Disorientation.
    D. Hallucinations.

18. People suffering from neuroses usually complain of:
    A. Hallucinations, delusions, and fatigue.
    B. Fatigue, fears, and physical complaints.
    C. Fatigue, rejections, and dissociation.
    D. Flight of ideas, illusions, and disorientation.

5

Legal Considerations

OBJECTIVES: Student will be able to:
1. Define and state an example of a voluntary admission.
2. Define and state an example of an involuntary admission.
3. List the rights of a voluntarily and involuntarily admitted patient.
4. State three specific things one can do in caring for the mentally ill which will reduce the likelihood of becoming involved in litigation due to improper patient care.

Some experts call the present period in American history the "Age of the Consumer." Since Ralph Nader's rise to fame, more people are insisting that they receive quality products and services for the money they pay.

One may wonder what consumer's rights have to do with the mentally ill. Consider for a moment that patient care provided by a hospital or clinic is a service, and a costly one at that. Hospital room rates alone may run over two hundred dollars per day. These prices often do not include special treatments, medications, or psychotherapy. Since mentally ill patients frequently are hospitalized for weeks at a time, it is not difficult to understand why people are demanding the best care. Many patients or their families will readily seek legal advice if the care that they receive is not satisfactory.

The fear of a lawsuit, however, should not be the motivating factor in providing quality care to patients. Rather, the obligation to honor the trust placed in one by patients is the professional ethic and commitment. Honoring this trust would practically eliminate lawsuits.

A major responsibility of any member of the mental health team is to help other team members create the type of environment that provides for both physical and emotional safety and comfort of patients. One step toward the attainment of this type of environment is to treat all patients as unique individuals, taking measures to preserve their dignity and to respect the rights and privileges guaranteed them by law.

Most lawsuits involving members of the mental health team center around a negligent act (negligence being seen as willful neglect, abuse, harassment, or failure to attend adequately to a patient). For example, if a patient who is experiencing post-ECT confusion is allowed to take a shower unattended and subsequently falls and breaks a hip, the patient would very likely win a negligence suit.

The objective of this chapter is to provide basic guidelines to follow when working with mentally ill patients. These guidelines should help the mental health worker to avoid legal entanglement which might otherwise arise when providing patient care. Mental health workers must make themselves aware of the laws pertaining to the care of the mentally ill for the state in which they practice since such laws vary considerably from state to state.

Make sure that you are familiar with the job description for your position. Know what you can legally do and then learn to perform those procedures in a correct and skillful manner. Ask questions and tactfully refuse when asked to do any task for which you have not been prepared. Be sure to read carefully the rules and regulations of your hospital or clinic and thoroughly commit to memory those which are specific to the unit upon which you will be employed. You should also familiarize yourself with the information in the procedure manual. Discuss with your supervisor any part of the procedure manual that you do not understand completely, for in many states you can be held legally responsible for any rules, regulations, and procedures that apply to patient care on your unit or the hospital in general. This is true even if you do not "know" about a particular rule, regulation, or procedure. Make it your business to know . . . Be informed!

Familiarize yourself with the laws of your state regarding treatment of the mentally ill. In most states there are two main ways in which mentally ill patients are admitted for psychiatric care. When a person agrees that medical assistance is needed and agrees to be admitted to the hospital, it is said to be a *voluntary admission*. If an unwilling patient must be forced to enter the hospital, it is an *involuntary admission* (involuntary admission and involuntary commitment are considered to be interchangeable). Involuntary admissions require legal action. A judge or doctor (it varies according to state law) who determines that a person is in danger of harming himself or others has the responsibility of deciding whether or not to admit the person to a psychiatric hospital or unit for treatment.

The main reason for being aware of the difference between these two procedures is best illustrated when one is faced with a patient who has decided to leave the hospital. In the case of a voluntary admission, the patient should be allowed to leave if the patient has decided not to continue treatment. Most hospitals will ask patients to put their intentions in writing and then wait 24 hours before leaving. Patients who refuse to do this are usually asked to sign a legal form which states that they know they are leaving against medical advice and that the hospital is not responsible for their actions. In most states, however, patients cannot be required to sign such a form. If the person in charge of the unit believes that these patients are likely to harm themselves or others if they leave, the charge person may detain such patients against their will for a period of 24 hours. During this time, legal procedures must be started in order to change the patient's admission status from voluntary to involuntary. A patient who has been involuntarily admitted should not be permitted to leave the hospital unless officially discharged by the attending physician. Commitment is legally ended upon discharge.

It is important for all members of the psychiatric team to remember that patients admitted to the hospital on an involuntary basis do not necessarily lose all of their civil and legal rights. These patients do lose the right to leave the hospital without permission but in many states retain the right to vote, make contracts, drive a car, marry, divorce, write letters, and seek legal advice. As out-of-date laws are repealed in more states, the only way a patient can lose civil and legal rights is to be declared *incompetent*. This is a special legal procedure, *not* a routine matter for patients hospitalized on an involuntary basis. Once a patient is declared incompetent it takes another legal procedure to declare them competent. Discharge from the hospital is not enough.

The issue of confidentiality is also being legally challenged. Court decisions uphold the belief that the "protective privilege of confidentiality ends where the public peril begins." If you have patients who make threats to harm themselves or others, report this to your supervisor immediately. They in turn will have to act upon this information in accordance with procedures outlined by the agency or institution for which you work.

Since the early 70s, more and more of the court suits filed by mental health patients have dealt with what they considered to be infringements upon their basic human rights and freedoms, as guaranteed to them by the Bill of Rights and the Civil Rights Amendments. Since hospitalized patients tend to be more vulnerable, they are more likely to have their rights violated.

Because of recent court rulings, thousands of patients have been released from state institutions in the last 10 years and returned to a society ill-prepared to meet their needs. This has led to conflict between society and the medical and legal professions. The law governing mental health practices is in a state of flux and many laws currently on the books are being challenged on the grounds that they are unconstitutional because they do not provide for due process.

Be careful not to let your attention wander, be distracted, or be manipulated from your duties. Be especially careful when you are taking a patient or a group of patients off the unit or when a suicidal patient is under your supervision. A good rule to follow is that if you have more than one patient going off the unit, you should have more than one mental health worker with the group. Then, if something happens to a patient, one staff member can stay with the group while the other staff member goes for help. It is generally not a safe practice to try to manage patient groups larger than ten.

Patients have a right to refuse treatment or to withdraw from treatment once it is started. The constitutional basis for this is the patient's fundamental right to privacy and personal autonomy. Todays mental health professional walks a fine line between providing for a patient's well-being and protecting their rights.

Except in extreme psychiatric emergencies, the mental health professional must explain all procedures and drugs to the patient in such a manner that the patient can make an intelligent, informed choice as to whether or not to allow it. The patient's agreement must be written. The patient should be given information regarding expected outcomes, potential risks, and alternative treatment modalities.

Informed consent is not valid if a patient is coerced or is under the influence of drugs or alcohol, or is in such a state of agitation that it prevents free choice. If the staff feels a patient cannot make rational decisions regarding care, the proper authorities should be notified and incompetency proceedings started.

If you must place a patient in seclusion, remember that it is not a punishment but a protective device and is used only when other methods (medication, talking, and so forth) fail. If such an order is given, make sure the patient is checked at least every 20 minutes. Stay with the patient yourself if at all possible or try to find a staff member or a family member who can stay.

If working on a hospital unit, help the medication nurse by observing that each patient receiving medication actually does swallow the pills and does not hoard them. This can be accomplished by giving the patient something to drink immediately or if you suspect a patient of hoarding, staying with the patient for 15 minutes or so.

One should be constantly alert for potentially dangerous items on the unit. Remove the item when possible and report any hazards to the supervisor. For example, one should pick up a nail file left by a visitor or report a torn screen to the head nurse.

EXERCISES

The following situations provide an opportunity to apply the information learned in this chapter to situations which one is likely to face when assuming duties on a psychiatric unit. The five statements below describe actions taken by a mental health staff member. Some are appropriate and some are inappropriate. Mark an A by those believed to be appropriate and an I by those believed to be inappropriate.

_____ 1. A patient approaches the staff member saying that he is tired of being "cooped up" and that he is going to leave the hospital. The staff member immediately notifies his supervisor, checks the patient's chart and finds that the patient is a voluntary patient. The staff member then notifies the patient's physician who asks the patient to sign a statement saying that he is leaving the hospital against medical advice. The patient signs the form and is permitted to leave.

_____ 2. Mr. Colbert is allowed to continue to carry his small pocket knife even though he had threatened to use it on a fellow patient. The team member assigned to care for Mr. Colbert decided that the patient had just been angry and had not really meant what he said.

_____ 3. A patient, being very angry, screamed and yelled and called one of the staff several bad names. An hour later the patient became totally unmanageable and had to be restrained. In helping to apply the restraints, the staff member that had been verbally abused used more force than necessary in order to get the patient to settle down. Later, when the patient's arm began to swell, the staff member decided on his own to apply hot compresses to the area to reduce the swelling.

_____ 4. The staff member assigned to Mr. Goldstead, a patient who was confused as a result of a series of ECT treatments, was helping him to bathe. Another staff member opened the door and asked the attendant to come help him move another patient, stating it would only take a minute or two. Mr. Goldstead's attendant asked the other staff member to find someone else to help.

_____ 5. A staff member who happened to be a very good bowler was demonstrating his bowling techniques to the ten patients that he had taken to the bowling alley. When a patient asked if he could return to the unit, he was permitted to do so in the company of another patient.

After responding to the above statements on your own, discuss what makes each of them appropriate or inappropriate with your classmates.

ANNOTATED BIBLIOGRAPHY

Cushing, M.: *A judgment on standards.* American Journal of Nursing, 1981, 81(4):797–798.

Researches legal findings involving cases where psychiatric patients were placed in seclusion.

Hemelt, M.D., and Mackert, M.E.: *Your legal guide to nursing practice.* Nursing '79, 1979, 9(10):57–64.

Explores the legal aspects of nursing practice, including informed consent and administration of medications.

Horsley, J.E.: *Short staffing means increased liability for you.* RN, 1981, 44(2):73–82.

The nurse is in an increased ability situation when short-staffed. This article describes how to avoid the legal pitfalls of this situation.

Hull, R.T.: *Responsibility and accountability analyzed.* Nursing Outlook, 1981, 29(12):707–712.

Describes how the principles of responsibility and accountability affect the liability of the nurse.

Laken, D.D.: *Protecting patients against themselves.* Nursing '83, 1983, 13(1):90–94.

Explains and provides examples on how to deal with the patient who refuses treatment. Discusses the health care worker's legal and moral obligation to explain the nature and purpose of proposed treatments. The author recommends listening carefully to the patient and explaining in a nonthreatening manner.

Moskowitz, L.D., and Moskowitz, S.: *Therapeutic role of the legal process.* Journal of Psychosocial Nursing and Mental Health Services, 1981, 19(10):33–36.

This viewpoint advocates the legal process in medicine, stating that it assures quality care and promotes a consumer-oriented system.

Regan, W.A.: *You don't have to tolerate substandard hospital practices.* RN, 1981, 44(2):73–82.

Describes how the nurse can legally promote improved care standards within the hospital.

Shindul, J.A., and Snyder, M.E.: *Legal restraints on restraint.* American Journal of Nursing, 1981, 81(2):393–394.

Relates the circumstances whereby restraints may and may not be used. Particularly addresses the use of restraints on the mentally ill.

POST-TEST

Chapter 5

Legal Considerations

True or False. Circle your choice. (Answers may vary according to the laws of your state. Have you read the laws of your state?)

T F 1. A patient cannot be legally detained in the hospital if he admitted himself voluntarily even though he is still very ill.

T F 2. Involuntary admission and commitment are considered the same thing.

T F 3. A patient under a voluntary admission can be held against his will for 72 hours.

T F 4. When a patient is admitted involuntarily, he automatically loses his civil and legal rights.

T F 5. It is not necessary for a patient admitted involuntarily to give his consent to special treatment or procedures.

T F 6. A temporary commitment permits a patient to be hospitalized from 90 to 180 days.

T F 7. Patients have the right to be present at the court hearing for their commitment.

T F 8. A patient who is committed by court action retains all of his civil rights except the right to vote and the right to leave.

T F 9. A legally committed patient has the right to conduct business.

T F 10. A guardian is always assigned to a person that is declared legally incompetent.

T F 11. Malpractice is a kind of negligence.

T F 12. Communication between husband and wife is not considered privileged.

T F 13. A patient who enters a psychiatric hospital voluntarily retains all legal and civil rights except the right to leave.

T F 14. The patient's nearest relatives may institute a commitment proceeding.

Matching. Select the appropriate term from Column B for each statement in Column A.

	Column A	*Column B*
_____	1. Violation of Civil Rights.	A. ECT

_____ 2. Does not have right to leave hospital without physician's permission.

_____ 3. Must have special signed consent form for voluntary patient.

_____ 4. May leave hospital without physician's permission.

_____ 5. Special court procedure.

B. Restraining patients
C. Involuntary patient
D. Reading patient's mail
E. Incompetency hearing
F. Voluntary patient

Short Answer. Answer the following questions as briefly and specifically as possible.

1. Negligence is defined as _____

_____

2. Define the difference between involuntary and voluntary admission.

_____

_____

_____

3. If you are unable to answer a patient's question correctly, the best thing to do is:

_____

_____

_____

4. What would be the main reason for placing a patient in seclusion?

_____

5. Most lawsuits involving members of the mental health team are usually centered around:

_____

Part 2

THERAPEUTIC TREATMENT ACTIVITIES

6

Communication

OBJECTIVES: Student will be able to:
1. Define communication.
2. Differentiate between verbal and nonverbal communication.
3. List major objectives in developing a therapeutic relationship.
4. List 10 techniques useful in communicating more effectively with patients.
5. List at least eight major factors that should be used to maintain accurate and complete charting.

Communication, a key factor in the development of any therapeutic relationship, occurs on both a *verbal* and a *nonverbal* basis. Verbal communications are transmitted through the spoken or written word and nonverbal communications are transmitted through behavior. Regardless of the mode of transmission, the aim of all forms of communication is to provide information, receive information, or exchange information.

WRITTEN COMMUNICATION

When using written communication, the writer provides information without the benefit of feedback; therefore, if the one to whom the message is written does not understand the message, successful communication has not been achieved. For example, if a staff member charts that a patient is "hostile" and Dr. Jones reads the chart after that staff member has gone off duty, he really doesn't know what happened and probably will not have a clear understanding of what the staff member meant by "hostile." This is especially true if Dr. Jones sees the patient sitting calmly in the day room visiting and chatting with other patients. In order to discuss the behavior with the patient, Dr. Jones must understand what the staff member meant by "hostile."

One means of clarifying and making written communication more explicit is to use *descriptive writing*. Instead of saying that the patient is "hostile," it would be better to write exactly what the patient said or did. For example, "The patient is walking up and down the hall cursing" or

"When another patient walks by, Mr. Brown screams at them and tries to hit them." This tells the doctor exactly what the patient has been doing. Since unclear written communications are likely to result in either no information or misinformation, the use of descriptive writing is extremely important.

VERBAL COMMUNICATION

Most people know how to communicate verbally since we all converse daily. Unfortunately, we frequently do not think before we talk and are unaware of what we are communicating to other people. Verbal communication, therefore, is largely effective because it is easy to talk and feedback can alert one to the possibility that the desired message is not being communicated. For example, a person listening to a speaker may question what has been said, may challenge a statement that was made, may ask for clarification of a point, or may add to a statement, thus facilitating effective communications.

A frequent error made by people when they are communicating verbally occurs when they say things that they do not mean. A mother says to her son who has misbehaved, "I'm not going to love you any more." Obviously the message being sent is not true. A mother is not going to stop loving her child because he misbehaved. The message she wanted to communicate was, "I do not like the way you are behaving. I love you, but I want you to change your behavior." When we say things we do not mean, the messages we send are misunderstood and may cause interpersonal relationship problems. Communications such as these, if consistent over a long enough period, may lead to mental illness.

NONVERBAL COMMUNICATION

Some authorities believe that nonverbal communication is the most accurate of all forms of communication. People communicate nonverbally via their behavior and their body posture. If someone is depressed, they may slump, walk with their head down, and have a gloomy look on their face. These behaviors send a message to all those who come in contact with this person. The message is, "I don't feel well; I'm depressed." Remember the song that says, "If you're happy and you know it, then your face will surely show it"? Well, it is true that when people are happy, their faces generally show it. They also express their feeling of well being when they walk at a brisk pace with their head up and shoulders thrown back.

One's behavior thus often indicates one's state of mind, and mentally ill patients are no exception. Their behavior infers a great deal about their feelings. When a nurse walks into Mr. Brown's room and says, "How are you feeling this morning?", the patient may respond by saying that he feels fine. If, however, he is lying in a fetal position with the covers drawn up to his shoulders and refuses to have his room light turned on, his nonverbal behaviors would indicate that he is not feeling well.

Why would Mr. Brown respond to you with "I am feeling fine" when obviously he is not? There are several possibilities. Perhaps Mr. Brown is afraid that if he says that he is not feeling well, the doctor won't let him go home on Friday as planned. Mr. Brown may have heard a nurse standing outside his door complaining to another staff member about the floor being overloaded with patients thus causing the staff to be overworked; therefore, Mr. Brown is afraid to say he feels bad because that might put another burden on the nurses.

We have all said things that we didn't mean and patients are no exception. Since nonverbal communications convey attitudes, feelings, and reactions much more clearly than verbal communications, they are generally more accurate. We must, therefore, always be alert to nonverbal clues which may actually be a better indication of the patient's true feelings than what he says.

STAFF-PATIENT RELATIONSHIPS

In establishing a therapeutic relationship, the first step is to make initial contact with the patient. Obviously in talking to a patient for the first time, one cannot expect that patient to relate their life history. People are generally cautious about meeting someone new. They are not sure what the new person's attitude will be toward them and are uncomfortable if the new person is too pushy, overly friendly, or too inquisitive. Mentally ill people are often very sensitive individuals who have been hurt by their interpersonal relationships many, many times. The people they have trusted have let them down. They have shared their personal problems with individuals who seemed to care but instead they have been laughed at, ridiculed, degraded, or have had unkind remarks made to them. They may not trust people because their experiences have taught them that people cannot be trusted.

It follows then that a primary objective of early staff-patient contacts is to establish a relationship which promotes mutual trust. A step is made in that direction when a staff member is honest and straightforward with patients. For example, if staff members do not know the answer to a patient's question, they should tell the patient that they don't know the answer, but that they will try to find the answer for them. When a staff member makes such a promise, care should be taken to be certain that adequate follow-up is made. Staff members should consider carefully what they tell patients they will do for them. Casual remarks and half-hearted offers are often taken seriously. Since one can never be sure what the events of the day will bring, a thoughtful response to make to a patient who asks to go for a walk might be, "It looks as though my schedule is free this afternoon and unless something unusual interferes, I will go for a walk with you around 4:00." If something does interfere, one might say to the patient for example, "I am really sorry but Dr. Jones is making rounds and I can't leave the unit now" or "I have been called to a staff meeting so we can't go for a walk this afternoon. I will be back around 5:00" or "Is there something special you wanted to talk about with me? If not, we will really try to take that walk tomorrow."

When a staff member is beginning to develop a trusting and therapeutic relationship with a patient, it is probably best to have frequent contacts of short duration. At the first meeting, one should introduce oneself and tell the patient one's title (nurse, nursing assistant, social worker, and so forth). Then explain one's purpose for approaching the patient. A mental health worker on a hospital unit might say, "I am Jane Doe, a mental health technician. I work the 3 to 11 shift and I'm assigned to take care of you this evening. If you need anything, want to talk, or have any questions, I will be happy to help." Then engage the patient in a discussion of some neutral topic. If the patient was watching television or reading the newspaper, one could make some comment about the TV program or some very neutral comment about a sporting event or weather forecast reported in the paper. Try to have a short, pleasant conversation and then leave the patient for a while. Later, try to interest the patient in some social activity such as playing cards, checkers, or having a cup of coffee with another person.

Staff members should work toward helping all patients realize that the staff is sincerely interested in them and their problems. Patients need to feel important and there are two key approaches to helping make them feel that way. First, the very fact that a staff member would want to spend time with them helps patients to feel important. Mental health workers are often seen as authority figures and as special persons by patients. Thus, many patients are surprised when a staff member says, "I would like to sit and talk with you for a while." Their self-esteem is so poor that they have a difficult time believing that someone as important as a staff member would want to talk with them or could really be concerned about their problems.

As a staff member, another way to help a patient feel important is to make sure one's time with him is not spent in talking about one's own personal life. Talking about oneself or unloading one's own personal problems on a patient says to that patient that the staff member is not really interested in anyone but himself.

84

There are other reasons, of course, why staff members should not talk about their own personal life. Mentally ill patients sometimes use the personal information given them to justify ill feelings toward the very staff member who shared with them. They may also use the information to gossip with other patients. If one tells a depressed patient one's own burdens in an attempt to help them understand that they are not the only person with problems, it may make them even more depressed. They may even feel that they should not add to the staff member's load by discussing their own problems.

It is not a good idea to tell a patient one's address or telephone number even if the patient insists. When a patient makes such personal inquiries, one might respond by saying, "What makes you ask?" and then attempt to involve the patient in a discussion directed toward his own problems. One might also say, "This time is for you to talk about your problems" or "It would be more helpful if you would talk about yourself." This is especially important in the first few patient-staff contacts when the patient may be unclear about the relationship and the purpose of the discussions. If all else fails, one may simply say that one is not permitted to discuss personal information.

Dating patients is also an unwise practice for staff members, even after the patients have been discharged from the hospital. One never knows when a patient might need to return to the hospital, and it is difficult to mix personal and professional relationships. If a patient's efforts to establish a social relationship persist, one might need to respond in the following manner: "I am sorry but it is hospital policy that staff members not see patients socially." A hospital is an impersonal object and a patient may ventilate anger toward it without causing any great harm.

Since spending time with patients is one of the most therapeutic activities in which a staff member can engage, it is important to make the most of each opportunity. A five minute visit may seem much longer to the patient if the staff member seems relaxed, unhurried, and discusses topics which are important to the patient.

When talking with patients, one should pull a chair close or sit beside them on the sofa. Pay attention to what the patient is saying. Don't fidget in the chair, tap one's feet, or wring one's hands. Adopt a pleasant, sincere, interested attitude which says to the patient, "I am here to talk to you and I am interested in what you have to say." Try never to stand over a patient. To do so makes one appear rushed and the patient may become anxious and uncomfortable. If one is in a hurry, let the patient know when there will be time to talk.

Since time with patients is limited, it is important that one's verbal communication be as effective as possible. The use of *goals* can help. Such goals are determined by the purpose of one's contact with a patient and may be further influenced by the amount of time one has to spend, the nature of the information to be communicated, and one's attitude toward the patient. For example, if a staff member is to tell Mr. Jones about a test he is going to have the next day, then the goal of the conversation is to familiarize Mr. Jones with that test. The patient will need to be told when the test is scheduled and whether he has to have any special preparations for the test. He should then be allowed to ask questions for clarification and to express any feelings or concerns he might have about the procedure.

The goals for the conversation described above would be quite different from the goals of a conversation one might have with a patient who is depressed and just wants someone to sit and listen. In this situation, the staff member's goals would probably be aimed toward supporting the patient while allowing the patient an opportunity to talk.

COMMUNICATION TECHNIQUES

So often when patients try to tell their doctor, their nurse, their social worker, or the mental health worker assigned to their case about their problems, their illness or their inexperience at being effective communicators causes them to leave out important details and/or to skip from one subject to another before completing their original thought. Listed below are some techniques which staff members find useful in helping mentally ill patients communicate more effectively.

1. The high anxiety level experienced by many mentally ill patients plus their preoccupation with the things that are upsetting and making them anxious greatly decreases and narrows their attention span. They may appear confused and may hear very little of what is said to them. It may be necessary to repeat one's name several times or to reintroduce oneself each time the patient is approached. Staff members, therefore, should observe for behavioral or verbal clues that would indicate that a patient has not understood the intended message and thus cannot respond appropriately. On the other hand, some patients are acutely aware of all that is happening in their environment and would feel greatly insulted if a staff member kept repeating things over and over again.

2. It is important for staff members to use simple, direct statements and questions. Long, involved sentences and explanations may just confuse patients. Use the simplest language possible to convey the message. Avoid the use of abstract statements such as, "It's raining cats and dogs outside." If this was said to an hallucinating patient, the patient might take it seriously and run to the window saying, "Where, where?"

3. Do not use indefinite pronouns such as she, he, they, and so forth. Be specific about the person being discussed. Encourage the patients to do the same. Ask for clarification about the identity of the person the

patient is discussing. For example, a patient might say, "She always belittles me. I can never do anything right." The staff member might respond by saying, "Who is she?" or "Who is it that you feel belittles you?"

4. Psychiatric patients sometimes have difficulty trying to describe or explain things that happen to them. Since their interpretation of their experiences may be very different from what actually occurred, it is helpful to such patients if a staff member can help them to more objectively describe their experience and then consider alternatives which were previously overlooked. If Mr. Green is unfriendly one morning, Mr. Jones may become upset because he believes that Mr. Green is angry with him. If a staff member helps Mr. Jones see that Mr. Green is upset about a personal problem, Mr. Jones may be able to relax and feel less anxious.

5. It is often necessary for staff members to help patients maintain an orientation to the "here and now." Patients sometimes try to escape a problem by denying its existence or by talking about getting out of the hospital, Aunt Bee's new hat, or the possibility that a rich uncle may die and leave them a fortune. It is more beneficial for patients to deal with their real problems in an open manner than to smooth over them with wishes, dreams, and fantasies.

6. Open-ended type questions should be used when one wishes to engage a patient in conversation or obtain general information. If one asks a patient, "Are you married?" the probable response would be "Yes." The question is answered, but the conversation is over. On the other hand, if one uses an open-ended statement such as, "Mr. Jones, tell me about your family", the patient cannot answer with a simple "yes" or "no." He will have to elaborate on his response and one can begin a conversation which may lead to further discussion of related topics. Questions such as "Tell me about yourself," "What happened to bring you to the hospital?", "What have you done today?" are all examples of open-ended type questions. This type of question also allows the patient some freedom in choosing what to discuss. Mr. Brown may choose a neutral topic when asked, "What has happened since we talked last week?" He may say that he got a nice birthday card from his mother, or that he had a date, or that it was a nice week—all very safe subjects. On the other hand, he may choose to tell you that he had a terrible fight with his girlfriend. In either case, Mr. Brown chose the topic and is, therefore, less likely to feel that the staff member is prying or pushing him to discuss something that he is not ready to discuss.

7. Mentally ill patients may use mental health staff members as role models and pattern much of their behavior after that of the staff. Likewise, they may pattern their communication style after the style of the person with whom they are working. Therefore, it is important to give patients a good role model.

8. Since patients sometimes take cues about staff members' expectations from the way a statement is phrased, words such as *can, could,* and *would* may create problems. A sentence beginning with *can* or *would* may lead patients to believe that they have some choice in the matter when they really do not. If one says to a patient, "Can you get up?" or "Would you come with me?" the patient may say "No." If a patient must go somewhere for a treatment, it is probably best to say, "It is time for your treatment. Come with me." From that statement, it is obvious that the patient is expected to cooperate. Most authorities agree that it is better not to offer a patient a choice when there is none. Offering a nonexistent choice may only anger the patient and create animosity.

9. Whenever possible, the patient should be consulted when the staff is developing the patient's care plan. If Mr. Jones likes to take his bath in the evening and there are no valid staff objections, his preference should be honored. This consideration helps Mr. Jones feel that the staff sees him as an individual and that his personal concerns are important. As a general rule, no one is more interested in his well being than the patient himself. Most patients feel better when they have some say in and control over their own life, even when they are sick.

10. Mentally ill patients sometimes have difficulty focusing on one topic at a time or may skip from one subject to another without ever finishing a thought. This may occur because their anxiety level is high, making it difficult for them to concentrate, or, by skipping from subject to subject, they may avoid talking about a particular topic which makes them feel anxious. It is important to help patients improve their ability to discuss one topic at a time, especially if the topic involves an area of conflict. If the topic of conflict can be discussed fully, the patient may gain a better understanding of it and may even uncover some of the reasons behind the conflict.

11. One should realize that patients often relate to mental health staff members as authority figures and, therefore, may want staff members to make all their decisions for them. One should be careful not to allow that to happen. Having someone else make decisions for them does not help patients learn to deal more effectively with their problems nor does it help them learn to be more responsible for their lives. Also, if a patient does not like the outcome of a discussion made for him by a staff member, the staff member will likely receive the blame.

12. Silences often provoke anxiety and both patients and staff members are likely to feel uncomfortable when they occur. It is helpful to remember that both patients and staff members sometimes need a brief period of silence in order to collect their thoughts. When talking with Mr. Green, a patient who is anxious, he may need time to organize what he is going to say or to decide exactly how he feels about something. Mental

health workers need to be good observers in order to be able to determine whether patients are silent because they are out of contact with reality or because they simply need to collect their thoughts.

13. A good technique to use when working with patients who are communicating on a nonverbal basis is to help them identify their feelings. A staff member might say something like the following to a patient: "Are you feeling anxious?" If the patient responds, "No, what makes you ask?", one might say, "Well, I noticed that you were swinging your foot and that you have smoked six cigarettes in the last 20 minutes." Helping the patient to become aware of nonverbal cues of anxiety may lead to the patient becoming able to discuss such feelings verbally. It is also necessary to remember that just as staff members observe patients for their nonverbal communications, patients also notice the nonverbal communication of staff members. If during a conversation, one swings one's leg or twiddles a piece of clothing, the patient may believe that the staff member is bored, in a hurry, or wishes that the patient would get on with the topic of discussion.

14. When they discuss painful or embarassing subjects, patients need support and encouragement. If one looks at the patient in a helpful, interested, concerned manner, the patient is encouraged to continue. In addition, one might occasionally say, "I see" or "Go on" or "I can understand that." Such statements also encourage the patient to continue talking and let the patient know that the staff member is listening and attentive to what is being said.

15. If one does not understand something that was said by a patient, it may be that the patient is not clear about the subject either. Ask for clarification, "I'm sorry, but I didn't hear the last thing you said" or "I don't understand what you mean. Please explain it to me." Do not make statements such as, "You talk so low I can't understand what you are saying" or "The last statement you made was mean." Statements such as these make patients feel intimidated and inferior, thus lowering their self-esteem and, therefore, possibly blocking further attempts to communicate.

16. Mental health workers should avoid using emotionally charged words and incriminating statements. Statements such as, "You know smoking can cause lung cancer" may cause a patient to become unduly upset. One should also avoid leading questions such as, "It doesn't hurt when you bend over, does it?" Such questions imply that a particular answer is expected and predispose the patient to admit or deny symptoms.

Communication is something we have practiced all our lives. Some of us just happen to be better at it than others. Fortunately, it is a skill which can be improved if one will take time to learn and practice a few basic techniques such as the ones discussed in this chapter.

REPORTING AND RECORDING

One of the most important uses for good communication skills is in the reporting and recording of information concerning patients. Pertinent information is kept in a legal document called the patient's record or the patient's chart. Each patient's record should contain everything of significance pertaining to that patient. Accurate and complete charting and verbal reporting of observations encourages continuity of patient care by providing usable information about the patient to other team members.

The suggestions about effective communication techniques in this chapter along with the specific instructions regarding charting listed below should be helpful when reporting or charting one's observations about patients.

1. Write or print legibly in ink. Be sure that notations are made on the correct patient's chart and that all notations are dated and signed.

2. Do not erase. If a mistake is made, draw a line through it and print the word ERROR above the line.

3. Be concise, yet make the meaning of each sentence clear.

4. Be objective by providing a description of what the patient has said or done. Try to avoid interpreting the patient's behavior. Remember that behaviors taken out of context may seem bizarre, but when described in the situations where they actually happened, may be quite normal and appropriate.

5. Use only the abbreviations approved by one's institution.

6. Chart medications and treatments after they are given, not before. If a patient refuses to participate in an activity, take a medication, or allow a treatment, be sure to chart the refusal. Whenever possible, the patient's reason for the refusal should also be noted.

7. Report and record any sudden change in the patient's behavior.

8. Always record the time of occurrence of the event being recorded. It is a good idea to record events as soon after they happen as possible since important details may be forgotten if one waits several hours to write the report.

9. Accidents should be reported and recorded according to the policy of one's institution. Thoroughness in writing such reports is extremely important since legal action may later require detailed information about the accident.

The following charts are provided as a guide to some of the factors that need to be observed and recorded when working with mentally ill patients. Many hospitals and clinics routinely use similar charts.

BEHAVIORS TO BE OBSERVED

Appearance	Personal Hygiene: clean ____ dirty ____ body odor ____ bathes self ____ requires help with bath ____ Dress: appropriate ____ inappropriate ____ neat ____ unkept ____ dresses self ____ requires help dressing ____
General Behavior	cooperative ____ helpful ____ dependable ____ quiet ____ loud ____ excitable ____ overactive ____ bitter ____ sullen ____ angry ____ depressed ____ listless ____ irritable ____ verbally aggressive ____ anxious (specify: _____) complaints (specify: _____) physically aggressive ____ temper tantrums ____ bites nails ____ uses obscene language ____ shows fear of others ____ pacing ____ seems overtly nervous ____ masturbates ____ sexually interested in staff ____ in other patients ____ expresses suicidal impulses ____ homicidal impulses ____
Body Behavior	staring into space ____ rigid, stiff movements ____ obviously tense ____ jerking spastic movements (tics) ____ frequent startled responses ____ holds one position for prolonged periods ____ seems to be in a trance ____ coordinated motor behavior ____ staggers ____ falls ____ slumps when sitting ____ good general posture ____ poor general posture ____
Verbal Behavior	Speech: slow ____ rapid ____ slurred ____ otherwise impaired ____ unintelligible ____ rambling ____ dramatic ____ talks to self ____ repeats words or phrases over and over ____ talks compulsively or constantly ____ talks very little ____ not at all ____

BEHAVIORS TO BE OBSERVED—*Continued*

Thought Processes	Answers to questions: relevant ___
	irrelevant ___
	rambling ___
	incoherent ___
	Hears voices: threatening ___ ordering ___
	accusing ___
	Has visual hallucinations (specify: _____
	_____)
	Has visions (specify: _____
	_____)
	Has peculiar bodily sensations (specify: _____
	_____)
	Has delusions (specify: _____
	_____)
	Ideas of: reference ___ persecution ___
	conspiracy ___
	people controlling ___
	outside forces controlling ___
	body destruction ___
	famous person ___
	having unusual powers ___
	having a divine mission ___
Orientation	Oriented to: time ___ place ___
	person ___ date ___
	month ___ year ___
	Able to recognize: staff ___
	other patients ___
	own room ___
	Short-term memory: good ___ poor ___
	bad ___
	Long-term memory: good ___ poor ___
	bad ___ frequently
	forgets who he(she)
	is ___

PHYSICAL SYMPTOMS

Vital Signs	Temp. _____ Pulse _____ Respiration _____ B/P _____ Weight _____
Neck, Face, and Skin	Appearance: pale _____ rosey _____ clammy _____ hot _____ cold _____ sweaty _____ acne _____ scars _____ red spots _____ bruises or lacerations _____ smooth texture _____ rough texture _____
Mouth	Teeth: Natural _____ dentures _____ clean _____ good hygiene _____ poor hygiene _____ Gums: good color _____ smooth _____ irritated or inflamed _____ bloody _____ pus _____ Tongue: coated _____ uncoated _____ inflamed _____ wet _____ dry _____ chewed or bitten _____ Breath: clean _____ sour _____ fruity _____
Urine	Color: pale yellow _____ bloody _____ pus _____ dark _____ Odor: essentially odorless _____ foul odor _____
Urinary Habits	Voiding: voids easily _____ trouble voiding _____ voids too often _____ incontinent for urine _____
Stool	Consistency: liquified _____ soft _____ hard _____ normal _____ Color: (brown, etc.) _____ Unusual odor _____ blood _____ mucus _____
Pain	Area (leg, etc.) _____ sharp _____ dull _____ stabbing _____ throbbing _____ intense _____ mild _____ occasional _____ frequent _____ continuous _____ first noticed (time) _____ How long has patient had the pain (days, hours, etc.) _____

Vomiting	Time (1:00 A.M., etc.) _____
	Color (yellow, etc.) _____
	Amount: little____ moderate____ much___
	Consistency: watery____ average____
	thick____ bloody____
	Material vomited (breakfast, etc.) _____
	_____
Cough	When: continuously____ moderately____
	occasionally____ mostly A.M.____
	P.M.____ day____ night____
	Type: dry____ sputum produced____
	blood____ loud____ soft____
	hacking____ whooping____
	hoarse____
Sleep	Amount (7 hrs., etc.) _____
	day____ night____ sound____
	moderate____ light____ fitful____
	disturbed____ restless____ up a lot____
	sleeps easily____ sleeps with difficulty____
	needs sleep medication____
Eating Habits	Appetite: very good____ good____ fair____
	poor____
	eats without assistance____
	needs assistance____ throws food ___
	Table manners: good____ fair____ poor ___
Medicines	Takes meds without complaints____
	"cheeks" meds____ hoardes meds ____
	refuses meds____ no side effects noted ____
	side effects (specify: _____)

BEHAVIORS AND PROBLEMS FREQUENTLY SEEN

Anxiety Disorders

1. Increased heart rate, palpitations, increased blood pressure
2. Muscular tension
3. Increased respirations to the point of hyperventilation
4. Weakness
5. Dilated pupils
6. Constipation
7. Dry mouth
8. Anorexia
9. Urinary frequency, diarrhea, parasympathetic responses
10. Headaches
11. Nausea and vomiting
12. Decreased sexual functioning
13. Restlessness
14. Tremors
15. Accident proneness.

Dysthymic Disorders or Major Depression

1. Poor personal hygiene
2. Decreased motor activity
3. Fatigue
4. Anxiety — restlessness
5. Low self-esteem
6. Decreased mental processes
7. Constipation
8. Increased or decreased appetite
9. Sleeping disturbances — increased or decreased sleep, early morning awakening
10. Suicidal verbalization or gestures.

Manic Disorders

1. Increased agitation
2. Hyperactivity
3. Loose associations
4. Insomnia
5. Hostility
6. Acting-out
7. Hallucinations
8. Delusions
9. Sexual acting-out
10. Rapid speech.

Psychotic Disorders

1. Hallucinations
2. Delusions
3. Inappropriate affect
4. Regressive behaviors
5. Withdrawn behaviors
6. Sleep disturbances
7. Disorganized, illogical thinking
8. Acting-out
9. Aggressive or destructive behaviors
10. Suicidal verbalization or gestures
11. Poor personal hygiene.

Neurologic Disorders

1. Short attention span
2. Disorientation
3. Confusion
4. Confabulation
5. Poor immediate recall
6. Inappropriate or dramatic changes in social behavior
7. Poor judgment
8. Anger, hostility, or combativeness
9. Withdrawal
10. Inability to complete a task
11. Impaired ability to take care of activities of daily living

ANNOTATED BIBLIOGRAPHY

Anderson, M.L.: *Nursing interventions: What did you do that helped?* Perspectives of Psychiatric Care, 1983, 21(1):4–8.

Acquaints the reader with over 40 specific therapeutic communication techniques (including Broad Openings, Consensual Validation, Reinforcement, etc.), and defines each technique.

Brockopp, D.Y.: *What is NLP?* American Journal of Nursing, 1983, 83(7): 1012–1014.

Explains the rationale of the neuro-linguistic programming techniques. Describes the three areas of communications; auditory, kinesthetic, and visual.

Forsyth, D.M.: *Looking good to communicate better with patients.* Nursing '83, 13(7):34–37.

Instructs the health care worker on how to convey the desired meaning of communication through non-verbal expression.

Knowles, R.D.: *Building rapport through neuro-linguistic programming.* American Journal of Nursing, 1983, 83(7):1010–1014.

Illustrates the use of Bandler and Grinder's NLP techniques in verbal and non-verbal communication.

Mansheim, P., and Cohen, C.M.: *Communicating with developmentally disabled patients.* Journal of Psychosocial Nursing and Mental Health Services, 1982, 20(6):9–11.

Describes the most common problems of communicating with developmentally disabled and mentally retarded patients. Recommends strategies for improving communication.

Sloan, M.R. and Schommer, B.T.: *Want to get your patient involved in his care? Use a contract.* Nursing '82, 1982, 12(12):48–49.

Relates the benefits of contracting in establishment of a time frame for goals and assessing the achievement of goals.

Topf, M., and Dambacher, B.: *Teaching interpersonal skills: A model for facilitating optimal interpersonal relations.* Journal of Psychosocial Nursing and Mental Health Services, 1981, 19(12):29–33.

On the basis of several recent research studies, this article explores three principles of interpersonal communication including interpersonal complementarity, interpersonal versatility, and interpersonal influence.

True or False. Circle your choice.

T F   1. The two basic forms of communication are verbal and nonverbal.

T F   2. A common problem associated with verbal communication is the sending of messages one does not really mean.

T F   3. Some authorities believe that nonverbal communication is the most accurate of all forms of communication.

T F   4. In establishing a therapeutic relationship with a patient, the first step is to read their chart very carefully.

T F   5. People communicate nonverbally via their behavior and their body posture.

T F   6. Nonverbal clues may be a better indication of a patient's true feelings than what the patient actually says.

T F   7. A patient who is highly anxious is usually a better listener than one who is relatively calm.

T F   8. One should not offer a patient a choice if in reality he does not have a choice.

T F   9. If a patient appears to be having difficulty making a decision, a staff member should make it for him.

T F 10. The patient should be involved as much as possible in planning his own care and treatment plans.

Multiple Choice. Circle the letter you think represents the best answer.

1. The manner in which questions are asked can be improved by all of the following *except:*
   A. Listening before asking.
   B. Phrasing questions clearly and concisely.
   C. Asking only questions pertinent to the subject at hand.
   D. Phrasing questions so that a "yes" or "no" will suffice for the answer.

2. If verbal communications are difficult, it is sometimes helpful and therapeutic to:

A. Digress from focusing on the patient and his problems and mention similar problems of your own.
B. Ask the patient direct questions that require concrete answers.
C. Ask several nonproductive questions that will not make the patient feel threatened.
D. Engage in a social activity with the patient while he talks so that he will feel more comfortable.

3. The mental health worker's ability to effectively interpret communication is most dependent on:
A. Sources available for validation of communication content.
B. The immediacy with which the staff member attempts interpretation.
C. The staff member's understanding of psychiatric terminology.
D. How well the staff member listens and observes.

4. When observing behavior, the staff member should remember that behavioral symptoms:
A. Have meaning.
B. Are purposeful.
C. Are multidetermined.
D. All of the above.

5. Accurate recording of observations made in psychiatric settings includes:
1. Employing psychiatric terminology whenever possible.
2. Recording data as soon as possible.
3. Expressing personal opinions and interpreting behavior.
4. Using common, everyday descriptive language.
    A. 4 only.
    B. 1 and 3.
    C. 2 and 4.
    D. 1, 2, and 3.
    E. All of the above.

6. The main purpose for record keeping (charting) in the psychiatric setting is to:
A. Provide a subjective report of the patient's behavior.
B. Provide an objective report of the patient's behavior.
C. Provide a description of the patient's environment.
D. Note behavior signs of a specific illness.

7. If a patient becomes silent for a few seconds during an interaction, the staff member should probably:
A. Interpret this as an indication that the patient is ready for the staff member to depart.
B. Ask him a simple, nonthreatening question to get the conversation going again.

C. Remind him that you can best help him if he shares his feelings with you.

D. Remain with the patient and be quietly attentive.

8. The therapeutic relationship is enhanced when a staff member uses verbal and nonverbal communication to:
   1. Give attention and recognition to patients.
   2. Foster a patient's self-esteem.
   3. Indicate understanding.
   4. Communicate a feeling of acceptance and security.
       A. 4 only.
       B. 2 and 3.
       C. 1 and 4.
       D. 1, 2, and 4.
       E. All of the above.

9. Miss Long, a social worker, approaches one of her patients and starts a conversation. The patient says, "I don't want to talk today." What response by Miss Long would indicate that she understood and accepted her patient's behavior?
   A. "You say you don't want to talk?"
   B. "I'll sit here with you for a while."
   C. "There is no need for you to talk."
   D. "Why don't you want to talk today?"

10. Mrs. Adams tells a staff member that she is feeling depressed about the recent death of her father. Which of the following responses would communicate understanding and acceptance?
    A. "I know just how you feel."
    B. "Everyone gets depressed when they lose a loved one."
    C. "This must be very difficult for you."
    D. "Try to think positive. He was ill only a short time and didn't have to suffer long."

11. Which of the following responses could prevent effective communication?
    1. "What you should do is . . ."
    2. "In my opinion . . ."
    3. "Try not to worry; everything will be all right."
    4. "Why did you do that?"
        A. 4 only.
        B. 1, 2, and 4.
        C. 1, 3, and 4.
        D. All of the above.

12. While communicating with a schizophrenic patient, the mental health worker should:
    A. Sit quietly and do not encourage the patient to verbalize.

B. Talk with the patient as one would a normal person.

C. Allow the patient to do all the talking.

D. Use very simple, concrete language in speaking to the patient.

13. When talking to a patient for the first time, the staff member must realize:

A. That hostile behavior in a patient indicates that the staff member's initial approach has been inadequate.

B. That the case history should be read before talking with the patient.

C. That the patient's physical appearance provides an accurate index as to whether or not he will be receptive.

D. That the patient is a stranger to the staff member and the staff member is a stranger to the patient.

7

Drug Therapy

OBJECTIVES: Student will be able to:
1. Identify the desired effect and side effects of major tranquilizers.
2. List 10 of the most commonly used major tranquilizers.
3. Describe the desired effects and side effects of minor tranquilizers.
4. Describe the goals of antidepressant therapy, sedative therapy, anticonvulsant therapy, and antiparkinson therapy.

In the mid-1950s, the development of a group of drugs known as phenothiazines revolutionized the care of the mentally ill. It was first thought that these drugs might actually "cure" mental illness, but this did not prove to be the case. However, these drugs did calm patients, decreasing the severity of symptoms to the point where they were responsive to other forms of therapy. Patients receiving phenothiazines became more aware of their surroundings, began to participate in daily activities, were more cooperative with hospital routines and, of most importance, began to communicate. These drastic changes in patient behavior allowed the staff to begin to help them establish interpersonal relationships and to cope more effectively with their environment.

Since this major breakthrough in drug therapy, many other drugs effective in the treatment of various psychiatric disorders have been developed. The two major classifications of the psychotropic drugs (drugs active in decreasing symptoms of mental illness) are the tranquilizers, which are further divided into major and minor groups, and the antidepressants. We also discuss the anticonvulsants, sedatives, hypnotics, and antiparkinsons, since they are also used in the treatment of psychiatric patients.

MAJOR TRANQUILIZERS

The word tranquilize means to make tranquil, i.e., calm and basically free from agitation or disturbance. This definition is exactly the effect

101

tranquilizers are intended to have on disturbed patients. Drugs designated as major tranquilizers not only calm patients but they also help to control severe agitation and reduce the frequency of hallucinations, delusions, thought disorders, and the type of withdrawal seen in catatonic schizophrenia. In other words, these drugs cause patients to exhibit more normal behavior. It may take several days of drug therapy before the symptoms mentioned begin to subside but during this time, the patient usually becomes less fearful and hostile and is less upset by his disturbed sensory perceptions. As the patient's disturbed thinking and behavior improve, he becomes more receptive to psychotherapy and other forms of treatment.

The phenothiazine derivatives are the largest group of antipsychotic drugs. All the drugs in this group have essentially the same type of action on the body but vary according to strength and the type and severity of their side effects. Although rarely serious, phenothiazines produce several side effects which may cause discomfort. The patient should be observed carefully on a regular basis for the possible occurrence of the side effects listed below. Since early detection is important, it is desirable for all members of the treatment team to become thoroughly familiar with these major side effects.

Side Effects

Extrapyramidal Symptoms. There are three major types of extrapyramidal symptoms: 1) pseudoparkinsonism—restlessness, mask-like facial expression, drooling, and tremors; 2) akathisia—inability to sit still, complaints of fatigue and weakness, and continuous movement of the hands, mouth, and body; and 3) dyskinesia—lack of control over voluntary movements. For example, the patient might want to reach for something but be unable to do so. The patient may have a protruding tongue, a drooping head, and may become very frightened if stiffness of the neck and swallowing difficulties develop. Immediate action must be taken to combat extrapyramidal side effects and administration of antiparkinson drugs usually produces a dramatic reduction in symptoms.

Autonomic Reactions. This group of side effects includes dry mouth, constipation, excessive weight gain, and edema. Strict attention must be paid to the patient's personal hygiene and they should be informed of the possibility of these side effects and should be given suggestions as to how to combat them. Increasing the patient's intake of fluids, especially water, will help the mouth dryness and will also trigger the body's mechanism to reduce water retention thus reducing the edema. A drug called urecholine is also now being used to decrease mouth dryness. Since excessive weight gain is a potential problem, patients should be cautioned to lessen their intake of fattening foods and increase their intake of salads, fruits, etc. This will also help reduce constipation problems.

Postural Hypotension. This is a drop in blood pressure when a patient moves from lying flat in bed to a standing position. Symptoms include dizziness, heart pounding, and a "faint" feeling. Since patients could faint and injure themselves when first getting up, they should be cautioned to sit on the side of the bed first and dangle their feet a while before standing. Patients receiving a high dose of a phenothiazine drug should have their blood pressure checked on a regular basis. Any time a patient is given a large oral or IM dose of one of the phenothiazines, it is wise for them to lie in bed for about an hour.

Allergic Reactions. These are rare but serious when they do occur. If the patient develops dermatosis, jaundice, or ulcerative lesions in the mouth or throat, the drug will usually have to be discontinued. Thus, if a patient complains of a sore throat or other signs of infection, the physician should be notified immediately.

Sedation. If a patient receiving phenothiazines is lethargic and wants to sleep a great deal, the dose of medicine may be too high and need adjustment.

Decreased Sexual Interest. The possibility of this side effect needs to be explained so that the patient will know what is happening if sexual interest diminishes. Women patients may exhibit some of the signs and symptoms of pregnancy such as absence of menstrual cycle, false positive pregnancy tests, and weight gain. If the patient is checked further and there are no positive signs of pregnancy, she should be assured that the medication is the causative factor.

Photosensitivity. If this side effect occurs, the patient is especially sensitive to light and prone to sunburn and visual problems. Therefore, lengthy periods of direct sunlight should be avoided or protective clothing and glasses should be worn.

Other Side Effects. Patients on phenothiazines often experience blurred vision and drowsiness and should not drive or use dangerous equipment. Patients on phenothiazine therapy should be cautioned about taking other medications without their physicians' permission since phenothiazines may increase the action of other drugs, especially pain medications.

If any of the side effects discussed above cause the patient an unusual amount of difficulty or serious hazards, the physician may try one of the following three remedies: 1) the drug dosage may be decreased; 2) if symptoms persist, the medication may be completely withdrawn for 24 hours, then be restarted with a gradual buildup of the dosage; or 3) change the drug, choosing another phenothiazine derivative known to be less likely to produce the troublesome side effects.

TABLE 1. Major Tranquilizers
(Phenothiazine Derivatives)

Trade Name	24-Hour Dosage Range[†]
Permitil, Prolixin	1–20 mg.
Stelazine	2–20 mg.
Trilafon	6–64 mg.
Compazine	15–150 mg.
Dartal	15–100 mg.
Tindal	40–80 mg.
Vesprin	60–150 mg.
Thorazine	30–1200 mg.
Pacatal*	50–400 mg.
Mellaril*	30–800 mg.
Prolixin enanthate	25 mg. s.q. 1–3 weeks
Loxitane	20–250 mg.
Serentil	100–400 mg.
Repoise	15–30 mg.
Haldol	2–8 mg.
Proketazine	25–50 mg.
Navane	6–60 mg.
Taractan	30–100 mg.
Mobane	5–200 mg.

*These have the lowest extrapyramidal symptoms.

†Dosages are highly variable. Much higher or much lower dosages may be given.

Table 1 lists some of the major phenothiazine-type tranquilizers. Knowing these trade names will alert you to the fact that a patient is taking a phenothiazine drug and should be carefully observed for side effects.

MINOR TRANQUILIZERS

The minor tranquilizers reduce anxiety and the muscle tension associated with it. They are primarily useful in treating patients with psychoneurotic and psychosomatic disorders. When given in small doses, they are relatively safe and have few side effects. Unlike the major tranquilizers, however, some of the minor tranquilizers tend to be habit forming. If the drug is discontinued, the patient may experience severe withdrawal symptoms which may even include delerium and convulsions. They differ from barbiturates in that they produce a much lower degree of drowsiness.

Side Effects

Patients are occasionally hypersensitive to the minor tranquilizers and may have rashes, chills, fever, nausea and vomiting. They may also cause

TABLE 2. Minor Tranquilizers

Trade Name	24-Hour Dosage Range
Sparine	50–1500 mg.
Librium	15–300 mg.
Tranxene	15–60 mg.
Atarax	50–400 mg.
Equanil, Miltown	200–1200 mg.
Serax	30–120 mg.
Valium	4–40 mg.
Vistaril	50–400 mg.
Suavitil	3–10 mg.

headaches, poor muscle coordination, some inability to concentrate, and dizziness. Patients taking these drugs should be cautioned against driving or performing any task that requires careful attention to detail and mental alertness. Excessive amounts of these drugs may lead to coma and death; however, death is much less likely to occur with an overdose of a minor tranquilizer than with an overdose of barbiturates. Table 2 lists many of the minor tranquilizers commonly used.

ANTIDEPRESSANTS

These drugs have been called psychomotor stimulants and those commonly used are divided into two groups: the monamine oxidase (MAO) inhibitors and tricyclic compounds. The goal of antidepressant drug therapy is to elevate the patient's mood, increase the patient's appetite, and increase the patient's mental and physical alertness. They also help decrease the patient's preoccupation with his own feelings of worthlessness, inadequacy, and hopelessness.

MAO Inhibitors

The value of the MAO inhibitors is being questioned by many authorities in the field of psychiatry because they tend to produce a number of severe side effects. Many of these side effects have led to fatalities or prolonged and serious medical problems. Since these drugs are primarily used to treat depressed patients who often have suicidal tendencies, another drawback occurs. It takes one to two weeks of drug therapy before MAO inhibitors effect behavior changes. The suicidal patient needs faster acting medicine.

Hypertensive (high blood pressure) crises have occurred after patients receiving MAO inhibitors have consumed certain foods such as cheese, bananas, avocados, or beverages such as beer and Chianti wine. Patients taking MAO inhibitors must also avoid certain other drugs used for relieving colds, hay fever, and nausea. Hypertensive crises may cause severe headaches and intracranial bleeding. Nausea and vomiting, chills and fever, neck stiffness, sensitivity to light, chest pain, and heart arrhythmias may also occur. When any of these symptoms appear, they should be reported immediately and the drug should be discontinued by the physician.

MAO inhibitors are contraindicated if the patient suffers from any severe major medical problem and especially if there is a history of impaired kidney function. MAO inhibitors should not be mixed with other MAO inhibitors and should not be given if the patient is taking alcohol, barbiturates, or morphine-like drugs since they potentiate the action of these drugs.

MAO inhibitors include Marplan, Nardil, Niamid, and Parnate.

Tricyclic Antidepressants

These antidepressants are used to elevate the patient's mood and to stimulate the patient's activity level. Like the MAO inhibitors, drugs in this group tend to take one to four weeks of therapy before significant changes occur in the patient's outlook. Antidepressants are sometimes given in large doses in the afternoon or evening since their sedating effect may facilitate the patient's ability to sleep. Since these drugs sometimes excite patients rather than sedate them, patients must be observed closely for individual reactions.

Common side effects include dry mouth, fatigue, weakness, blurring of vision, constipation, parkinsonian syndrome and increased perspiration. Most, if not all, of these symptoms can be controlled by lowering the dosage of the medication. Table 3 lists some commonly used tricyclic antidepressants.

TABLE 3. Tricyclic Antidepressants

Trade Name	24-Hour Dosage Range
Tofranil	25–300 mg.
Norpramin	25–300 mg.
Aventyl	25–300 mg.
Elavil	25–300 mg.
Vivactil	5–60 mg.
Norpramin	25–300 mg.
Sinequan	150–300 mg.

SEDATIVES AND HYPNOTICS

The barbiturate hypnotics, nonbarbiturate hypnotics, and other seda-tives are considered similar in effect to the minor tranquilizers in that they act to reduce anxiety. A main difference in their action is that these drugs tend to cause the patient to be more sleepy than the tranquilizers. Barbiturates, however, are much more dangerous since an overdose, whether accidental or planned, can cause death. The barbiturates are also highly addictive and greatly potentiate the action of drugs such as alcoholic beverages and narcotics. Since these drugs along with the minor tranquilizers are often used in depressed patients, one should observe the patient closely for suicidal intentions, and only small amounts of these drugs should be given in order to avoid the deliberate taking of a massive overdose (especially if the patient is an outpatient). It may even be necessary to carefully check the hospitalized patient's mouth to make sure the medication has been swallowed and is not being saved until enough is collected to constitute a deadly overdose. Never leave the medication with a patient to take when he is "ready."

Compared with barbiturate hypnotics, the nonbarbiturate hypnotics have less toxic effects if an overdose occurs, are less habit forming, and result in fewer "hangovers." They are also less likely to cause "paradoxic excitement" (i.e., excite rather than calm) in patients who have unusual reactions to drugs. Patients can also develop tolerance or allergic reaction to barbiturates thus making them ineffective. When this occurs, non-barbiturate hypnotics can be safely substituted.

After the administration of these drugs, the patient should be observed closely for any reactions. If he falls into a deep sleep, he should not be awakened for the next dose. If the patient seems unusually non-responsive, the next dose of medication should be withheld and the patient's physician notified at once. It is also important to remember that the elderly patient, especially if cerebral vascular disease is present, may react to sedatives and hypnotics in a manner opposite to the desired effect. He may become excited, confused, and even try to get up. Safety must be maintained and this may require staying with the patient, talking to him in a quiet, calm manner, and repeating his name and telling him where he is in order to reorient him to his environment.

Barbiturates and sedatives, when abused, can cause a certain degree of euphoria and, therefore, a patient with a history of alcoholism or drug abuse should be carefully observed when taking any of these drugs over a long period. Staff members might suggest and help the patient learn alternative methods of handling nervousness such as listening to music, taking a warm bath at bedtime, or developing a hobby in order to help the patient gradually give up sedatives and tranquilizers. Table 4 lists frequently used sedatives and hypnotics.

TABLE 4. Sedatives and Hypnotics

Trade Name	24-Hour Dosage Range
Barbiturates	
Amytal	50–200 mg.
Perichloz	300–600 mg.
Delvinal	100–200 mg.
Butisol	45–120 mg.
Seconal	50–200 mg.
Nembutal	50–200 mg.
Nonbarbiturates	
Placidyl	100–1000 mg.
Paraldrhyde	8–15 ml.
Dalmane	15–30 mg.
Noctec	250 mg.–2 gm.
Doriden	125–1000 mg.
Valmid	500–1000 mg.
Noludar	50–400 mg.

ANTICONVULSANTS

These drugs are used to treat various kinds of convulsive seizures and phenobarbital and Dilantin are the most commonly used of all anticonvulsant drugs. Phenobarbital often has to be given in doses so large that it produces sleepiness and lethargy. Dilantin is not a hypnotic and is often used in conjunction with phenobarbital in order to allow better control of seizures with less sedative side effects. However, Dilantin may cause gastric irritation, dizziness, nausea and vomiting, blurred vision, nervousness, and excessive growth of gum tissue and hair, especially facial hair. Some patients are particularly sensitive to the drug and develop skin rashes, dermatitis, fever, and some may have difficulty breathing. Such serious side effects as hallucinations, psychosis, hepatitis, and lupus erythematosus have been reported due to Dilantin therapy.

ANTIPARKINSONS

The three antiparkinson drugs frequently used in treating psychiatric patients are Benadryl, Cogentin, and Artane. The drugs are used to combat the parkinson-like side effects often produced when the patient is receiving tranquilizers or other antipsychotic drugs. They reduce muscle rigidity, excessive drooling, and sweating. If the dosage is too high, the patient may have difficulty voiding, blurred vision, and dry mouth. Sucking on hard candies is one way the patient can avoid oral discomfort.

OTHER DRUGS

Some other drugs are used quite often in the treatment of psychiatric patients and, therefore, are included here.

Indoklon. This drug is a central nervous system stimulant administered by inhalation and used instead of ECT to produce convulsions in depressed patients.

Lithium Carbonate. This drug is used in the treatment of manic depressive psychoses since it is effective in decreasing the manic patient's excessive motor activity, talking, and unstable behavior by acting on the patient's brain metabolism. Patients should be observed for the following signs of lithium intoxication: nausea, vomiting, diarrhea, sudden loss of appetite, drowsiness, muscle weakness, and motor uncoordination. If these symptoms occur, discontinuation of the drug is required. Knowing that this drug acts on the brain metabolism and seeing it drastically improve patient behavior leads many authorities to believe that many of the psychiatric disorders may be due to faulty metabolism and thus may someday be curable through the use of drug therapy.

Brevital. This is a rapid acting, ultrashort acting barbiturate administered IV and used to induce light surgical anesthesia before ECT treatments.

Succinylcholine Chloride (Anectine). This drug is used to produce skeletal muscle relaxation prior to ECT treatment.

GENERAL CONSIDERATIONS

Drug therapy is not a cure for mental illness; at best it is only an adjunct to psychotherapy. It is important, however, since it allows many patients to control symptoms to such a degree that they can still function as effective members of society. Just as diabetics have to take insulin for the rest of their lives in order to survive, many mentally ill patients will have to take psychotropic drugs on a long term basis.

Since most of these drugs are relatively new, it is extremely important that these patients be watched for unexpected side effects and complications. The family is usually interested in the patient's progress and should be actively involved in the care plan. Patients should assume the responsibility for taking their own medication when at home and should learn the correct amount and frequency of doses from the staff. The staff should also explain to the patient that many of the medications taken are effective because a certain amount of the drug (blood level) is constantly in one's system. If one skips a dose or stops taking the medication, the blood level drops and the medication is ineffective. Many patients stop taking their medications as soon as they feel better because they feel that they are cured. Unfortunately, they fail to realize that the medication has brought about much of their improvement and a relapse will occur if they stop taking their prescribed drugs.

Patients and their families should be well informed concerning possible side effects and know to report them to the staff as soon as they appear. Most patients will cooperate about taking medication if they know how it will help and why it is being given.

SPECIFIC NURSING CONSIDERATIONS

MAJOR TRANQUILIZERS
1. Responses are highly individualized and it is important to find the lowest effective dose for the patient. Also, many signs and symptoms are dose-related.
2. Bed rails may be needed for the first few days of therapy because of hypotensive reactions, drowsiness, and dizziness that may occur in initial attempts to stabilize a dosage.
3. Phenothiazine drugs are not stable when mixed with other medications. Do not mix.
4. When giving phenothiazines IM, give them deep to prevent tissue irritation and avoid injection into the subcutaneous tissue, and inject them slowly.
5. Urinary retention and constipation may occur. Record intake and output.
6. Upon discharge, explain the following to the patient:
   a. importance of taking medication as ordered to maintain a therapeutic blood level
   b. tolerance can develop but medication does not produce physical dependence
   c. refrain from activities requiring mental alertness and coordination until re-evaluation by the physician
   d. if in liquid form, medication is sensitive to light and must be kept out of direct sunlight
   e. medication may turn urine pink to reddish-brown
   f. patient should carry identification that he is receiving phenothiazine medication
   g. patient and family should understand side-effects and how to reach attending physician if necessary.

MINOR TRANQUILIZERS
1. Unlike major tranquilizers, the possibility of physical and psychologic dependence is always present.
2. Alcohol should be avoided when taking these drugs because they augment the depressant effects of alcohol.
3. In prolonged Librium therapy, periodic blood cell counts and liver function tests are recommended.
4. Prepare IM Librium immediately before administration and dispose of unused portion.
5. IV Valium cannot be mixed with other drugs or any type of solution. It therefore cannot be added to intravenous fluids. Administer IV Valium slowly, taking at least one minute for each 5 mg. (1 cc).

110

6. After prolonged administration of Valium or Librium, withdrawal symptoms may occur.

ANTIDEPRESSANTS
1. Instruct patient on what foods to avoid when taking MAO inhibitors.
2. Warn patient against mixing medications with over-the-counter items such as cough syrup, etc.
3. Monitor effectiveness of the drug as evidenced by patient's renewed interest in self and surroundings. This is especially important because therapeutic response is so variable, occurring anywhere from 2 days to 2 months.
4. When the patient begins showing renewed interest, evaluate and supervise patient because the risk of suicide increases when the medication helps the patient to feel strong enough to carry out suicidal plans.
5. Patients may require assistance in getting in the upright position during the initial stage of therapy because of orthostatic hypotension.

SEDATIVES AND HYPNOTICS
1. Barbiturates, especially short-acting ones, may cause dependence; if this occurs, withdrawal may be very serious.
2. Patient should be informed that the use of these drugs with each other or with alcohol may be fatal and should be completely avoided.
3. Barbiturates significantly reduce the effectiveness of the oral anticoagulants and these drugs should not be given together.
4. Discourage the patient from mixing these drugs with any over-the-counter drugs, especially drugs such as antihistamines that can give additive central nervous system depression.
5. Caution patient against abruptly discontinuing these drugs since withdrawal symptoms may occur.
6. Encourage the patient to do some type of relaxation exercises before using these drugs since they are habit forming.
7. Warn patient receiving barbiturates not to drive a car or operate machinery.
8. If the patient is discharged with a prescription for sleeping pills, encourage the patient not to leave the pill bottle at the bedside. This may help avoid an accidental overdose.

ANTICONVULSANTS
1. Include patient and family in health teaching on use of medication as a part of therapeutic regimen.
2. Warn that excessive use of alcohol may interfere with drug action.
3. To avoid GI problems, take medication with fluids or food.
4. Stress the necessity of continuing under medical supervision after discharge.
5. Stress that patient should not alter the dosage. If medication is not controlling the seizures, the physician should be notified.
6. Warn the patient of things that lower the seizure threshold, such as fever, low blood sugar, etc.

ANTIPARKINSONS
1. It sometimes takes two or three days for these medications to show effects.
2. These drugs have a sedation effect.
3. Monitor intake and output because oliguria can interfere with the excretion of these drugs.
4. Most antiparkinsons drugs should be given after meals.

ANNOTATED BIBLIOGRAPHY

Battle, E.H., Halliburton, A., and Wallston, K.A.: *Self-medication among psychiatric patients and adherence after discharge.* Journal of Psychosocial Nursing and Mental Health Services, 1982, 20(5):21–28.

Research study on causes of noncompliance of self-medication in outpatients.

Betemps, E.: *Management of the withdrawal syndrome of barbiturates and other central nervous system depressants.* Journal of Psychosocial Nursing and Mental Health Services, 1981, 19(9):31–34.

Lists withdrawal symptoms of various barbiturates and CNS depressants and includes implications for nursing management.

Boettcher, E.G., and Alderson, S.: *Psychotropic medications and the nursing process.* Journal of Psychosocial Nursing and Mental Health Services, 1982, 20(11):12–16.

Explains use of nursing process in administration and evaluation of psychotropic medications.

Neizo, B., and Murphy, M.K.: *Medication groups on an acute psychiatric unit.* Perspectives in Psychiatric Care, 1983, 21(2):70–73.

Addresses the problems of noncompliance, fear, and patient teaching on a psychiatric unit when giving medication. Relates the solution of one hospital to the medication problems.

McDermott, J.: *Ready or not, here comes your patient on lithium.* Nursing '83, 1983, 13(8):45–48.

Relates action of lithium in manic depressive disorders. Includes side effects, drug interactions, dosages, serum level monitoring, and case study.

Rosal-Greif, V.L.F.: *Drug-induced dyskinesias.* American Journal of Nursing, 1982, 82(1):66–69.

Describes symptoms of tardive dyskinesia induced by major tranquilizers and levodopa. Provides tool for assessment of dyskinesias and outlines care and management.

Vernon, A.W.: *Classification of psychotherapeutic drugs.* Journal of Psychosocial Nursing and Mental Health Services, 1981, 19(11):15–17.

Discusses classifications and categories of psychotropic drugs, including antipsychotics, antidepressants, antimanics, and antianxiety drugs.

POST-TEST

Chapter 7

Drug Therapy

Matching. Match the letter of the appropriate item in Column B with the descriptive statements in Column A.

	Column A	*Column B*
_____	1. Helps control severe agitation.	A. Antidepressants
		B. Lithium
_____	2. Helps elevate the patient's mood.	C. Major tranquilizers
		D. Indoklon
_____	3. Combats parkinson-like side effects.	E. Antiparkinson
		F. Anectine
_____	4. Used in treatment of manic depressives.	
_____	5. Produces skeletal muscle relaxation prior to ECT.	

Match the letter of the appropriate item in Column B with the drugs in Column A. (Letters in Column B may be used more than once.)

	Column A	*Column B*
_____	1. Valium	A. Major tranquilizer
_____	2. Tofranil	B. Antiparkinson
_____	3. Dalmane	C. Anticonvulsant
_____	4. Vistaril	D. Antidepressant
_____	5. Cogentin	E. Minor tranquilizer
_____	6. Compazine	F. Sedative-hypnotic
_____	7. Dilantin	
_____	8. Aventyl	
_____	9. Mellaril	

True or False. Circle your choice.

T   F   1. Phenothiazines are a cure for mental illness.

T   F   2. The phenothiazine derivatives are the largest group of anti-psychotic drugs.

T F 3. Increased sexual interest is a major problem with patients receiving phenothiazines.

T F 4. One of the main difficulties in using minor tranquilizers is that they tend to be habit forming.

T F 5. MAO inhibitors are usually given with another MAO inhibitor to achieve the desired effect.

T F 6. Patients no longer need to take their medication when they feel better.

Short Answers. Answer the following questions as briefly and specifically as possible.

1. What effect might one expect the tranquilizers to have on a patient?

_____

_____

_____

2. If a patient is having an autonomic reaction to his medication, what is the nursing responsibility?

_____

_____

_____

3. What are the two categories of antidepressants?

1. _____

2. _____

4. What are the common side effects to watch for in a patient receiving a tricyclic antidepressant?

_____

_____

_____

Multiple Choice. Circle the letter you think represents the best answer.

1. Which side effects are characteristic of lithium carbonate?
    1. Diarrhea.
    2. Nausea and vomiting.
    3. Excessive thirst.
    4. Muscle weakness and motor incoordination.
    5. Loss of appetite.
        A. 2 and 4.
        B. 1, 2, and 3.

C. 1, 4, and 5.

D. All of the above.

2. Parkinson-like symptoms which occur as a side effect of the phenothiazine drugs can best be controlled by:

1. Mellaril.

2. Colace.

3. Artane.

4. Congentin.

5. Compazine.

    A. 1 only.

    B. 2 and 5.

    C. 3 and 5.

    D. 2 and 4.

    E. 3 and 4.

3. Jaundice, photosensitivity, and parkinsonian syndrome may occur in patients receiving:

A. Valium.

B. Elavil.

C. Miltown.

D. Thorazine.

4. Which of the following are true of extrapyramidal symptoms?

1. They may appear after a single dose of the phenothiazines.

2. They may appear after prolonged administration of the phenothiazines.

3. They indicate that the phenothiazines are affecting the deeper brain centers.

4. They are not controllable.

5. They are fatal.

    A. 1, 4, and 5.

    B. 1, 2, and 3.

    C. 1 and 4.

    D. 2 and 3.

    E. 1 and 3.

5. The time required to reach an effective blood level of antidepressant medication is:

A. 24 hours.

B. 2 days.

C. 2 weeks.

D. 20 days.

6. Side effects from antipsychotic agents such as thorazine include:

1. Extrapyramidal symptoms.

2. Mental confusion.

3. Hypotension.

4. Habituation.

5. Dryness of the mouth.

A. 1, 2, and 3.
B. 1, 3, and 4.
C. 1, 2, and 4.
D. 1, 3, and 5.
E. All of these.
7. In administering medications on a psychiatric service one should:
   1. Check identification by reading the identification bracelet.
   2. Carry only one drug at a time on a tray.
   3. Mix poorly accepted medications in food or drink.
   4. Inspect the mouth of the patient who is likely or suspected to hoard medications to be sure the medications are swallowed.
      A. 1 and 2.
      B. 1 and 4.
      C. 1, 3, and 4.
      D. All of the above.

8

Electroconvulsive Therapy

> **OBJECTIVES:** Student will be able to:
> 1. Describe two theories about why ECT works.
> 2. List diagnostic tests necessary before administering ECT.
> 3. List general guidelines for caring for the patient before ECT.
> 4. List general guidelines for caring for the patient after ECT.

The purpose of this section is to familiarize the reader with the technique of electroconvulsive shock therapy, sometimes called ECT or EST. This technique of treating patients was introduced by Dr. Ugo Cerletti and Dr. Lucio Bini of Rome, Italy in the late 1930s. In the last eight to ten years, physicians have refined this treatment technique and now administer muscle relaxants and anesthesia prior to the actual treatment to reduce the violent aspects of the patient's convulsion. This is done to prevent fractures and contusions which often occurred before such medications were used. When treatments are given using muscle relaxants and anesthesia, all one observes is a slight tremor in the patient's hands and feet lasting approximately one to two minutes. Patients do not remember treatment activities and the only pain experienced by patients is an occasional post-ECT headache.

Although we are not certain why ECT works, two theories are frequently offered. The first of these theories suggests that ECT works by breaking up neural patterns or memory traces in the brain, thus permitting the patient to forget or at least think less about the painful aspects of his life experiences. The second theory suggests that patients who receive ECT treatments perceive them as a form of punishment and thus improve after treatment because they feel they have been punished for their actions. This latter theory gains much of its support from the idea that ECT seems to work most effectively with depressed patients. As previously discussed, depressed patients frequently have severe guilt feelings. Perhaps ECT reduces guilt by causing the patients to feel that they have "paid" for all their sins.

Although ECT treatments are done on a routine basis in many hospitals, it is important to remember that the procedure is a potentially dangerous one and that a great deal of care must be exercised when administering it. All of the following tests should be completed on any patient scheduled for ECT *prior* to the first treatment:

1. A thorough physical examination.
2. A thorough mental examination.
3. An EKG (electrocardiogram) since ECT places a great deal of strain on a patient's heart.
4. Chest and lumbosacral (spinal) x-rays along with routine blood studies are usually obtained to determine if any abnormalities exist.
5. An EEG (electroencephalogram) to determine whether or not there are any abnormal electrical activities already occurring in the patient's brain. If the possibility of organic brain disease exists, a complete skull x-ray series is also completed along with a brain scan.

If any significant abnormality is discovered, the physician will likely choose another treatment method. However, in some cases (e.g., chronic suicidal patients), a physician may decide that the need for the treatment outweighs the potential risks involved.

Depressed patients, patients with involutional melancholia and manic-depressive patients seem to be most effectively treated with ECT. These same patients are the ones who are most likely to experience significant guilt feelings and to be anxious and worried. Since they may have heard inaccurate and terrifying stories about ECT and because of the real dangers which have been explained to them by their physician, these patients are often extremely anxious about having ECT treatments. They require a considerable amount of support and encouragement from the staff and will likely need to spend a good bit of time just talking about the procedure. This affords them the opportunity to openly explore their anxieties and feelings with a staff member who is familiar with the procedure and who can be friendly, informative, supportive, and attentive. This pre-ECT care and support is a vital aspect of the total treatment procedure.

Below are some questions frequently asked by persons who are to receive ECT treatments. We have provided a possible answer to each question but one should remember that the answer given is by no means the only appropriate answer. Answers may also vary in order to comply with the rules and procedures of a particular institution.

Will I feel any pain?

The only discomfort you might feel would be from the shot which will be given to you immediately prior to the treatment. You will not feel the electricity and you will not remember anything that happens. You may feel some muscle stiffness for a few hours after the treatment but usually a warm bath and a little exercise will make you feel much better. Some patients have a post-ECT headache which lasts for a few hours.

Will I die?

No. There is some risk associated with any treatment procedure but this treatment is safe because we take a great deal of care to be sure that you are able to tolerate the treatment.

Is there a possibility that I could be electrocuted?

It is not possible for you to be electrocuted. The machines used produce only a very small amount of electrical current and it is not enough to electrocute you.

How many treatments will I have to take?

The number of treatments you will receive will depend on what your doctor thinks is best and on the progress you make after each treatment. Usually between 8 and 12 treatments are used.

Will I lose my memory?

People usually do not remember the treatment itself and may be confused for a few hours or even a few days after ECT treatments; however, there is rarely any permanent memory loss and you will probably remember everything that you want to remember within a few days to a few weeks after treatment.

Will my mind be ruined?

No. Most people are able to do things as well or better than they could before the treatment. Immediately following the treatments you may be confused, but the confusion will go away within a short period of time.

PROCEDURAL GUIDELINES

Presented below are the major tasks which need to be accomplished when a patient is to receive ECT. These are general guidelines and the particular policies and procedures of each institution must be taken into account.

Pretreatment

1. At some point prior to the ECT treatment, written consent will have to be obtained from the patient. Legally it is the responsibility of the treating physician to explain the procedure to the patient and to be sure that any questions the patient might have are answered. The physician then has the patient sign a written consent form giving permission for the ECT treatment. An ECT treatment should never be administered without the patient's written consent except in the case of an involuntary admission. Even then, the laws for one's particular state

119

should be checked regarding the legality of administering ECT without the patient's written permission.

2. Several hours before the ECT treatment, the patient's chart should be checked to see that all laboratory work, x-rays, and pretreatment procedures have been completed.

3. The patient will need to be NPO (without food or water) for at least eight hours before treatment. This should be carefully explained to the patient.

4. Patients should be given ample opportunity to ask questions and express their anxieties. It is important to keep in mind that patients are likely to be quite anxious and upset prior to treatment and may ask the same questions several times. Members of the treatment team must be supportive during this period and patiently answer any questions a patient might ask regardless of how many times the question is repeated.

5. Just prior to the treatment, ask the patient to void. This will help to reduce any discomfort and embarassment that the patient might experience from becoming incontinent during the treatment. All watches, rings, hairpins, jewelry, and so forth should be removed from the patient and placed in a valuables envelope. Such items may cause burns or may be lost during or after the treatment procedure. Post-ECT confusion prevents many patients from remembering what they do with their valuables. Care should be taken to protect their valuables and to reassure them that they are not lost.

6. All objects which are removable should be taken from the mouth (e.g., chewing gum, bridges, or dentures). This is to prevent the patient from aspirating these items during the treatment. Contact lenses should be removed also.

7. Pre-ECT medication is administered by the member of the treatment team responsible for that particular task. It is important that this medication be the accurate amount and that it be given as close to the time specified by the order as possible. The patient may complain of a dry mouth.

Treatment

1. All equipment to be used during the treatment should be carefully checked to make sure it is available and functioning properly. This includes the ECT machine, oxygen equipment, the emergency cart, and any emergency trays that might be necessary in case complications occur during the treatment. The patient should be accompanied to the treatment room and asked to lie on the stretcher or operating table where the treatment is to be given. The safety straps should be secured. The straps should be snug enough to keep the patient from falling from the table but

120

loose enough to allow for slight movement when the seizure occurs. Some institutions may require the patient to wear a hospital gown during this procedure.

2. The patient's temporal area where the surfaces of the electrodes will be placed should be cleaned prior to treatment. Since cleansing solutions may vary, check your institution's procedure manual for specific instructions. Usually a special paste is applied to the skin of the temporal area in order to keep the electrodes from burning the skin when the electrical activity occurs. After the treatment, this paste will need to be removed with warm water to keep it from caking on the patient's hair and skin.

3. After the operative medication is administered, an airway of some type is generally put into the patient's mouth in order to assure that the patient will continue to have an open airway.

4. A physician should administer the shock. As soon as the electrical current hits the brain, the patient will have a grand mal type seizure. Thanks to the use of muscle relaxants and anesthesia, the seizures are generally very mild. However, two health workers should be present to help hold the patient on the stretcher or table. Care should be taken not to constrict the patient's movements any more than is necessary to insure that the patient does not hurt himself by either hitting himself or by falling off the table.

5. After the patient has regained consciousness and the physician has determined that the patient is having no difficulty breathing, the patient should be removed to a recovery area. Someone should stay with the patient at all times until he is fully conscious.

Post-Treatment

1. After the patient has regained consciousness and is able to stand up and move about, a warm bath or mild exercise may help relieve soreness in his muscles and joints. Patients should also be given a light breakfast such as coffee, juice and toast since they were NPO several hours prior to treatment. **Many physicians routinely request that 10 grains of aspirin be given to their patients as soon as they are fully recovered. This is done to relieve post-ECT headaches.**

2. Patients may be confused after ECT treatments and thus require a great deal of supervision, assistance and reassurance. Answer any questions and be as supportive and attentive as possible.

3. Sometimes, even after one or more treatments, patients may be very uncertain of themselves and may develop or retain anxieties about having ECT treatment. In such cases, continual reassurance, support and attentiveness will be necessary in order to help the patients deal with their anxieties about ECT treatments.

ANNOTATED BIBLIOGRAPHY

Ahern, L.: *Electroconvulsive therapy: An effective treatment.* Association of Operating Room Nurses, 1981, 34(3):463–470.

Advocates the use of ECT in specific mental disorders. Describes in great detail the procedure of modern ECT.

Beardshaw, V.: *A question of conscience.* Nursing Times, March 9, 1982, 78:349–51.

Discusses the pros and cons of administering ECT and the issues which confront nursing.

Bevilacqua, J.: *Voodoo—Myth of mental illness?* Journal of Psychosocial Nursing and Mental Health Services, 1980, 18(2):17–23.

Includes the treatment of a catatonic adolescent Haitian girl with ECT. Describes the patient's reactions to ECT.

Campkin, P. *Endogenous depression: Moody blues ECT.* Nursing Mirror, February 19, 1981, 152:43–44.

Parsons, L.: *Why ECT is an ethical issue.* Nursing Times, March 3, 1982, 78:352.

A British nurse relates his personal feelings and the social issues which lead to his decision not to participate in ECT in a nursing capacity.

Psychiatry. A shock to the system . . . pros and cons of ECT. Nursing Mirror, April 2, 1981, 152:20–22.

POST-TEST

Chapter 8

Electroconvulsive Therapy

True or False. Circle your choice.

T F 1. ECT is a simple procedure with no risks involved.

T F 2. Legal consent is not necessary from the patient before ECT is administered.

T F 3. It is necessary for the patient to go without food or water for eight hours before an ECT treatment.

T F 4. When the electric current reaches the brain, the patient will have a petit mal type seizure.

T F 5. After an ECT treatment, a patient may be confused and need a great deal of supervision, assistance, and reassurance.

T F 6. If a patient seems very embarassed to remove his dentures before an ECT treatment, it is all right for the patient to leave the dentures in rather than to cause the patient embarrassment.

Short Answer. Answer the following questions as briefly and specifically as possible.

1. Give the two commonly accepted theories as to why ECT is effective.

   1. _____

   2. _____

2. Why is an EKG completed before the patient receives ECT treatment?

   _____

3. Which psychiatric diagnostic category seems to show the best improvement after receiving ECT?

   _____

4. Why is it necessary to remove dentures, bridges, etc., from the patient's mouth prior to ECT?

   _____

Multiple Choice. Circle the letter you think represents the best answer.

1. Mrs. Jones is a patient who is scheduled for shock treatment. Miss Smith, a student nurse, becomes very anxious and is unable to help with the treatment. What mental mechanism is she using?
   A. Identification.
   B. Denial.
   C. Regression.
   D. Suppression.

2. Which of the following physical complications never occurs as a result of electric shock therapy?
   A. Dislocated jaw.
   B. Compression fractures.
   C. Respiratory arrest.
   D. Electrocution.
   E. Cardiac arrest.

3. Electroshock therapy is most effective in the treatment of:
   1. Depression.
   2. Neuroses.
   3. Catatonic schizophrenia.
   4. Personality disorders.
      A. 1 and 2.
      B. 1 and 3.
      C. 2 and 3.
      D. All of the above.

4. An appropriate approach to a patient complaining of amnesia following ECT is to:
   A. Explain that forgetting is the usual reaction and will clear up after the treatments are finished.
   B. Help him remember those things he has forgotten.
   C. Tell him that the amnesia will subside in a few hours.
   D. Tell him that the amnesia is selective and he will not forget important things.

5. If Mr. Brown is treated with convulsive therapy, the nurse should:
   1. Take measures to prevent physical injury, especially fractures.
   2. Provide a secure pre- and post-treatment environment.
   3. Monitor vital signs.
   4. Remain with the patient during his confused state.
   5. Assure the patient that he will not notice any memory loss.
      A. 1 and 3.
      B. 2, 3, 4, and 5.
      C. 1, 2, 3, and 4.
      D. All of the above.

9

Other Therapies

TALK THERAPIES

Psychotherapy, as the talking therapy is generally called, can either be done on an individual basis or in groups and may be under the direction of a physician, clinical psychologist, or other therapist. In any case, the aim of the therapy is the same, that is, to help patients gain understanding and/or insight into their problems so that they can learn to deal with them more effectively. Psychotherapy may be used in conjunction with drug therapy, electroconvulsive shock therapy, art therapy, recreational therapy, and occupational therapy. Frequently, a combination of two or more types of therapy will yield best results.

Although there is a great deal of argument about the effectiveness of psychotherapy, and for that matter many other forms of therapy, it is probable that three things are necessary for an improvement in the patient's ability to cope with the stresses of life. First, the patient must want to get better. Second, the patient must come to a better understanding of what is causing his problems and in turn learn methods or techniques for dealing more effectively with them. Third, an environment in which it is possible for change to take place must be provided.

In many cases, the third task is the most difficult one to accomplish. Although most treatment teams are successful in creating a therapeutic environment in which desirable changes can occur, when the patient goes back home to a nonsupportive environment, it often happens that the best insight and the best treatment available is insufficient to overcome the adverse effects of the patient's environment. In such cases, family therapy is advisable. Otherwise, it is quite probable that the patient will have to return for further treatment.

As a member of a treatment team, one needs to support and reinforce the efforts of the team members who are responsible for individual or group psychotherapy. The skills and techniques presented in the chapter on communicating with patients should be helpful in developing support skills for the talking therapies.

BEHAVIOR MODIFICATION

Behavior therapy is a term used to specify a particular kind of treatment wherein no claim is made to do anything other than change or modify the behavior of the patient. For this reason, it has been called simplistic by many of its critics.

Essentially, behavior therapy consists of deciding which behaviors exhibited by a particular patient are desirable and which are undesirable and then trying to increase the frequency of the desirable behaviors and eliminate or decrease the frequency of the undesirable behaviors. This method of treatment has been particularly effective in the treatment of children and mentally retarded persons.

There are advocates and critics of behavior therapy. The movie "Clockwork Orange" presented both the capabilities of behavior therapy as well as some of the drawbacks. In this particular movie, a young sociopathic person (one who engages in acts that society considers wrong) was conditioned against responding to anything in a hostile or sexual way. He had been a very hostile young man who had beaten and mugged several persons and sexually assaulted several others. After he was conditioned not to react to any stimulus in a hostile or sexual manner, he was returned to his community. Of course, being unable to respond in a hostile manner, his former enemies and even his friends quickly began to take advantage of him. In the end, he was taken back and deconditioned because of the public uproar over the treatment he had received. Members of his community considered the conditioning technique to be barbaric and inhuman. This points out the fact that just because a particular technique works, it may not be fully utilized because of social pressures.

Basically, conditioning operates on the idea that people will behave in ways that get them what they want. Each of us responds in this manner every day of our lives. For example, you are reading this book because you wish to gain more knowledge about the subject matter. It may be that you need this knowledge to obtain a degree in some particular area, to get a better job, to be a better mental health worker, or simply because you are curious about the treatment of the mentally ill. You would not be reading this book would it not help in some way to get you something that you want. The factory worker who works 40 hours a week at a job he finds boring usually does so because working at the factory gets him the money he needs to obtain other satisfactions in life. Such conditioning factors operate in our lives in other ways. If a four year old realizes that in order to get mother's attention, he must lie down on the floor and kick his heels and scream at the top of his voice, he will then engage in that type behavior whenever he wants his mother's attention. The same is true for the young man who goes to medical school, not because he wants to be a doctor but because it gains him the approval he so desperately wants and needs from his parents. Sometimes individuals engage in self-destructive behavior in order to gain some apparently superficial end, yet that end has a great deal of meaning to that individual. The idea again is that people behave in ways that get them what they want although they may not always be aware of the long term consequences of the behavior or even aware that their behavior often appears inappropriate to other people.

In behavior therapy, an effort is made to ascertain which behaviors exhibited by an individual are desirable and which are undesirable, and then to reward selectively the desirable behaviors and ignore the undesirable behaviors. This is done to increase the desirable behaviors and decrease the undesirable behaviors. Little thought is given to the causes of the behavior or to the dynamics of the behavior in the traditional psychotherapeutic sense. A behaviorist will not ask why a patient is hostile, because hostility is not a concept with which he is willing to deal. Rather, he asks in what behaviors one wishes the patient to engage. He wants to know what *behaviors* make the patient appear hostile. The behavior therapist argues that the patient only seems hostile because he is engaging in certain behaviors and that if the patient ceases to engage in those behaviors, he will not be called hostile.

While some rather astonishing behavioral changes can be made in a relatively short period of time, this method of treatment has some definite drawbacks. For one, a great deal of control is required over the patient's behavior. It is necessary to be able to control the environment in such a way as to prevent unwanted reinforcement or rewarding of certain behaviors and to be certain that the desired behaviors are rewarded. There is also a problem of maintaining the frequency of the desired behaviors once the patient leaves the controlled environment and the systematic application of reinforcement is no longer possible.

THE AUXILIARY THERAPIES
(Occupational Therapy, Recreational Therapy, Art Therapy, Music Therapy)

It has been said that man is a social creature and, therefore, must respond to a wide range of situations. In order to successfully meet the demands of today's complex and ever changing society, man must indeed possess a good deal of flexibility.

By and large, mentally ill patients have developed maladaptive ways of responding to their environments and thus, to some extent, lose their social adaptability. Their range of interests and activities becomes quite constricted and they may or may not lose contact with reality. In general, these patients experience some degree of personality disorganization.

In order to assist the mentally ill patient in his attempts to interact effectively with other people again, occupational, art, recreational, and music therapists provide a wide range of activities. These activities require the patient to become involved in something outside himself, thus affording the patient less time to dwell on his problems. These activities also require interaction with the therapist and possibly with one or more other patients who are also in the treatment program. If patients are given interesting and challenging projects at a level of difficulty which is appropriate for them, they benefit from their participation. By having to collect their thoughts, organize their actions and use their own initiative, they can be led to become active once again in their own lives as well as the lives of their families and friends. Hopefully, the successful completion of projects will enhance the patient's self-concept and afford him a sense of pride or accomplishment which often has been lacking for quite some time. Success also tends to encourage the patient to respond to his environment and the people in it in a more healthy fashion.

Not all patients are delighted about the opportunity to participate in such therapeutic activities. Often they prefer to remain in their rooms or to engage in some solitary activity. It is important that they be gently, but firmly, encouraged to participate in therapeutic activities. If patients receive repeated invitations to join the group and are not rejected when they refuse to participate, they may later become more willing to join in such activities. Frequently patients do not wish to participate because they have experienced so many failures, they are certain that they will only fail again. Their anxieties should be taken into account and an effort made to understand them. As is generally the case with mentally ill persons, a great deal of understanding, reassurance, and patience is required in order to help the individual feel comfortable enough to engage in any new activity.

It is always important to be certain that once patients agree to participate, they are not expected to engage in some activity which is likely to cause them to be humiliated in front of others or in which they are likely to fail. Activities must be carefully selected and expectations kept in line with their capabilities. If at all possible, conferences between the various members of the treatment team, including those from the various auxiliary therapies, should be held to discuss the patient's progress, treatment goals, capabilities, and needs.

Perhaps the most important thing to keep in mind regarding the various therapeutic activities is that these auxiliary therapies should provide the patient with an opportunity to relax, to engage in something which is enjoyable, and provide a break in the regular therapeutic routine. It should be a time of fun for the patient and the patient should be encouraged to participate as freely and as spontaneously as possible.

ANNOTATED BIBLIOGRAPHY

Baker, B.S.: *The use of music with autistic children.* Journal of Psychosocial Nursing and Mental Health Services, 1982, 20(4):31–34.

Describes four stages of utilizing music therapy with autistic children; breaking the shell, shifting of awareness, building competencies, and building relationships with others.

Carser, D.L.: *Primary nursing in the milieu.* Journal of Psychosocial Nursing and Mental Health Services, 1981, 19(2):35–41.

Explains the relationship between psychiatric care, milieu therapy, and primary care. Stresses wholistic care including family and community systems.

Devine, B.A.: *Therapeutic milieu/mileu therapy. An overview.* Journal of Psychosocial Nursing and Mental Health Services, 1981, 19(3):20–24.

Contains a condensed historical perspective. Also includes definitions, principles, a description of the role of nursing, and a review of research findings.

Hinds, P.S.; *Music: A milieu factor with implications for the nurse-therapist.* Journal of Psychosocial Nursing and Mental Health Services, 1980, 18(6):28–33.

Research study that revealed that the behaviors of school aged males with socialization disorders improved with the use of music therapy. The socialization and positive behaviors in these boys was enhanced over a 14-week period.

Impey, L.: *Art media: A means to therapeutic communication with families.* Perspectives in Psychiatric Care, 1981, 19(1):70–77.

Interactions with four families taking part in family therapy are utilized to illustrate the value of art therapy to enhance therapist-family and interfamilial communication.

Minshull, D.: *Counselling in psychiatric nursing.* Nursing Times, 1982, 78(28):1201–1202.

Briefly describes nine different approaches in talk therapy. Freudian approach, primal therapy, Rogerian counselling, behavior modification, reality therapy, rational emotive therapy, transactional analysis, six category intervention analysis, and Christian counselling.

Pothier, P.C.: *Implications for sensory motor therapy with emotionally disturbed children.* Journal of Psychosocial Nursing and Mental Health Services, 1980, 18(9):20–23.

Relates the characteristics of sensory motor dysfunction (SMD), the relationship of SMD to emotional disturbance, and the types of sensory motor therapy in current use.

POST-TEST

Chapter 9

Other Therapies

True or False. Circle your choice.

T F 1. Basically, behavior modification uses the idea that people behave in ways that get them what they want.

T F 2. Mentally ill patients to a large extent have lost their social adaptability due to their maladaptive ways of responding to their environment.

T F 3. It is the mental health worker's responsibility to see that all patients participate in every activity and not allow excuses from anyone.

T F 4. Occupational therapy is an important measure in the treatment of the psychiatric patient because it offers a means whereby the individual may achieve a feeling of accomplishment.

T F 5. If you were using behavior modification with a patient with poor table manners, you would just accept these manners without comment.

T F 6. Behavior modification is especially helpful in the treatment of children and mentally retarded persons.

Short Answer. Answer the following as briefly and specifically as possible.

1. What three essential things are necessary for an improvement in a patient's ability to cope with life's stresses?

1. _____

2. _____

3. _____

2. Which of the above three tasks is the most difficult to accomplish?

_____

3. What is the primary purpose of psychotherapy?

_____

_____

Multiple Choice. Circle the letter you think represents the best answer.
1. Which of the following will probably be most likely to get Mr. Cartwright, a patient on a behavioral modification ward, to change his eating habits:
   A. Accept his table manners without comment.
   B. Urge him to eat as the other patients do.
   C. Offer him a reward for each improvement in his table manners.
   D. Point out to him that his eating habits distress the other patients.
2. Limits should be set:
   1. To help the patient to reduce his anxiety.
   2. To help the patient to learn to control his behavior.
   3. To establish the authority of the staff over the patient.
   4. To punish inappropriate behavior.
   5. To protect people and property from injury.
      A. 1, 2, and 5.
      B. 1, 2, and 3.
      C. 2, 4, and 5.
      D. All of these.
3. Steps and techniques involved in setting limits are:
   1. Identify the need for the limit.
   2. Help the patient to understand the need for the limit.
   3. Allow the patient to verbalize his feelings about the limit.
   4. Consistency.
   5. Evaluate the limit frequently.
      A. 1, 3, and 5.
      B. 2, 3, and 4.
      C. 1, 2, and 4.
      D. All of these.
4. Which of the following are advantages of group therapy?
   A. Gives the therapists a chance to supply authorative answers to problems common to the group.
   B. Provides for the resolution of problems through group discussion and discovery of possible solutions.
   C. Gives the mentally dull an opportunity to reason and form judgments through group interaction.
   D. Allows the therapist to interact with several patients at one time so that they all have access to professional counseling.
5. Occupational therapy is an important measure in the treatment of the psychiatric patient because it primarily:

A. Offers the poor patient an opportunity to pay for part of his care by selling items he makes.
B. Provides an opportunity to keep the patient active.
C. Offers a means wherein the individual may achieve a feeling of accomplishment.
D. Offers an opportunity to observe the patient.

6. A therapeutic health promoting environment for patients (milieu therapy) provides for:
   1. A testing ground for new patterns of behavior.
   2. Acceptance as an individual.
   3. Unconditional acceptance of behavior.
   4. Protection from self-injury.
   5. A continuous appraisal of patient's needs.
      A. 2 only.
      B. 2 and 3.
      C. 1, 2, and 4.
      D. All the above.

7. Which of the following are true about psychotherapy?
   1. The aim of psychotherapy is to help the patient learn new patterns of behavior.
   2. Psychotherapy refers to a certain type relationship between one or more patients and a therapist.
   3. In family psychotherapy, the therapist treats only the neurotic or psychotic family member.
   4. Group therapy, psychoanalysis, and counseling are three common types of psychotherapy.
      A. 2 only.
      B. 2 and 3.
      C. 1, 2, and 4.
      D. All the above.

Part 3

CONSTRUCTIVE APPROACHES TO INAPPROPRIATE BEHAVIOR

10

Aggressive Patients

There are several groups of behaviors commonly associated with the aggressive patient. These include verbally abusive behavior, agitated or destructive behavior, demanding behavior, lying and stealing, fighting, arguing and irritating behavior and, finally, uncooperative behavior. It is important to keep in mind that although patients behave in an aggressive manner for various reasons, the management of the behavior is the same. The specific behaviors usually associated with the aggressive patient are presented individually and discussed in some detail.

VERBALLY ABUSIVE BEHAVIOR

Patients usually become verbally abusive because of frustrating circumstances which are beyond their control. They then displace the anger and frustration to other patients or staff members. Many verbally abusive patients have developed this pattern of behavior in response to the fact that they believe they are going to be rejected. In an attempt to reject before they can be rejected, they become quite hostile to others. Thus, others respond to them in a like manner and a vicious, self-defeating cycle begins. This is called a self-fulfilling prophecy. In order to break this cycle, it is imperative for staff members not to respond to a patient's verbal aggression in a punitive, hostile or rejecting manner.

Staff members must recognize that in most cases these patients do not mean anything personal by their abusive remarks. They are simply displacing their frustration and anger from the object or situation creating those feelings to the staff member. The ability to express negative feelings can be a healthy sign. It may also indicate that patients feel that the staff is capable of accepting the abuse and can deal with it in an effective manner. It also may mean that patients feel comfortable enough to express their frustrations because they know that if they lose control of themselves, the staff will take nonpunitive steps to help them regain control. These patients need to be accepted as they are and staff members must try to understand what the patient is saying from the patient's point of view. When limits must be set, it is important that the limits be on the patient's actions and behaviors, not the patient's feelings. The verbal expression of aggression is an important outlet for the frustrations and tensions which these patients feel.

A key to managing this type patient is to teach them how to find more socially acceptable ways of expressing their frustrations. Sometimes it is difficult to discourage a particular behavior without appearing to be rejecting; it may be necessary to actually tell patients that although the staff still accepts and cares about them, they are not willing to accept their verbally abusive behavior. Judgmental, moralistic, or disparaging remarks about the patient's behavior will only make matters worse.

Staff members should be careful not to let patients draw them into arguments. Any time a staff member argues with a patient, the patient wins. Aside from the fact that the patient will feel that he has one up on the staff member who has lost his temper, the staff member has provided an inappropriate role model for the patient. In many instances, patients are not able to utilize good judgment or act in a rational manner. Staff members, however, are expected to show good judgment, restraint, and socially appropriate behavior. One of the most important therapeutic tools that staff members have is their own behavior. If they provide an acceptable behavioral model, patients are likely to benefit by being able to identify with the staff member and pattern their behavior accordingly.

Since verbally abusive patients are quite upsetting to other patients, staff members need to remain calm and controlled when patients have emotional outbursts. If possible, accompany such patients to their rooms or to a more isolated area. There the staff member can reassure and calm the patient while allowing the patient time to regain control. Many patients are later embarassed by their outburst and may resent the staff for having permitted them to engage in behaviors which make them look bad in front of their fellow patients. Do not press patients for an explanation of their behavior when they are upset. They should be given time to calm down so that they will be able to discuss their situation in a more rational manner.

When patients become so upset that they have difficulty regaining control, they should be given their PRN medications. The dosage should not be enough to heavily sedate the patient, just enough to permit

138

resumption of the ability to relate to staff members who are trying to help.

When the patient is calm, the staff member can explore the kinds of responses the patient would likely encounter if the same behavior had occurred in everyday life situations. The staff member then has the opportunity to help the patient consider other ways of dealing with the feelings that caused the emotional outburst and the aggressive behavior. By discussing the negative results of previous outbursts, the patient may gain insight about the need for changing his behavior.

Finally, staff members should analyze their own response to these patients. If they have any negative or hostile feelings toward a particular patient, they should try to find effective ways of coping with those feelings. It is sometimes helpful to discuss such feelings with a fellow staff member or supervisor. Psychiatric patients are sensitive to the attitudes of others and a staff member's negative feelings may cause a patient to become even more abusive because he feels rejected.

VIOLENT, AGITATED, OR PHYSICALLY DESTRUCTIVE BEHAVIOR

There are probably few places that the old addage "an ounce of prevention is better than a pound of cure" applies more than in dealing with patients who are violent, agitated, or physically destructive. Violence usually occurs only when a patient feels threatened and unable to do anything else. Perhaps the most important single factor in dealing with such patients is to learn to recognize danger signals or behaviors which indicate that the patient is about to become agitated or violent. When the conditions are likely to lead to the patient becoming upset and combative, it is usually wise to use the patient's PRN medications and to try to remove the patient to an area where violent behavior could be more easily handled. Frequently, when patients are isolated with only one staff member, they are less prone to be physically assaultive because they are not stimulated by other patients who are becoming upset and by having a large number of people milling around trying to decide what to do. Patients usually calm down much more quickly when they do not have an audience.

Once such patients are in a quiet area and have been given any needed PRN medications, they should be encouraged to talk about their anger and to discuss the reasons they became violent. As with the verbally abusive patients, it is also important to explore with patients alternative ways of expressing their anger and hostility and also to help them explore similar kinds of behavior or incidents which might have occurred in the past.

Perhaps one of the most detrimental ways to approach patients who become upset and potentially combative is to try to manhandle them without giving them an opportunity to accompany a single individual on their own to a quieter, more secluded place. Frequently, when patients are very upset, the simple act of a staff member taking their arm is sufficient to cause them to completely lose control. Therefore, it is probably best never to touch patients who are agitated or out of control until all other approaches have failed. Threatening patients with various forms of punishment such as shots, locking them in the seclusion room, restraining them to the bed, or other such punitive acts will further increase the patient's agitation. If a staff member can approach potentially combative patients in a nonthreatening, calm, reassuring manner and if the staff member does not apear to be afraid of such patients, it is likely that the staff member will be able to relate to them in an effective manner. Arguing with these patients or otherwise irritating them will insure the patient's loss of control. One should try to reduce patients' perception of threat—not increase it.

It is frequently helpful with patients who tend to be physically abusive or combative to explain to them very clearly and directly what behaviors are expected of them and then to verbally praise and support patients who make an effort to engage in the expected behaviors. It is especially important that staff members be consistent in their expectations of patients and in reinforcing the expected behaviors. If patients are told that a particular consequence will follow a particular behavior, then it is of utmost importance that the behavior be dealt with in the way the patients were told it would be. Otherwise, patients cannot learn to trust the staff and may be tempted to engage in certain undesirable behaviors just to see if they can get away with them.

Another important way of helping patients learn to deal with their physically abusive or combative behavior is to have them understand the inappropriateness of the behavior and to confront them with it. This should never be done at the height of patient's agitation but rather after the patients have had time to calm down and can be fairly rational in looking at their behavior.

If all efforts to calm violent or destructive patients fail, it will be necessary to physically control their behavior. This is done only to protect the patients themselves, other patients, staff members, or to prevent the destruction of property. Even in these cases, only the minimum force necessary to control patients should be used. Staff members should use force carefully but as quickly and efficiently as possible. If a patient has become violent, first remove all other patients and unnecessary staff members from the area. Then collect enough staff members so that there is no doubt about who is going to win the confrontation. Sometimes this will further agitate patients but is necessary to assure the proper outcome. At least five people are needed. One for each arm and leg and one to give general assistance. One person should be in charge and receive instant response from the other staff members. Pillows or a blanket may be wrapped around staff members' arms to reduce blows and avoid injury from objects which are thrown. From that point, the proper procedure is to get the patient off his feet and gently placed face down on the floor. Every effort should be made to accomplish this without injuring the patient. Some authorities suggest using patients' clothing to restrain them. Others suggest that when using the patient's limbs to restrain him, grasp him near the major joints. This should reduce leverage and thus the likelihood of severe injury. When the patient is under staff control, the person in charge should decide whether to give a PRN medication and whether mechanical restraints are necessary. If mechanical restraints are used, care must be taken to see that they are not unnecessarily uncomfortable for the patient. They should be removed as soon as the patient regains control and the patient should be told that this is what will happen. Other patients who might have been involved should be reassured and given an opportunity to express their feelings about the incident. The staff should then discuss the incident and try to find ways of preventing future reoccurrences.

DEMANDING BEHAVIOR

One of the most difficult patients to deal with is the passive, whiney patient who constantly seeks a particular staff member's attention and who demands support and reassurance from that person. Such patients frequently become annoying in their demands because nothing the staff member does is enough. First they want their shaving kit, and then they want their toothpaste, and then they want their shoe polish, and then they want their medicine, and then they want to talk, and then they want to make a telephone call, and on and on. Frequently such patients will seek to control all of a particular staff member's time, unconsciously believing the amount of time spent with the staff member is an indication of their worth as a person. In other words, such patient's feelings of worth are directly related to how much contact they are able to establish with the staff. Usually, a staff member will find it impossible to attend to all assigned duties if constantly required to deal with a demanding patient. It is more helpful both to the staff member and to the patient if a structured program can be developed wherein the patient is guaranteed access to the staff member at certain times and the staff member makes frequent but brief contacts with the patient at times which are convenient for the staff member. In this way, the staff member takes the initiative for the contacts away from the patient which encourages the patient to be more adaptable in delaying immediate gratification of their dependency needs.

Sometimes the most effective thing a staff member can do is ignore the patient who makes constant demands. It is very important, however, that the staff member not show annoyance or anger toward the patient. It may be necessary at times to confront such patients with the fact that their behavior is inappropriate and to help them understand that it is necessary to learn other ways of meeting their needs. Frequently patients do not recognize the fact that they are unrealistically demanding and are not aware of the effect their behavior has on other people. Verbal reinforcement should be given to patients when they show independent activity and when they are able to meet their need for attention in acceptable ways.

LYING AND STEALING BEHAVIOR

Managing patients who lie and steal is among the most frustrating of all mental health tasks. Frequently, it is difficult to ascertain whether or not a patient is actually guilty of lying or stealing. When confronted with such behaviors, patients are likely to become quite agitated and upset.

One of the reasons that these behaviors are troublesome is that they often involve other patients. For example, one particular patient may steal from other patients which irritates and upsets them or a patient may lie about another patient or staff member to another patient, upsetting and irritating the other patient.

If a staff member is certain that Mr. Smith lied or stole something, it is probably best to simply confront him with the behavior rather than asking whether or not the behavior occurred. Asking about the occurrence of the behavior gives him more opportunity to get into trouble because he feels compelled to deny the behavior. The patient later may feel resentful that the staff member caused him to further compound his lies when the staff member was already aware of the truth.

In confronting the patient with lying or stealing behavior, it is important to be as nonpunitive and as accepting as possible. If the patient is aware that other patients and staff members know that the patient has a problem with lying or stealing, the patient may be encouraged to stop the behavior. It is also important to ask the patient to restore any property that may have been taken and to explore with the patient the reasons for the lying or stealing behavior. Frequently, it is important to discuss with patients the inappropriateness of such behaviors and the potential consequences of such behaviors in the environment outside the treatment center. Patients should be encouraged to verbalize appropriate behaviors and to explore the effect that these behaviors have on their feelings about themselves. It is important to confront patients at a time when other patients will not be able to observe the confrontation. Such confrontations should not be humiliating to patients. Staff behavior which is judgmental or moralistic is inappropriate, and trying to reason with patients on religious grounds is not an effective means of dealing with lying or stealing behavior.

ANTAGONISTIC, INTIMIDATING, OR PHYSICALLY ABUSIVE BEHAVIOR

As in dealing with patients who are likely to become physically abusive, one of the most important things to be done in preventing fights among patients is to recognize potential situations or conditions which are likely to cause patients' tempers to flare and to recognize personality conflicts among certain patients. Patients who have conflicts might be kept busy doing things which will not bring them into contact with each other frequently. Further, the staff should not permit patients who are likely to have conflicts to engage in activities which might cause their basic personality differences to be exaggerated.

If a fight does occur, it is important to separate the participants and to refrain from taking sides. The same is true for verbal arguments between patients. If the patients are actually involved in a physical fight, it is important to separate them so that each patient can be dealt with independently. If sufficient manpower is not available to physically separate the patients, then a staff member who realizes this might attempt to distract the patients in some way. After the patients have calmed down, it might help to have a therapeutic confrontation letting the two patients sit down with a staff member and discuss what upsets them about each other. It is sometimes helpful to explore the patients' feelings about themselves as well as their feelings about the other patient. The staff member might then be able to help both patients understand their conflict and to suggest alternative ways of dealing with their feelings about each other. Sometimes patients who have been antagonistic toward each other become good friends once they understand the differences that exist between them and the reasons for their behavior.

One of the most effective things that can be done to help avoid fighting and arguing is to plan a program of activities which will not permit the patients so much free time that they become bored. Group therapy for patients may be utilized to settle disagreements among patients before they reach the stage of serious arguments and fighting. Again, it is important that staff members provide a good role model and it is sometimes helpful for a staff member to play the part of the other patient when he is dealing with patients who have been separated after a serious argument or fight, and to respond in a manner which would be appropriate if the staff member were actually the other patient. Sometimes it helps to have patients switch roles with each other after they have had time to calm down.

Perhaps one of the most serious staff errors is to ignore or to accept behavior from a particular patient that is known to be annoying or upsetting to other patients. It is also important to remember that a staff member should not intervene in a constructive argument which is being appropriately handled by the patients involved.

UNCOOPERATIVE BEHAVIOR

In the case of uncooperative patients, it is important to be aware of the patient's diagnosis because in some cases a patient is significantly psychologically regressed and is not being intentionally uncooperative. In other cases, patients are uncooperative for what seems to them a legitimate reason. Some of these reasons include being afraid of hospitalization, of medications, or of unusual treatments (such as electroconvulsive shock treatments). One of the least constructive things to do is to approach such patients in a threatening manner and to threaten them with punishment if they do not obey orders or if they do not do what is asked of them. The patient's reasons for being uncooperative should be explored. The staff member should be reassurring and use a kind but firm approach. If a staff member calmly explains the reason patients are being asked to follow directions, they will usually comply. It is quite detrimental to try to *force* patients to do anything. Since a little humor goes a long way with patients, it can be used to avoid authoritative "orders" which may cause argumentative patient behaviors that sometimes lead to more serious conflicts.

It is sometimes necessary to make patient privileges dependent upon cooperation with the staff. Within reason, the patient must learn to live in accordance with unit policy and regulations. Whenever possible, however, patients should be given a choice of one or more alternatives. Giving patients a choice permits them to maintain a feeling of independence and to remain responsible for their behavior. When patients do not have a choice in the behavior requested, don't play verbal games with them. For example, if Mr. Smith has to take a certain medication, don't ask him if he would like to take his medicine. In asking that question, one leaves oneself open to a confrontation because Mr. Smith can simply say, "No, I don't want to take my medication." In such situations, it is better to say, "Mr. Smith, it's time to take your medicine. Would you rather have it with water or juice?"

Mentally ill patients will often test the limit set by staff members.

Highly manipulative patients especially need to know that the staff is in charge of the unit and that inappropriate behavior will not gain extra attention or special privileges for them. They need to know that they are expected to participate in ward activities, work assignments, and therapeutic activities. If patients do refuse to comply or are uncooperative, it is important that they not be rejected by staff members. Such patients should not be made to feel that the staff has a personal dislike for them or that they are annoyed or angry with them. Instead, the staff should stress that the patient is liked and accepted but that the uncooperative behavior is not acceptable.

While it is important to be firm in gaining patients' cooperation with the behaviors expected of them, it is also important to recognize that occasionally a patient has a legitimate reason for not cooperating and understanding is necessary when patients balk for good reason.

SEXUALLY AGGRESSIVE BEHAVIOR

Patients who are sexually aggressive seem to be especially upsetting to many mental health workers. Perhaps this is related to the staff member's moral beliefs. However, personal beliefs must be set aside when treating patients who are mentally ill. While it is not necessary to condone sexual misconduct, it is vitally important that a noncondemning, nonjudgmental, approach be used with sexually acting out patients.

Mentally ill patients have the same basic sexual needs as healthy individuals but they often find that appropriate outlets (husband or wife, boyfriend or girlfriend) for these needs are far removed, especially when the patient has been hospitalized for a long period of time. In some cases, patients feel too unattractive, too insecure, or too inadequate to find someone with whom they might develop an intimate relationship which might lead to appropriate sexual activity. In other cases, patients have such poor interpersonal relationship skills that they alienate appropriate sexual partners. The sexual frustration such patients feel often causes them to engage in inappropriate sexual activities such as the establishment of fleeting heterosexual relationships with other patients or making sexual advances toward staff members. Staff members need to discuss with these patients the inappropriateness of their actions, set limits on their acting out, and try to arrange for appropriate outlets. Very often, the simple arrangement of a weekend pass for a married person will eliminate such inappropriate behavior. Other patients, especially adolescents, have not yet learned to handle their affectionate and sexual feelings in socially acceptable ways. With adolescents and other patients who have sexual problems, it is important that staff members be firm but supportive when inappropriate behavior occurs. If the behavior cannot be ignored, the patient should be confronted and encouraged to discuss the behavior. If it is possible, the behavior might be temporarily ignored until the staff can have an opportunity to discuss the behavior and plan the patient's care accordingly. Motivational considerations other than sexual attraction may need to be evaluated. Sexual behavior may be exhibited by a patient as a way of getting a staff member's attention or as a way of embarrassing a staff member who has caused a patient to feel slighted in some way. It may also be a way of testing limits and a method of seeking reassurance that inappropriate behavior will be controlled by the staff. Finally, one must consider that such behavior is motivated by a patient's fear of rejection. Thus, the patient tries to provoke anger in an attempt to confirm rejection and reduce the anxiety of unconfirmed rejection.

Staff members must be careful that their warm, friendly, accepting attitudes toward patients do not become seductive. If Mr. Smith does mistake Miss Jones' warmth and acceptance for love or sexual feelings, he may begin to act out sexually toward her. If this occurs, Miss Jones should try to remain calm and say, "Mr. Smith, I like you as a person but it makes me uncomfortable when you say that you love me or when you try to touch me." If the behavior persists, Miss Jones should first be sure that her behavior toward the patient is not subtly encouraging him and then firmly tell him, "Mr. Smith, I have tried to be nice about this but you won't let me. Your behavior is inappropriate and must stop." If the patient persists further, Miss Jones should ask her supervisor to assign someone else to work with the patient.

Patients do not often act out sexually toward staff members but when they do, the behavior must be dealt with firmly and with the patient being able to perceive as little as possible of the staff member's anxiety.

ANNOTATED BIBLIOGRAPHY

Assey, J.L., and Herbert, J.M.: *Who is the seductive patient?* American Journal of Nursing, 1983, 83(4):530–532.

> *Relates the motivation of sexually aggressive behavior and describes constructive nursing response.*

Cohn, L.: *They all felt wounded.* Journal of Psychosocial Nursing and Mental Health Services, 1981, 19(7):34–36.

> *Explains the etiology of aggressive behavior in one particular patient and relates how it was effectively handled by the nursing staff.*

Gluck, M.: *Learning a therapeutic verbal response to anger.* Journal of Psychosocial Nursing and Mental Health Services, 1981, 19(3):9–12.

> *Based on the theory that appropriate therapeutic communication will re-*

duce angry aggressive behavior, this article provides guidelines for handling angry patients.

Knowles, R.D.: *Preventing anger.* American Journal of Nursing, 1982, 82(1):118.

Offers alternative behaviors in dealing with patient's anger.

Maagdenberg, A.M.: *The "violent" patient.* American Journal of Nursing, 1983, 83(3):402–403.

Describes nursing actions that may provoke assaultive behavior and recommends alternative approaches to potentially violent patients.

Pisarcik, G.: *Facing the violent patient.* Nursing '81, 1981, 11(9):62–65.

Guidelines for anticipating, preventing, and coping with the violent patient. Chemical and physical restraints are discussed and a chart of "Dos and Don'ts" is provided.

Self, P.R., and Viau, J.J.: *Four steps for helping a patient alleviate anger.* Nursing '80, 1980, 10(12):66.

Recommendations to identify the patient with concealed anger and encourage constructive ventilation.

Smitherman, C.: *Your patient's angry—What should you do?* Nursing '81, 1981, 11(11):96–97.

Suggestions using therapeutic communication in dealing with anger.

Stockard, S.: *Caring for the sexually aggressive patient—You don't have to blush and bear it.* Nursing '81, 11(11):114–116.

Discusses dealing with sexual acting-out in the aggressive patient.

POST-TEST

Chapter 10

Aggressive Patients

True or False. Circle your choice.

T F 1. The key to managing aggressive patients is to teach them to find more socially acceptable ways of expressing their frustrations.

T F 2. It is appropriate and necessary for a staff member to argue with a patient if the staff member is right and the patient is definitely wrong.

T F 3. A staff member's own behavior is often his most therapeutic tool.

T F 4. Staff members should not press patients for an explanation of why they behaved in a certain manner.

T F 5. A patient usually becomes violent only when he feels threatened and unable to react in any other manner.

T F 6. Touching agitated patients tends to have a calming effect on them.

T F 7. Sometimes the most effective approach a staff member can have toward a patient who makes continuous demands is to ignore him.

T F 8. It is often necessary to force patients to comply to rules when they are resistant.

T F 9. An effective approach for dealing with a hostile patient is to accept his feelings without indicating approval, disapproval, or value judgments.

Multiple Choice. Circle the letter you think represents the best answer.

1. In dealing with a hostile patient, the staff member should:
   1. Understand that hostility is the result of a basic character defect.
   2. Be aware of their own reactions to the expressed hostility.
   3. Avoid reacting defensively toward the patient.
   4. Set limits on the patient's behavior.
      A. 1 and 2.
      B. 2 and 3.

C. 2, 3, and 4.

D. All the above.

2. Effective approaches for dealing with hostility include:
1. Recognize the patient's feelings of hostility.
2. Allow the patient to set the pace in the establishment of staff-patient relationships.
3. Accept his feelings without indicating approval, disapproval, or value judgments.
4. Convey to the patient that it is wrong to feel hostile.
5. Plan approaches to meet the patient's individual needs.

    A. 1, 2, and 3.

    B. 2, 4, and 5.

    C. 1, 3, and 5.

    D. 1, 2, 3, and 5.

    E. All of these.

Situation: Mrs. Jones tells you in a loud, angry tone of voice that she is very irritated by the incompetencies of the medical and nursing staff. You say, "You sound angry." Mrs. Jones says, "Wouldn't you if you had to fight for everything you get?" The next two questions apply to this situation.

3. What would be your most supportive response to Mrs. Jones?

A. "Yes, I guess I would."

B. "Tell me about the things that are irritating and make you feel angry."

C. "The doctor and nurses are trying to help you. Please cooperate."

D. "You'll have to learn to control your anger."

4. What would be your most nonsupportive response to Mrs. Jones?

A. "Yes, I guess I would."

B. "Tell me about the things that are irritating and make you feel angry."

C. "The doctor and nurses are trying to help you. Please cooperate."

D. "You'll have to learn to control your anger."

5. Mrs. White, a staff member has been talking to a patient and as she gets up to leave, he puts his arms around her and tries to kiss her. She should:

A. Kick him in the groin.

B. Tell him his behavior is inappropriate.

C. Tell him that she is going to tell his wife if he doesn't stop.

D. Tell him that his behavior makes her uncomfortable and ask him to stop.

Short Answer. Answer the following as briefly and specifically as possible.

1. If a staff member is certain that a patient has stolen an article from another patient, how should the staff member handle the situation?

   _____

   _____

2. What is one of the most effective ways to keep patients from fighting and arguing?

   _____

   _____

3. When does a patient usually resort to physical violence?

   _____

   _____

4. Why is it a good idea to try to isolate a patient that appears to be becoming physically destructive?

   _____

   _____

11

Anxious Patients

> **OBJECTIVES:** Student will be able to:
> 1. Differentiate between behavioral manifestations of anxiety seen in a healthy person as related to those behaviors seen in a mentally ill patient.
> 2. List techniques used in working with patients exhibiting compulsive behaviors and patients exhibiting phobic behaviors.

We have already talked about the fear and anxiety felt by many patients. Some worry constantly and many have specific phobias. A large number of patients show restless, somewhat agitated behavior while others show compulsive, ritualistic behavior. For a review of symptoms see Chapter 4. In practically all cases, the behavior associated with the anxious patient is aimed at reducing the subjective feeling of anxiety which is experienced by the patient. Anxiety tells the patient and the staff that something needs to be done. The patient's difficulty often lies in the fact that he is so anxious he cannot make a decision. This may occur because the patient sees so many possible solutions that no single solution seems appropriate. It may also be that the patient cannot find even one solution which is acceptable. Thus, nothing is done and the anxiety continues. This chapter discusses many of the behaviors which might be expected from such patients and explores some ways of managing those behaviors. It should be understood that drug therapy is often used in conjunction with the management techniques presented here.

It is often the case that very anxious patients are upset by new and unfamiliar surroundings. They become more frightened, agitated, and sometimes withdrawn when they do not know what is expected of them and how they should behave. Uncertainty and conflict are the primary causes of anxiety. Therefore, it is important that a new patient who is anxious, worried, or upset be introduced to the unit by very carefully explaining what is expected of him, where he will sleep, how he will get his meals, when his doctor will come, and what he should do if he needs help. These patients frequently need someone to talk to them to reassure them and simply to provide company. They may have many questions, some of which will be repeated more than once. These questions should always be answered carefully and fully, and the patient should be reassured that someone will be available to help if he needs anything.

On an open unit, anxious patients can frequently be seen moving about searching for someone to talk to about their fears. It is important that staff members take time to talk to such patients and try to help them understand and recognize their fears. Patients can usually be helped to calm down by gradually easing them off the subject of a particular fear or worry and then getting them to talk about things which do not arouse their anxiety or fear and thus are not upsetting to them.

It sometimes happens that highly anxious patients are afraid of other patients on the unit. It may be helpful to introduce such patients to other patients on the unit and to encourage them to talk with some of the other patients. It is sometimes helpful to point out to the anxious patient that all the patients are there for the same reason, to receive help for their difficulties, and that the staff is there to see that everybody receives whatever help they need. Try to avoid situations where one patient is made to express a view or opinion which may conflict with other patients' views.

Frequently, anxious patients will become upset over something that has a great deal of importance to that particular patient but which may be of little or no importance either to other patients or to staff members. In such cases, it is helpful to the patient if some specific concession is made which will permit the patient to decrease his anxiety or fear by engaging in some particular behavior which would have a calming effect on the patient. For example, it is frequently the case that when a patient is about to go on leave or is about to be discharged, that patient is quite afraid that no one will come to pick him up and he may want to call his family to be reassured that someone is coming for him. The patient might be quite relieved and thus more calm if he is allowed to call his family and reassure himself that someone will come to pick him up.

RESTLESS, AGITATED BEHAVIOR

Patients who are restless are frequently reassured and calmed by having a mental health team member take them for a brief walk or by simply taking them to a quiet place and sitting down to talk with them. Usually if agitated, restless patients are allowed to say what is on their minds, they are able to settle down more quickly and to feel more reassured. Unless patients are allowed to say what is on their minds and to express the things that are troubling them, a great deal of unnecessary angry and frustrated acting out may occur. For example, in one case

154

three attendants were used to restrain one female patient who insisted on being allowed to go into another patient's room. Since nobody thought to ask why the patient wanted to go into another patient's room, she was simply told that she could go into her own room but not into the other patient's room. After a great deal of acting out behavior and after the patient had been restrained by the three attendants, a nurse asked the girl why she wanted to go into the other patient's room. The patient explained that she had dropped her ring and it had rolled into the other patient's room. When the ring was retrieved, the patient calmed down and was released. The problem could have been prevented by simply asking the patient why she wanted to go into the room in the first place.

If patients are allowed to discuss their anxieties and feelings, much of the emotional pressure they feel seems to be relieved. This is particularly the case at bedtime for patients with anxiety problems. It is usually not a good policy to insist that patients go to bed whether they are sleepy or not. Frequently, patients who are forced to go to bed become quite agitated and restless and are much more likely to act out than if they are taken to a quiet area where they will not disturb other patients who may be trying to sleep and are allowed to stay up and discuss their feelings with a staff member. As soon as the patient calms down, he may then be returned to his room and encouraged to try to go to sleep. Other patients may be able to go to sleep without leaving their rooms if a mental health team member will simply come and sit with them or if they are allowed to leave a light on. Sometimes patients will agree to going to bed if they are given some small favor such as a glass of juice, a drink of water, a cup of decaffeinated coffee, or simply a chance to walk around for a few minutes before going to bed. PRN medications should also be considered for such patients.

Occasionally, patients seem to become more anxious if staff members or other patients are friendly and supportive of them. In these cases, it is best to maintain a businesslike manner. Such patients need time to accept the idea that others can like them and be interested in them without expecting something in return.

COMPULSIVE BEHAVIOR

One form of anxious behavior which is sometimes difficult to control is compulsive behavior, which may or may not include ritualism. Some patients carry these behaviors to such extremes that they create significant physical problems. One of the most common ritualistic behaviors is that of hand washing. Some patients have been known to wash their hands more than a hundred times a day and continue to wash them despite the fact that their hands are cracked and bleeding from the soap

155

and water and scrubbing. Such patients should never be approached in a demanding and threatening way since such behavior will only increase the patient's insecurity and anxiety thus creating more need for the ritualistic behavior.

For many compulsive or ritualistic behaviors it is possible to talk with patients about their behavior and encourage them to try other ways of controlling their anxiety. Sometimes it is possible to help patients begin reducing a ritual by leaving off one of the components of the ritual, and the next day, leaving off another component, and the following day, leaving off another component, until the ritualistic behavior is eliminated or stopped. By trying to reduce the compulsive behavior a little at a time, the patient is permitted to adjust to the new conditions slowly rather than having to suddenly deal with all the anxieties that the ritual helped to control.

It is never helpful to be critical of a patient's ritualistic behavior. It is important to remember that while the behavior may be quite silly to an observer, it has a very real meaning to the patient. The most important thing is to let patients feel that they and their problems are accepted by the staff members. This usually does more to relieve patients' anxieties than reassurance that "everything is going to be all right." The patient doesn't think that things are going to be all right and feels rejected if that is all he is offered in the way of reassurance. Instead of saying, "don't worry so much" to a patient, say "I can see that you are upset about this. Why don't we talk about it?" Other reassuring statements include, "You seem to feel hurt about Mrs. Jones saying she hates you. Let's talk about it." or "Let's talk about why you feel that people don't like you." or "I have noticed that you always wring your hands and seem upset when your mother calls." Such statements give patients an opportunity to talk if they want to. It is not useful, however, to insist that they talk when they obviously do not want to. More often than not, patients like to talk and a staff member who listens well will be highly valued by patients.

PHOBIC BEHAVIOR

Phobic patients have specific fears or anxieties and may become quite upset, frightened, or agitated when confronted with the phobic or feared object. Frequently these patients seek reassurance by asking repeatedly whether or not one will be able to help, whether or not they are going crazy, and whether or not they are going to be able to recover from their illness. Perhaps the best reply to such requests for reassurance is to simply tell the patient that one will be happy to talk with the patient about problems any time that one is free. The patient may also be told that talking about problems is often the best way to solve them.

In managing anxious patients, it is most important that staff members remain calm and restrained. Anxious patients frequently try to provoke anxiety in staff members. If they are successful then they feel that their own anxiety is justified. If they are not successful, then they tend to be reassured. When anxious patients perceive uncertainty or conflict among staff members or other patients, they are likely to respond by becoming even more anxious themselves.

ANNOTATED BIBLIOGRAPHY

Hagerty, B.K.: *Obsessive-compulsive behavior: An overview of four psychological frameworks.* Journal of Psychosocial Nursing and Mental Health Services, 1981, 19(1):37–39.

Places the obsessive-compulsive phenomenon in the context of several psychological theorists: Erikson, Freud, Horney, Fenchil, and Shapiro. Includes defense mechanisms most commonly utilized by the obsessive-compulsive personality.

Heidt, P.: *Effect of therapeutic touch on anxiety level of hospitalized patients.* Nursing Research, 1981, 30(1):32–37.

Research study discovered that the use of therapeutic touch significantly reduced anxiety for inpatients.

Knowles, R.D.: *Dealing with feelings—Managing anxiety.* American Journal of Nursing, 1981, 81(1):110–114.

An analytical approach to the subject of anxiety. Suggests alternative behaviors and coping mechanisms.

Knowles, R.D.: *Overcoming guilt and worry.* American Journal of Nursing, 1981, 81(9):1663.

Discusses guilt and worry as the etiology of anxiety. Suggests alternative coping strategies.

Mitchell, R.G.: *Anxiety states and phobias.* Nursing Times, 1983, 79(7):50–52.

Correlates various anxiety states to specific mental illnesses.

Ricci, M.S.: *An experiment with personal-space invasion in the nurse-patient relationship and its effect on anxiety.* Issues in Mental Health Nursing, 1981, 3:203–218.

Detailed research study that investigates the relationship between personal space and patient anxiety.

Smitherman, C.: *Your patient's anxious—what should you do?* Nursing '81, 1981, 11(10):72–73.

Practical suggestions for dealing with both situational and free-floating anxiety.

POST-TEST

Chapter 11

Anxious Patients

True or False. Circle your choice.

T F   1. Anxious patients are frequently upset by new and unfamiliar surroundings.

T F   2. Phobias are unusual in truly anxious patients.

T F   3. An anxious patient's ritualistic behavior is aimed at reducing his objective feelings of anxiety.

T F   4. Uncertainty and conflict are the primary causes of anxiety.

T F   5. An anxious patient should be encouraged not to talk about his fears because they are unrealistic.

T F   6. An agitated, restless patient should not be allowed to say what is on his mind because he may upset other patients.

T F   7. It is a good policy to insist that patients go to bed whether they are sleepy or not.

T F   8. Sometimes a friendly, supportive staff member can cause a patient to become more upset and anxious.

T F   9. Excessive handwashing is a sign of anxiety.

T F 10. The most effective way to discourage ritualistic behavior is to gently criticize the behavior to the patient. By doing so, the patient will recognize that his behavior is not helping and that it makes him look bad in front of others.

Multiple Choice. Circle the letter that represents the best answer.

1. An anxious patient:
   1. Feels threatened by unknown danger.
   2. Is unable to concentrate.
   3. Displays indecision.
   4. May make many demands for attention.
      A. 1 and 3.
      B. 2 and 4.
      C. 1, 2, and 3.
      D. All of the above.
2. The characteristic which distinguishes fear from anxiety is that fear:

A. Usually has a specific object.
B. Evokes a milder degree of emotion.
C. Persists over a longer period of time.
D. Occurs in the absence of real danger.
3. Which of the following are characteristic of anxiety:
   1. Feeling of helplessness.
   2. Reaction to evident danger.
   3. Reaction to future danger.
   4. Man attempts to alleviate by use of defense mechanisms.
   5. Leads to a neurosis if not halted.
      A. 1, 2, and 4.
      B. 1, 3, and 5.
      C. 1, 3, 4, and 5.
      D. 3, 4, and 5.
      E. All of the above.
4. The individual suffering from normal anxiety:
   1. Is able to focus on what is happening.
   2. Is able to recognize and face the threat realistically.
   3. Sometimes uses mental mechanisms for relief.
   4. Hears voices.
      A. 1 only.
      B. 1 and 3.
      C. 1, 2, and 3.
      D. All of the above.
5. Reassurance can be given to the anxious patient by:
   1. Remaining calm and confident with the patient.
   2. Guessing what the patient is worried about and getting him to talk.
   3. Giving correct information when the patient needs it.
   4. Remaining with the patient.
      A. 1 only.
      B. 1, 3, and 4.
      C. 3 and 4.
      D. 2, 3, and 4.
6. A characteristic of anxiety is:
   A. Feeling of helplessness.
   B. Anticipation of pleasure.
   C. Decrease in muscular tension.
   D. Relationship to specific objects.

Situation: Mary Jane, age 18, an honor student at Haven College, is admitted to the hospital during exam week in a state of extreme anxiety. She tells the staff member that if she flunks out, she won't be able to go to medical school as her parents want her to. The next two questions apply to this situation.

160

7. As Mary and the staff member enter the day room, Mary tries to break away and appears terrified of the group of patients. The staff member should take the following action.
   1. Gently steer Mary to her own room and stay with her.
   2. Call for the orderly to drag Mary away forcibly.
   3. Talk quietly and calmly to Mary as they proceed to her room.
   4. Warn Mary she will be put in restraints if she doesn't behave.
      A. 1 only.
      B. 2 only.
      C. 1 and 3.
      D. 2 and 4.
8. The next day Mary is calmer. She tells the staff member how disappointed her parents will be if she flunks. The staff member:
   A. Tells Mary she is sure her parents will love her anyway.
   B. Allows Mary to explore her feelings about this.
   C. Advises Mary to study hard so she can pass.
   D. Ignores the remark.
9. When a patient has an anxiety attack at night and refuses to remain in his room because he is afraid, you should:
   A. Explain that there is nothing to be afraid of.
   B. Let him sit out in the hall by the nurse's station.
   C. Leave a light burning in his room.
   D. Place him in seclusion room.
10. Which of the following responses is most appropriate in relation to a patient who is pacing the halls, wringing her hands and crying?
    A. "You seem all upset right now, but I'm sure you won't feel this way much longer."
    B. "Sit here a minute and I'll get your nerve medicine."
    C. "I'll stay with you; perhaps I can help."
    D. "Sit down a while; you'll feel better in a little while."
11. The *primary* defense mechanism used against anxiety is:
    A. Reaction formation.
    B. Denial.
    C. Suppression.
    D. Compensation.
    E. Repression.

12

Suspicious Patients

OBJECTIVES: Students will be able to:
1. Describe behaviors associated with the suspicious patient.
2. List the major defense mechanisms used by the paranoid patient.
3. List effective ways of dealing with the suspicious or paranoid patient.

In addition to the fearfulness and distrustfulness shown by the suspicious or paranoid patient, there is a tendency for such patients to be quarrelsome and aloof. Such behaviors often evoke a great deal of anger in other patients and staff members. This leads to rejection of the patient, causing him to respond with hostility and confirming his negative expectations about interpersonal relationships. Such patients, therefore, feel ill at ease in interpersonal relationships and tend to interpret minor oversights as significant personal rejections. In fact, they often find slights or injustices where none exist. They are likely to overreact to seemingly insignificant occurrences and are unable to control their feelings and their behaviors in situations where restraint and understanding are appropriate responses. Such patients are frequently over-concerned with fairness and with being certain that they are treated as everyone else is treated.

Projection is the major defense mechanism used by paranoid patients. Without realizing it, paranoid patients project their own hostility and aggressive impulses onto other people. The projection causes the patient to perceive hostility and rejection from others. Thus the patients become fearful, agitated and overly concerned about their rights. Since they see themselves as the focal point of everybody's behavior, they interpret anything that happens in their environment as having special meaning for them. Another point to remember in dealing with these patients is that they frequently show good ego strength. That is, they appear to be capable people and feel they do not need to rely on anyone other than themselves. They tend to be opinionated and stubborn and react with hostility when their opinions are challenged.

Dealing with the suspicious or paranoid patient requires a considerable amount of diplomacy. It is not in the best interest of the patient or the staff member to argue. In an argument, paranoid patients may perceive that they must defend their position and will feel quite self-righteous about venting their hostility, anger, and frustration. They tend to believe that they are defending their position for the benefit of mankind, thus justifying their unreasonable anger.

Paranoid patients sometimes try to get staff members on their side because they see staff members as authority figures. If they succeed, they feel their position is justified to some extent. Again, a great deal of tact and preparation is necessary in order to deal effectively with this situation. If a staff member tells a patient that he does not agree with the patient's position, that staff member is inviting an argument which the staff member will almost always lose because such patients usually have an extreme commitment to their position. On the other hand, making an appropriate interpretive statement may encourage the patient to talk and provide an opportunity to move him to an area where his anger and frustration can be vented in privacy. For example, if an angry patient shouts, "You had better not touch me!" it would probably be best to respond by saying to the patient, "It seems to bother you that I might touch you" rather than saying to the patient, "I don't intend to touch you" or "I will touch you if I have to" or "Don't be so afraid of being touched." The first suggested response leaves room for the patient to talk about his reasons for not wanting to be touched and to allow the staff member an opportunity to enter into a discussion with him. This might later lead to the establishment of a relationship wherein that patient might learn to trust the staff member.

Since a basic sense of worthlessness and inadequacy underlies much of the paranoid patient's behavior, it is usually not helpful to use flowery language, flattery, or an overabundance of praise in an effort to improve the patient's poor self-concept. Such staff behavior may reinforce patients feelings of grandiosity and may at best be inappropriate therapy for them. A staff member also runs the risk of having paranoid patients reject such verbalizations outright thus breaking off the potential for establishing therapeutic relationships.

Staff members and patients alike are frequently intimidated or made to feel extremely uncomfortable when the suspicious patient appears to be visually locked in on them. The "paranoid stare" occurs when patients stare intently trying to observe everything that is occurring in their environment. The fact is that such patients miss very little. For example, when staff members or others look away from staring patients, the patients sometimes feel that others are afraid of them or that they

164

cannot stand the scrutiny of such a righteous person. If a staff member is in a visual confrontation with a paranoid patient, it is best not to avoid the stare but to observe the patient closely for a brief period. The patient may then decide that the staff member is not afraid and is willing to pay close attention to what he has to say. A long staring duel may be avoided by staff members if they move quickly to distract the patient by suggesting some diversional activity.

Paranoid patients seem to have a great many religious delusions. A staff member should listen quietly as the patient talks about his delusion and take the first opportunity to ask him to help with some particular task or to engage him in a more reality oriented conversation. Make as little reference as possible to the delusional concerns. Argument is inappropriate and useless because the patient will feel compelled to defend his delusions.

The suspicious or paranoid patient has a strong fear of developing a close relationship with another person. This is caused by a fear of being rejected, and the patient can only feel rejection if close relationships are established. These patients are most likely to establish a relationship with a staff member who is honest and forthright. If Mr. Jones believes that you are going to hurt him, simply reassuring him that you are not going to hurt him will not allay his suspicions. However, if a staff member recognizes Mr. Jones' suspiciousness by saying, "I know that you don't trust me and that is all right. I just want to talk." the patient may be helped to understand that he is not going to be rejected because he is distrustful.

Another way of managing patients who present outlandish demands or who demand acceptance of obviously delusional ideas is to say to the patient, "I know you believe that you have a light bulb turned on inside your head but I do not see it; therefore, I must assume that you do not."

A reason for not agreeing with a patient's delusions is that patients frequently retain some contact with reality and will be quite mistrustful if able to convince the staff member that a delusion is true. If Mr. Jones has convinced the staff member of the truthfulness of his delusion, he may feel that the staff member is not as mentally healthy as he is.

To sum up these last few comments, a rule of thumb may be appropriate: Don't participate in a patient's mental games because you don't know the rules and, therefore, cannot hope to win. Finally, it is important to realize that a patient's suspiciousness and attentiveness to the things going on around him frequently make him a source of anxiety and provocation for staff members. A paranoid patient may make offensive, yet accurate, criticisms of staff members, ward policies, and ward procedures. It is of absolute importance that staff members not respond to these criticisms by becoming anxious or by rejecting the patient. This is a difficult lesson to learn. The paranoid patient is likely to be kind at times and vicious at others. This inconsistency in behavior makes the paranoid patient difficult to manage. It is the staff's responsibility to provide such patients with firm, consistent, supportive care.

ANNOTATED BIBLIOGRAPHY

Epstein, L.J.: *Paranoid illness in the elderly.* Consultant, 1980, 20(9):95–102.

Relates range of etiologic factors contributing to paranoid behavior in the elderly. Author states opinions on the goals of treatment.

Kolb, L.C.: *Paranoid psychoses.* In *Modern Clinical Psychiatry.* W.B. Saunders, Philadelphia, 1973, pp. 387–98.

Covers etiology, psychopathology, psychodynamics with a case presentation, prognosis, and treatment of a paranoid patient.

Mereness, D.A., and Taylor, C.M.: *Patients whose behavior is characterized by pathological suspicion.* In *Essentials of Psychiatric Nursing.* C.V. Mosby, St. Louis, 1974, pp. 187–96.

Covers causative factors, development of projective patterns of behavior, and how to meet the nursing needs of the suspicious patient.

Mitchell, R.G.: *Breakdown—Commonsense psychiatry for nurses. The schizophrenics.* Nursing Times, 1982, 78(49):2071–2074.

Includes discussion of paranoid schizophrenia with etiologic factors and nursing care.

Neadley, A.W.: *Paranoid depression.* Nursing Times, 1977, 73(41):1590–1592.

Case history of paranoid behavior. Relates the nursing care and clinical course of a particular patient.

POST-TEST

Chapter 12

Suspicious Patients

True or False. Circle your choice.

T F 1. Usually a patient's delusions have some basis in reality.

T F 2. It is therapeutic for a patient to discuss his delusion at length.

T F 3. The paranoid patient is likely to be warm and kind one moment and then become very vicious the next moment.

T F 4. The major defense mechanism used by the paranoid patient is projection.

T F 5. Suspicious patients often interpret minor oversights as personal rejection.

T F 6. Since a basic sense of worthlessness and inadequacy underlies much of the paranoid patient's behavior, it is helpful to use flattery and a great deal of praise to improve the patient's self-image.

T F 7. Paranoid patients may have a great many religious delusions.

Multiple Choice. Circle the letter you think represents the best answer.
Situation: Mr. White is a 49-year-old man who has spent much of his life drifting from place to place. He was admitted to the hospital because of extreme suspiciousness of others and visual hallucinations. The next four questions apply to Mr. White's situation.

1. Which approach by the staff would be the most threatening to Mr. White?

   A. Forthright and honest.

   B. Friendly and emotionally detached.

   C. Warm and nurturing.

   D. Permissive and reserved.

2. Mr. White is sitting quietly next to a staff member in the dayroom. He seems to be mumbling to himself. Which comment would best serve to get the patient's attention?

   A. "Tell me what you are thinking, Mr. White."

   B. "Why are you mumbling, Mr. White?"

   C. "I understand you are angry, Mr. White."

   D. "Let's look at this magazine, Mr. White."

3. You are talking with Mr. White and suddenly he says, "What are you asking me all this for. I've already told this to my doctor. I suppose you're trying to find out if my answers will be the same." Which of the following responses would be best?
   A. "Why do you think I would do that?"
   B. "I'm only trying to help you."
   C. "It seems to you I've been prying."
   D. "I'm sorry you feel that way. Let's talk about something else."
4. The chief mental mechanism Mr. White is using is:
   A. Rationalization.
   B. Reaction formation.
   C. Projection.
   D. Introjection.
   D. Conversion reaction.

Situation: Mr. Green has voluntarily admitted himself to the state hospital upon the urging of his physician. Mr. Green has lived alone most of his life and has no known friends. Recently, he had been phoning his neighbors, accusing them of "bugging" his house and plotting to kill him. The next two questions apply to this situation.

5. During the admission procedure, Mr. Green refuses to take off his clothes and get into bed. Which approach by the staff member would be most helpful at this point?
   A. Get another staff member to assist in removing the patient's clothes.
   B. Leave the room and send an orderly to undress the patient.
   C. Find out why the patient does not want to undress.
   D. Let the patient keep on his street clothes.
6. Mr. Green in angrily telling you about what people have been doing to him. Your best response is:
   A. To say nothing.
   B. "I don't blame you for being angry. That's a terrible thing for them to do."
   C. "Why are you angry at me? I haven't done anything to you."
   D. "It doesn't really make any sense, does it, that your neighbors would be doing this?"
   E. "It must be difficult to feel all alone and threatened like that."

13

Depressed Patients

OBJECTIVES: Student will be able to:
1. Identify symptoms of depression.
2. List techniques for dealing with the depressed patient.
3. Identify different modes of treatment for depression.

The depressed patient is the patient who usually gets the most sympathy from a therapeutic staff. However, if a patient's depression does not lift as treatment progresses, he may experience a great deal of rejection and hostility from staff members.

The depressed patient has such a multiplicity of symptoms and problems that effective management is difficult. These patients frequently have a decreased appetite, a significant weight gain or loss, a loss of interest in activities of daily living, difficulty sleeping and many other physical problems. Usually their self-esteem is poor and, when depression is severe, personal hygiene is neglected. A depressed patient is likely to be tearful, upset, and apathetic. Since their activity level is low, there is a predisposition to certain physical problems. Bed sores, skin rashes, boils, scalp infections, constipation, and nutritional deficiencies may occur. These problems may be reduced or prevented by attentive staff although extra effort is required.

The treatment of the depressed patient requires a great deal of careful observation and supportive therapy. Frequently the patient's life is at stake because of suicidal feelings. These patients often have exaggerated feelings of guilt and believe that their life is not worth living. Sometimes their feelings of uselessness and worthlessness are such that they feel that they do not deserve to live and would rather die. During this time, it is important to prevent these patients from destroying themselves while trying to help them understand that times and circumstances change as does the availability of love objects and that they may hope for a better situation at some time in the future. Most depressed patients, however, are strongly oriented to the present and have very little wish to consider a future for themselves. Inexperienced staff members sometimes allow themselves to become trapped by agreeing not to disclose a patient's suicidal thoughts. One should never agree to keep anything concerning a patient's welfare from other staff members or from the patient's physician. If, in reality, the patient did not want the information known, it is unlikely that he would share it with anyone.

It is important to recognize that depressed patients frequently deny their need for human company and for the support of persons in their environment. Although depressed patients may indicate that they do not want to talk and do not want company, they are usually comforted by someone paying attention to them and by knowing that someone is willing to talk to them. This subtly bolsters their self-esteem and helps them to feel that they are worthwhile individuals. Even if patients do not appear to notice that a staff member is present, it is quite likely that they take comfort in the knowledge that someone cares enough to sit with them in their misery. If at all possible, patients should be encouraged to talk about their feelings and problems. The patient's verbalizations should be responded to in an understanding and nonjudgmental way. Patients should be supported in their efforts to talk about their problems and should be permitted to express their discomfort and hurt by crying if they feel the need to cry. Patients should never be told not to cry.

Sometimes a crying or weeping patient causes discomfort among staff members. A crying patient, however, will usually respond to a calm, soothing voice and an arm around the shoulders. Comments such as "everything will be all right" and "the sun will shine tomorrow" are not comforting to the patient because they are not consistent with the patient's feelings. Instead, depressed patients should be encouraged to talk about what makes them feel like crying. Comments such as, "You seem to feel very sad. Would you like to talk about what is making you cry?" or "Something must be hurting you very much." may encourage the patient to talk.

Depressed patients also suffer from sleep disturbances. They may require medication for sleep and may need to talk or sit with someone before they can calm their fears and become sleepy. In other cases, depressed patients may sleep 12 to 14 hours a day as a means of escaping from feelings of guilt and depression.

Since depressed patients have low activity levels, it is often necessary to encourage them to participate in a wide range of activities so that they may begin to reestablish social relations which have been neglected. Involvement in as many activities as possible should be encouraged. This is particularly true of activities which will permit the establishment of social relationships which increase the patient's confidence and improve self-esteem. Depressed patients usually need to begin to establish relationships on a one-to-one basis. As their condition improves, they should be encouraged to become involved in group interactions. Sometimes when depressed patients do not believe they can help themselves, they will willingly do things to help others. Such interactions may prove to be quite therapeutic.

Depressed patients should be encouraged to get out of bed, to go to breakfast, to go to all their meals, to make up their beds, and to attend to matters of personal hygiene.

Staff members can help depressed patients regain pride in their personal appearance by making sure that they are provided with clean, attractive clothing and that they are neatly dressed and well groomed. Family members should be encouraged to bring favorite articles of clothing or perhaps a new shirt or a new dress. Barbers and beauticians may be needed to help with improving patients' physical appearance. Staff members, however, should be careful not to overwhelm depressed patients with too many extravagances since the patient may respond by withdrawing further, believing that he is not worthy of all the attention.

Small meals selected from favorite foods and presented attractively help to restore lost appetites and to improve nutrition. It may be helpful to sit with such patients and to offer verbal encouragement. Sometimes it is necessary for staff members to feed severely withdrawn patients.

It is important not to be critical of the level of involvement that a patient might show in some particular activity. Proficiency will improve with regular exposure and a developing interest in the activity. In the beginning, praise, and reinforcement for simply showing up at a particular activity is important and any efforts made toward becoming involved in activities should also be praised. Frequently, efforts to get a particular patient involved in activities will require a number of attempts. Staff members should not become discouraged or irritated if that patient will not respond immediately to their efforts. Persistence and kind, gentle persuasion will often result in the desired involvement. Force is not helpful. It will instead produce resentment or guilt feelings and more withdrawal. New patients especially need time to adjust to the clinic or ward routine and to learn what is expected of them.

On occasion, a crying, whiney patient will become attached to a particular staff member and will make the staff member's life miserable. In such cases, it is helpful if other staff members will approach that patient with suggestions for activities and with requests for assistance at some minor task. This encourages interaction with other staff members. Encouragement to become involved in activities which will require spending some time doing something independently or with another patient is desirable.

It is likely that there will be a few patients who will remain withdrawn despite the intensive efforts of the staff to draw them out and to get them involved in activities. In such cases, visits at regular intervals by particular staff members enable these patients to look forward to having company. This should be done even if it results in no conversation or interaction with the staff members. During such visits, staff members might perform small tasks for the patient which let the patient know of their care and concern. If the patient is in bed, a staff member might smooth the bedcovers, quickly brush the patient's hair, suggest some makeup, a change of bedclothes or some other aspect of personal care. Without appearing overly cheerful, a positive outlook on life and a discussion of activities which might interest the patient is helpful. Patients should be encouraged to attend activities which are of interest and even to attend some activities which may not be of interest but would simply help pass the time.

In talking with the depressed patient, a staff member might try a broad range of topics of possible interest. Usually even severely depressed patients are interested in something. The trick is to discover what that something is and then to use it to further the patient's interest in other activities.

It is critically important to remember that, although depressed patients may not show it, they want and are much in need of a relationship with another person. They are often afraid that they will not be able to fulfill their part of a relationship and thus are reluctant to become involved. Once involved, however, much therapeutic good can be accomplished.

Since depressed patients almost always have poor self-esteem, they may respond well to assisting staff members with minor tasks. This will make the patients feel somewhat special and important, thus improving their self-esteem. A patient may have a particular talent or characteristic which can be pointed to with respect and admiration by a staff member and by other patients. The ancilliary therapy activities, such as art, occupational, recreational, and music therapy frequently offer an opportunity for patients to do something which can be recognized and appreciated by staff members and patients.

Two other modes of treatment of the depressed patients are medication and electroconvulsive shock therapy (ECT). Since both of these treatment modes have been discussed in detail previously, they are not repeated here. It is sufficient to say that they require special attention and must be taken into consideration in treatment planning for a given patient. It might be helpful to review those procedures when beginning to care for depressed patients.

ANNOTATED BIBLIOGRAPHY

Harris, E.: *The dexamethasone supression test.* American Journal of Nursing, 1982, 82(5):784–785.

Describes the purpose and rationale of the DST. The DST differentiates the patients who are likely to respond to antidepressants or ECT and may also predict depressive relapses. (Note: There is now some question about the efficacy of the DST to accurately make any predictions).

Mellencamp, A.: *Adolescent depression: A review of the literature with implications for nursing care.* Journal of Psychosocial Nursing and Mental Health Services, 1981, 19(9):15–20.

Covers the losses of adolescence which contribute to depression, such as separation from parents, loss of self-esteem, and loss of sexual innocence. Differentiates between adolescent and adult depression and lists important points of nursing intervention.

Rosenbaum, M.S.: *Depression—What to do, what to say.* Nursing '80, 1980, 10(8):64–66.

Delves into the symptoms and etiology of depression. Techniques of treatment include spending time with the patient, permitting depression, maintaining contact, and encouragement.

Stuart, G.W.: *Role strain and depression: A casual inquiry.* Journal of Psychosocial Nursing and Mental Health Services, 1981, 19(12):20–28.

Stress associated with expected roles results in role strain. Article investigates models of depression and their significance.

Talley, J.A.: *Depression—Differentiate the endogenous variety from the look-alikes.* Consultant, 1983, 23(2):105–116.

Explores the differences between endogenous depression and other types of psychiatric disturbances. Includes the cardinal symptoms of depression and bipolar disorders.

vanServellen, G.M.: *Women treating women for depression.* Journal of Psychosocial Nursing and Mental Health Services, 1981, 19(8):22–24.

Psychodynamics of depression and the phenomenon of therapist-patient identification.

vanServellen, G.M., and Dull, L.V.: *Group psychotherapy for depressed women: A model.* Journal of Psychosocial Nursing and Mental Health Services, 1981, 19(8):25–31.

Includes tools for evaluation (global self-esteem scale, Beck depression inventory), and a format for group therapy.

POST-TEST

Chapter 13

Depressed Patients

True or False. Circle your choice.

T F 1. The depressed patient usually has a poor self-esteem.

T F 2. Often a depressed person feels so worthless that he feels he does not deserve to live.

T F 3. Depressed patients often convey a strong need for companionship.

T F 4. Upon approaching a tearful, depressed patient, it is helpful to remind him that things will be better tomorrow.

T F 5. Depressed patients frequently suffer from sleep disturbances.

T F 6. A high activity level is often seen in the depressed person.

T F 7. A staff member caring for a depressed patient should have a friendly, cheerful outlook in order to encourage the patient to feel the same.

T F 8. Two important modes of treatment of the depressed patient are medication and electroconvulsive therapy (ECT).

T F 9. Depressed patients should be encouraged to talk about their feelings and problems.

T F 10. Depressed patients should not be encouraged to participate in activities but should be left alone to participate at their own pace.

Multiple Choice. Circle the letter you think represents the best answer.

1. While planning activities for the depressed patient, the staff member should understand that the patient needs:
   A. Variety and challenge to lift him out of his depression.
   B. Competitive activities with the group.
   C. Activities which require exertion of energy.
   D. Simple and structured activities at first.

2. Which of the following are characteristic of depression:
   1. Early morning wakening.
   2. Good appetite.
   3. Lack of guilt feelings.

4. Worse in the late afternoon.
5. Enjoys life.
   A. 1 and 4.
   B. 1, 2, and 5.
   C. 3 and 5.
   D. 2, 4, and 5.
   E. None of the above.

Situation: Thirty-five-year-old Mrs. Brown, a mother of three, part-time bookkeeper, and part-time cosmetics salesperson, was brought to the hospital by her husband. She had become progressively unable to sleep, eat, talk, or perform housework. She sat for long periods of time, smoking one cigarette after another, seemingly unaware of people or things around her. The next two questions apply to this situation.

3. Mrs. Brown's depression is probably the result of:
   A. Paralyzing fear.
   B. Conflicting responsibilities.
   C. Physical exhaustion.
   D. Internalized aggression.
4. The feeling Mrs. Brown is most likely to demonstrate during her depression is:
   A. Suspicion.
   B. Fear.
   C. Loneliness.
   D. Worthlessness.
5. An attempt to commit suicide is most likely to occur during which of the following phases of hospitalization?
   A. Immediately following hospital admission.
   B. At the point of deepest depression.
   C. When depression begins to lift.
   D. Shortly before hospital discharge.
6. Mrs. Adams expresses to the staff member that she is feeling depressed about the recent death of her father. Which of the following responses by the staff member would communicate understanding and acceptance?
   A. "I know just how you feel."
   B. "Everyone gets depressed when they lose a loved one."
   C. "This must be very difficult for you."
   D. "Try to think positive. He was ill only a short time and didn't have to suffer long."

14

Patients Who Have Lost Reality Contact

OBJECTIVES: Student will be able to:
1. Identify behaviors associated with a patient who has lost contact with reality.
2. Define and give an example of a delusion, an illusion, and an hallucination.
3. Describe techniques for dealing with the patient who has lost contact with reality.

Patients who hallucinate or exhibit other bizarre behavior are usually suffering from one of the psychotic disorders (schizophrenia, senile dementia, affective psychosis, and so forth). Such behaviors, however, may occur if there is organic brain disease, traumatic injury to the brain, a high fever, or if the individual has taken certain drugs such as LSD. Regardless of the cause, these patients pose unique problems for staff members and can be quite upsetting to other patients.

If recognized soon enough, quiet attention and support from staff members can often keep this type of patient from losing control. Therefore, staff members must constantly be alert and attuned to behavioral clues that indicate impending problems. For example, a manic patient may first exhibit loud talk, rapid pacing, and grandiose ideas before becoming agitated and destroying the dayroom.

On the other hand, staff members must be careful not to reinforce bizarre behavior. This happens if the behaviors exhibited by patients get them what they want. For example, if a patient begins dancing up and down the hall with her dress tucked in her panties in order to get attention, the staff should kindly, but firmly, inform the patient to go to her room. When the patient has no audience, the behavior will cease. If the staff and other patients stop to watch, to clap, and giggle, the patient's inappropriate behavior will be rewarded and will most likely increase.

Patients who show bizarre behavior often need help in understanding why their behavior is inappropriate and what effect it has on others. They may benefit from appropriate confrontation with the fact that their behavior is not socially acceptable. Such confrontations should only be done by a staff member who is well trained and experienced in psychotherapeutic techniques.

Patients who are hallucinating or showing other bizarre behaviors do not respond well to demands or orders. They do, however, usually respond to kind yet firm reasoning.

Patients who are totally out of contact with reality exhibit behavior that is also bizarre, but which is far more disturbing. Staff and other patients are often at least tolerant of vulgar language, unusual makeup, or other inappropriate behavior, but they are often frightened by people who hear voices, see visions, and act in unusual ways because of their hallucinations. There are three types of reality distortions which indicate that a patient may have lost contact with reality. They are delusions, illusions, and hallucinations.

A *delusion* is a false belief that cannot be corrected by reason. For example, a delusional patient may believe that someone is trying to poison him by putting something in his food and, therefore, may refuse to eat.

An *illusion* is a false or misinterpretation of a real sensory impression or image. An example of an illusion would be when Mrs. Jones thinks she sees a man in her room when it is only the shadow of her bathrobe hanging on the door or Mr. Brown who thinks he hears a gunshot when he actually heard a car backfire as it passed his window.

A *hallucination* is an idea or perception which does not exist in reality. Patients who hear voices telling them to do things when no one is talking to them, or patients who see things which no one else sees are said to be hallucinating. The most common hallucinations are visual and auditory, but patients occasionally smell things (olfactory), taste things (gustatory), or feel things (tactile) that are not real.

These patients should be shown a great deal of kindness and concern, for their hallucinations, delusions, or illusions are often quite frightening. Voices may say scarey things to them or tell them to do dangerous or evil things. They may see snakes crawling on their beds or feel that there are lice all over their bodies. Although none of this is really happening, it is very real to the patients and they are often panic stricken. It is helpful to stay with these patients until their PRN medication can begin to calm them. Sometimes they will become quieter and more in contact with reality if they are simply removed from the environment (often busy, rushed, and overstimulating) in which they started to lose touch. Talking to the patient in a quiet, soothing manner is also helpful, especially if the nurse tries to steer the conversation back to reality. For example, Mrs.

178

Jones states that she just heard God telling her how to save the world. Instead of asking the patient to explain further (which would be focusing on the hallucination), the staff member should try to draw the patient's attention back to reality by commenting on the needlework the patient has been doing and asking to be shown how to do a particular stitch.

Patients who tend to lose contact with reality should not be allowed to spend a great deal of time alone since this encourages their bizarre behavior. Some authorities believe that hallucinations begin because a person is lonely and anxious and has no "real" person with whom to talk. Patients then "create" someone in their mind with whom they can have an interpersonal relationship. In the beginning, the imagined people or voices tell the patient what they want to hear and allow them relief from their anxiety. Thus, the patient begins to allow more time for their imagined relationship and less time for real people. They need to be around other people and, if possible, to sit and talk quietly with someone. A staff member who cares can help a great deal if the caring attitude and feeling are communicated to the patient. Staff members must begin to replace the imaginary people.

When a patient experiences an hallucination or delusion, they should be told that the staff member knows that the patient is upset and knows that the patient hears the voices or sees the snakes, but that the staff member cannot hear or see them. Staff members must serve as a healthy role model and someone with whom the patient can test what is real and what is unreal. For this reason, it is extremely important for staff members never to tell a patient they too can hear the voices or see the snakes.

Some authorities suggest that after a staff member has established a worthy relationship with a patient, they should tell the patient to dismiss the voices any time they are hallucinating. For example, the staff member might say, "Mrs. Jones, tell those "so-called voices" to go away. I'm real; they are not." Once again, focus the patient's attention on something else—something real.

Finally, it is important that staff members not argue with a patient who is hallucinating. Arguing forces patients to defend their false perceptions and may cause them to become violent. Avoid making statements which might be misinterpreted by patients and always try to be supportive of patients' feelings about their perception without supporting the misperceptions themselves. For example, the patient who says he is being chased by F.B.I. agents would not benefit from a staff member saying, "Mr. Jones, it is ridiculous for you to believe that F.B.I. agents are after you. That's nonsense. Just stop believing that and you will be all right." Neither would it be helpful to respond by saying, "Gee, that really sounds interesting, Mr. Jones. Please tell me more about it." It would be better to respond by saying, "Mr. Jones, I know you believe that

179

the F.B.I. is after you but it does not seem that way to me. It is a very pretty day. Why don't we take a walk." Then try to interest Mr. Jones in things that are reality oriented.

ANNOTATED BIBLIOGRAPHY

Epstein, L.J.: *Paranoid illness in the elderly.* Consultant, 1980, 20(9):95–102.

Discusses etiology of delusions and hallucinations in the elderly.

Hill, M.: *Care of a chronically ill psychiatric patient.* Nursing Times, 1983, 79(7):24–26

Case study relates the care of a hebephrenic schizophrenic experiencing delusions and hallucinations.

LaPorte, H.J.: *Reversible causes of dementia: A nursing challenge.* Journal of Gerontological Nursing, 1982, 8(2):74–80.

Discusses numerous causes of confusion and hallucinations and provides a ten-point plan to reorient patients to reality.

Mitchell, R.G.: *Breakdown—Commonsense psychiatric for nurses. The schizophrenias.* Nursing Times, 1982, 78(49):2071–2074.

Relates information about hallucinations and delusions in hebephrenic and paranoid schizophrenias. Includes recommendations for nursing care.

Mitchell, R.G.: *Confusion.* Nursing Times, 1983, 79(15):62–64.

Describes causes and nursing care of patients experiencing confusions, delusions, and hallucinations.

Todd, B.: *Could your patient's confusion be caused by drugs?* Geriatric Nursing, 1981, 2(3):219–222.

Describes the physiologic changes in the elderly that result in idiopathic drug reactions including hallucinations and delusions.

Winney, R., and Forrest, G.: *The reality game.* Nursing Times, 1983, 79(11):54–55.

The reality game is a technique devised by nurses to reinforce and orient schizophrenics to reality. Describes how the technique was developed and utilized.

POST-TEST

Chapter 14

Patients Who Have
Lost Reality Contact

True or False. Circle your choice.

T F 1. Patients who are hallucinating or exhibiting other bizarre behaviors respond best to direct demands.

T F 2. A patient who hears voices telling him to do things when no one is talking to him is said to be experiencing an illusion.

T F 3. The most common hallucinations are visual and auditory.

T F 4. Patients who tend to lose contact with reality should be left alone a great deal of the time because this tends to decrease their bizarre behavior.

T F 5. Some authorities believe that hallucinations begin because a person is lonely and anxious with no "real" person with whom to talk.

T F 6. A delusion is a false belief that cannot be corrected by reason.

Multiple Choice. Circle the letter you think represents the best answer.

1. Which of the following is *not* appropriate when responding to disoriented, confused, or incoherent patients?
   A. Giving the patient necessary information and assistance as needed.
   B. Assisting the patient to hurry through activities so he gets exposure to all areas of the ward routine.
   C. Be kind and firm yet help the patient when appropriate.
   D. Provide reality oriented conversation topics.

2. When working with a person who has a distorted perception of reality, the mental health worker will generally be most effective if he:
   A. Encourages the patient to discuss the voices he hears.
   B. Continually tries to draw the patient's attention to the here and now.
   C. Avoids all unnecessary physical contact.

3. In working with a patient who is hallucinating, appropriate approaches include:
   1. Carefully watching what one communicates nonverbally.
   2. Providing a structured environment.

3. Conveying to the patient that you believe the "voices" are real.
4. Asking concrete, reality-oriented questions.
5. Increasing social interaction rapidly.
   A. 1, 2, and 3.
   B. 1, 2, and 4.
   C. 2, 4, and 5.
   D. 3, 4, and 5.
   E. All of these.

Short Answer: Answer the following as briefly and specifically as possible.
1. List two psychiatric disorders mentioned in this chapter which are likely to have hallucinations as one of their major symptoms.

   1. _____

   2. _____

2. What behavioral clues would be indicative of a patient that is about to lose control?

   _____

   _____

3. List the three types of reality distortions which indicate that a patient has lost contact with reality.

   1. _____

   2. _____

   3. _____

4. Define an illusion:

   _____

   _____

5. Define hallucination:

   _____

   _____

15

Patients Who Have Neurological Deficits

OBJECTIVES: Student will be able to:
1. Define the terms JOCAM and affect.
2. Define and give an example of confabulation.
3. Give three examples of behavior that would be most effective with an organic brain syndrome patient.

Mental health professionals have coined the term JOCAM to describe the group of symptoms often shown by patients who suffer from neurological deficits. Of course, patients with other psychiatric illnesses may exhibit these same behaviors and one's approach to them may be the same. When used in reference to a patient, the term JOCAM means that the patient has difficulty in the following areas:

J = Judgment
O = Orientation
C = Confabulation
A = Affect
M = Memory.

When working with patients who exhibit behaviors that indicate problems in the above areas, staff members need to maintain a warm, accepting attitude. Since these patients often show poor judgment, they must be supervised closely to prevent them from bringing physical harm to themselves (e.g., wandering off or getting lost). Often these patients know that they are confused and become quite frustrated and agitated because they cannot correct the problem. Measures such as a supervised warm bath, a well lighted room that eliminates shadows which may be misinterpreted, playing soft music, or mild tranquilizers may be used to help these patients relax.

Some patients with neurological deficits have excellent memories for past events but forget new information and experiences rather quickly. It may be necessary for the staff to repeat information several times. The staff should use a kind, quiet tone of voice and give simple, short explanations and answers. This is especially important since the patient's attention span may be short. Loud voices and long explanations tend to bewilder these patients.

Since it is embarassing not to be able to remember, patients who are forgetful often make up information (confabulation) to fill in and cover up the things they have forgotten. It is important, therefore, to listen carefully to what the patient is saying. If the information is made up or incorrect, the patient should be corrected in a gentle, nonpunitive manner. A staff member might say, "I know you're having trouble remembering where you lived last year but your family says it was with your son, not in a home for the aging," or "I know you miss your mother, but she has been dead a long, long time." Calendars with large print and clocks with large numbers and hands help keep these patients oriented as to the date and the time. These should be placed around the unit in the areas where patients spend most of their time. Ideally there should be a clock and a calendar in every patient's room.

It may also be helpful to label certain areas such as the nurse's station, the bathrooms, and to even put the patient's names in big letters on their bedroom doors. Staff members should wear easy to read name tags at all times and it is helpful if the tag also states the person's position (e.g., R.N., Aide, Dietitian, Social Worker).

When patients with neurological deficits are admitted to the hospital unit or come to a community mental health center for treatment, they should be carefully oriented to their new environment. These patients are extremely sensitive to change and may become confused in new surroundings. They like to follow a stable routine and changes make them feel nervous and insecure. These patients should not be hurried and should be assisted whenever they need help. Since they may not always ask for assistance when they really need it, the staff must observe them carefully and give assistance when the situation warrants it. Mr. Green may be able to dress himself but may put his shoes on the wrong feet or may have forgotten how to tie his shoe strings. Mr. Jones may remember the general location of the bathroom but forget which is for the men and which is for the women. He may, therefore, use the wrong one. Patients with these problems should never be scolded or embarrassed in front of other patients or staff members. Instead, staff members should help them correct the inappropriate behavior or learn the necessary task. These problems occur because older patients who have brain damage often have trouble generalizing. For example, an older gentleman who learns to walk with the aid of a walker in physical therapy may be unable to remember how to use the walker when he returns home or to his room on the unit. Therefore, elderly patients have to be taught in a setting similar to the one in which they will use whatever skill is being learned or they should have supervised practice in that area.

184

When these patients talk in a nonsense manner, they should be told that the staff member does not understand what they are saying and the subject should be changed back to a reality oriented topic.

Confusion can be kept to a minimum by allowing patients to bring familiar objects from home such as a favorite chair, a nightstand, or pictures of their families. Also, it is helpful to place their personal items (clothing, toilet articles, and so forth) in an area to which the patient has easy access. If Mrs. Jones is found wandering around nude, she should be taken back to her room and helped to dress. The reason Mrs. Jones was wandering around nude may be that she was tired of wearing the same dirty dress and couldn't find her clean ones which were hidden away in her suitcase on the top shelf of the closet, out of reach and out of mind.

Another way to help decrease patient confusion and forgetfulness is to teach them to use lists and/or appointment books. If Mrs. Green has trouble remembering her daily schedule, help her write it down in a small notebook so that she can review it as needed. If she forgets and asks a staff member about a scheduled event, she can be referred to her notebook. A list taped next to the mirror in his bathroom may help Mr. Green remember to shave, comb his hair, and brush his teeth each day. Lists and appointment books are a socially acceptable means of keeping one from forgetting important matters and may even improve the patient's self-esteem.

Sometimes normal unit activities such as a sample birthday party for another patient can confuse a patient with a neurological deficit. If this happens, the patient should be removed to a quieter area. A staff member should stay with the patient while he eats his cake in peace and quiet so that he does not feel that he is being rejected or punished.

"Affect" means the feelings experienced with an emotion. Patients with problems of JOCAM are often described as having flat affects. They seem to be neither happy nor sad, they simply exist. Sometimes, however, their affect may be quite inappropriate. Patients may cry uncontrollably because they cannot get a letter open or may laugh when they hear that a friend has died. When such patients have reason to be upset, they need to express their feelings even if the wrong emotion is used. The appropriate emotion can sometimes be obtained by simply telling the patient, "I know you are upset. You might feel better if you cried." (or whatever the appropriate emotion might be). This technique structures the situation for the patient and gives information about the type of behavior expected. Another technique the staff can use in handling excessive emotional outbursts is distraction. Mrs. Brown, a patient who is crying uncontrollably, may be stopped by calling her attention to an interesting activity occurring across the room or by involving her in that activity.

The language of patients with neurologic deficits may also be inappropriate. If Mr. Jones swears and screams obscenities at a staff member who has moved his eyeglasses from their usual resting place, the staff member might respond in the following manner: "Mr. Jones, you're right. I should have put your glasses back where you keep them. I'm sorry, but screaming and saying what you did will only make people angry. Next time, try not to get so upset. Just ask for what you want and we will help you."

When a patient is being corrected, the correction should occur immediately after the inappropriate behavior takes place. Otherwise, the patient may not remember what he said or did that needs changing. When a patient acts in an appropriate way or learns a new task, be sure and give immediate feedback in the form of praise and approval.

It is the responsibility of staff members to recognize that brain damaged patients depend on routine and structure to help them stay oriented. Anything that disturbs their "world" is likely to upset them. In the situation discussed above, it was, in fact, the staff member who caused the situation leading to Mr. Jones' inappropriate behavior.

Patients who have neurological deficits are not hopeless. There are now drugs available which help clear the patient's thinking by increasing the brain's metabolism and use of oxygen. Further, great strides in helping such patients cope with their environment and illness can be made by a kind, understanding staff that rewards appropriate behavior and rechannels inappropriate behavior.

Staff members should remember that other physical problems such as infections, kidney problems, high fever, or adverse drug reactions may cause the behaviors described in this chapter. Staff members must be constantly alert for the possibility of such factors when JOCAM problems are discovered.

ANNOTATED BIBLIOGRAPHY

Charles, R., Truesdell, M.L., and Wood, E.L.: *Alzheimer's disease: Pathology, progression, and nursing process.* Journal of Gerontological Nursing, 1982, 8(2):69–73.

  Investigates the etiology of Alzheimer's disease and outlines a plan of nursing care.

Dietsche, L.M., and Pollman, J.N.: *Alzheimer's disease: Advances in clinical nursing.* Journal of Gerontological Nursing, 1982, 8(2):97–100.

  Explores such topics as stages of Alzheimer's, nutrition, activity, sensory changes, sleep disturbances, drug therapy, and family support groups.

Glaze, B.: *One woman's story.* Journal of Gerontological Nursing, 1982, 8(2):67–68.

Case history as related to the Congressional Subcommittee on Health, Education, and Welfare, by the wife of a man who suffered from organic brain syndrome. The patient was a former community leader and vice-president of his company until struck with Alzheimer's disease.

Mackey, A.M.: *OBS and nursing care.* Journal of Gerontological Nursing, 1983, 9(2):74–85.

Very thorough discussion of organic brain syndrome. Relates OBS to the DSM-III classifications. Provides tools to assess levels of disability.

Palmer, M.H.: *Alzheimer's disease and critical care.* Journal of Gerontological Nursing, 1983, 9(2):86–90.

Explores the etiology of Alzheimer's disease and discusses nursing care of Alzheimer's patients. Nursing implications include safety, trust, drugs, nutrition, and ongoing assessment.

Richardson, K.: *Hope and flexibility—your keys to helping OBS patients.* Nursing '82, 1982, 12(6):64–69.

Humanistic insight into the care and treatment goals of the OBS patient.

Steffl, B.M.: *Resources for teaching, learning, and dealing with cognitive changes in aging.* Journal of Gerontological Nursing, 1982, 8(2):101–103.

Extensive references for books, articles, videotapes, and films on Alzheimer's disease and other aging changes. Useful for teaching/learning of patients, families, and health care workers.

POST-TEST

Chapter 15

Patients Who Have
Organic Brain Damage

Multiple Choice. Circle the letter you think represents the best answer.

1. Organic brain disorders are caused by:
   1. Interpersonal traumas.
   2. Anatomic damage.
   3. Physiologic damage.
   4. Trauma to the psyche.
   5. A too strong superego.
      A. 1, 4, and 5.
      B. 2, 3, and 4.
      C. 4 and 5.
      D. 1, 2, and 3.
      E. 2 and 3.
2. Choose the items that can be features of organic brain disorders.
   1. Impairment of memory for past events.
   2. Impairment of judgment.
   3. Good control of emotions.
   4. Personality changes.
   5. Hallucinations.
      A. All of the above.
      B. 2, 4, and 5.
      C. 1, 2, and 3.
      D. 1, 2, and 5.
      E. None of the above.
3. Confabulation is:
   A. A type of hallucination.
   B. An effective medication.
   C. Fragmented thinking.
   D. Euholia.
   E. Filling in memory gaps.
4. In treating a patient with organic brain disorder caused by cerebral arteriosclerosis, the mental health worker should:
   1. Understand the patient's personality before illness.

2. Give individualized care.
3. Know that memory for recent events is better than memory for past events.
4. Provide a disordered environment.
5. Be optimistic, emphatic, and clear.
   A. All of the above.
   B. None of the above.
   C. 1, 2, 3, and 5.
   D. 1, 3, and 4.
   E. 1, 2, and 5.
5. The relatively permanent impairment of cerebral function that occurs in chronic organic brain damage produces defects in:
1. Memory.
2. Orientation.
3. Judgment.
4. Comprehension.
5. Affect.
   A. 1, 2, 3, and 5.
   B. 1, 2, and 3.
   C. 1, 2, 3, and 4.
   D. All of the above.
6. The premorbid personality of a patient with organic brain disorders:
   A. Usually has little to do with the type of illness he develops.
   B. Usually determines the behavior he shows.
   C. Is usually impossible to determine.
   D. Usually is the opposite of that shown.
7. A senile patient is withdrawn and negativistic. The best approach to the patient might be:
   A. "Would you like to go to your room where you can be alone?"
   B. "I need a partner to play checkers with me."
   C. "Your family will be terribly disappointed if you don't go to O.T."
   D. "Your doctor wants you to participate in activities."
8. Which of the following is *not* appropriate when responding to disoriented, confused, or incoherent patients?
   A. Giving patient necessary information and assistance as needed.
   B. Assisting the patient to hurry through activities so he gets exposure to all areas of ward routine.
   C. Be kind and firm yet help patient where appropriate.
   D. Provide reality oriented conversation topics.

True or False. Circle your choice.

T F 1. Organic brain disorders (chronic type) can be reversible.

T F 2. Good psychologic adjustment to life prior to the onset of cerebral arteriosclerosis is a determining factor in the prognosis of the disease.

T F 3. Patients with organic brain damage often have short memory spans.

T F 4. It is frequently helpful to "make an example" for other patients by choosing a particular brain damaged patient to keep correcting until he does almost everything in the desired manner.

T F 5. Patients should not be allowed to bring personal items from home because it only makes them cry and want to go home.

Short Answer. Answer the following as briefly and specifically as possible.

1. Fill in the term which corresponds to the letter given:

J = _____

O = _____

C = _____

A = _____

M = _____

2. The best way to explain something to an organically impaired person is

_____

3. Brain damaged patients often have difficulty with maintaining a good orientation to a new environment. List five things a mental health worker can do to reduce disorientation.

    1. _____

    2. _____

    3. _____

    4. _____

    5. _____

4. When it is necessary to correct a patient, why should it be done immediately following the inappropriate behavior?

_____

_____

5. The two most important factors in helping brain damaged patients to stay oriented are:

    1. _____

    2. _____

16

Patients Who Abuse
Alcohol and Other Drugs

OBJECTIVES: Student will be able to:
1. Identify factors that influence the use and abuse of alcohol.
2. Identify Jellinek's four stages of alcoholism.
3. Define the term cross tolerance.
4. Identify methods of treatment for alcoholism and other drug abuse.

The abuse of alcohol and other drugs represents a significant problem for health authorities in the United States. In fact, alcohol abuse alone has been said to be the third largest health problem in America. When abusers of other drugs are added to the ranks of those who abuse alcohol, the problem becomes even more devastating. Although many people believe that only members of the lower socioeconomic groups abuse alcohol and other drugs, statistics indicate that both abuses are found in all socioeconomic groups.

Although the deaths of persons tripped out on LSD or other hallucinogens frequently make the headlines and large heroin and marijuana busts make sensational news stories, alcohol remains the most commonly abused drug in the United States. Alcohol is more readily available than other drugs, it is legal, and its use is socially accepted by our society. In fact, the drunk seems to occupy a special place in our society. If our friend, John Smith, gets drunk at a party, he is laughed at when he stumbles over a table, curses loudly, or makes a pass at a friend's wife. All of his behavior is forgiven since he is not considered to be responsible because of his drunkenness. If Mr. Smith engaged in these behaviors under other circumstances, he would quickly become a social outcast.

We are a nation of drug takers. The television daily presents the virtues of every conceivable form of pain relief, sleep inducer, muscle relaxer, and vitamin supplement. If creatures from outer space were to observe our television commercials and report back to their leaders, they probably would say that we are a nation of people who never sleep, who suffer constant low back pain, nasal congestion, bronchial spasms, gastric indigestion, tension headaches, aching feet, bloodshot eyes, and premenstrual pain and tension. They might also say that the life-sustaining substances on earth are so poor that they must be supplemented daily with many different kinds and colors of special vitamin tablets and that indeed things are so bad that humans even have to have special foods for their animals which include the same kinds of supplements. Television commercials market all these various pills, along with alcoholic beverages, as a sure means of making life more tolerable and thus more pleasurable. Most drug abusers (remember that alcohol is a drug) drink or take pills in an attempt to withdraw or sedate themselves to escape from the realities of the world in which they live.

Unfortunately, the most significant impact created by media advertising of alcohol and pills lies in the promotion of an attitude rather than promotion of the products themselves. For the most part, the products are not harmful. On the other hand, the attitudes created by the media indicate that it is okay for people to seek happiness, escape, or pleasure from a pill or a bottle with seemingly little regard for the possible psychologic or physical addiction which may occur as a consequence of their drug taking behavior.

The following sections present information related specifically to abusers of alcohol and other drugs. Although there are similarities and differences between the two groups (Table 1), they will be presented separately in order to emphasize differences in treatment and management approaches.

ABUSE OF ALCOHOL

People who abuse alcohol are known by a variety of names ranging from problem drinkers to alcoholic, wino, lappster, derelict, or bum. The term *problem drinker* is usually applied to a person who does not have the obvious symptoms associated with clinically diagnosed alcoholics. Individuals are diagnosed as *alcoholics* when they have lost control of their drinking to the extent that interpersonal, family, and community relationships have become seriously threatened or disturbed. Although superficial alcoholics can be witty, charming, and friendly, a great number of them are destructive and aggressive when they have been drinking.

Long term alcoholics tend to be pale, skinny and poorly nourished since they spend their money on alcohol rather than food and because they forget to eat when they are drinking. Long term male alcoholics may have dilated blood vessels in their faces and a bulb-like, fleshy nose which is frequently referred to as a "whiskey nose." The alcoholic individual often has bloodshot eyes and a general disheveled appearance. Poor personal and dental hygiene is likely as is a hoarse voice, hand tremors,

TABLE 1. Comparison of Alcohol and Other Drug Abusers

Similarities	Differences
1. Addicts in both groups come from all sociologic and economic levels.	1. Men outnumber women 3:1 in drug abuse. The ratio of men to women for alcohol abuse is 1:1.
2. Basic personality structures for both include dependency, low self-esteem, inability to tolerate tension, immaturity, and difficulty in accepting responsibility for their own actions. Often blame their problems on someone else or on some event in their life.	2. Average age for alcoholic is substantially higher, being 30 to 55 years for the alcoholic and 16 to 25 years for other drug abusers.
3. Both cause psychologic and physical dependence with psychologic dependence occurring first.	3. Alcohol is much more socially acceptable than other drugs.
4. Often start habit for same reason—to feel accepted or to gain a feeling of social well being.	4. Usually takes longer to become addicted to alcohol than other drugs. Person may become psychologically dependent on other drugs after first dose; not so with alcohol.
5. Both begin behavior leading to addiction because of psychologic maladjustment and access to drugs and alcohol.	5. Alcohol withdrawal symptoms may appear from one to eight days after last drink; drug withdrawal symptoms begin to occur 12 to 16 hours after last dose.
6. In advanced stages, both present basically poor general appearance and look extremely malnourished because they spend money on their habit rather than food.	6. Persons withdrawing from alcohol have tremors, increasing jitters, spasmodic gait, nausea and vomiting, loss of consciousness, convulsions, hallucinations and death. Persons withdrawing from drugs other than alcohol often have teary eyes, persistent yawning, runny nose, increasing restlessness, hostility, and severe abdominal cramps.
7. Both cause severe economic problems for the addict and the addict's family due to cost of addiction.	7. Alcoholic withdrawal is frequently a more acute medical problem.
8. Both have impaired judgment.	8. Alcohol is taken by mouth; other forms of drugs can be taken by mouth but are frequently taken intravenously or subcutaneous (skin popping) to increase and speed up the desired effect. Other drugs may also be sniffed or snorted.
9. Both types of addicts initiate treatment because of an acute medical problem or the concern of someone else for them—rarely of their own initiative; both use massive denial.	9. Unpredictable bad trips are often seen with drugs other than alcohol.
10. In treating, both need patience, understanding, consistency, a structured environment, and empathy—not sympathy.	10. Blood pressure, pulse, and respiration are depressed with overdose of drugs other than alcohol; alcohol overdose—pulse rapid (over 100), respiration increased (often exceeding 30), blood pressure frequently normal.
11. Both need increasingly larger doses of their drug to produce the desired effect, with the end result being an increased intake not to feel good but to keep from feeling bad and to prevent withdrawal symptoms.	11. Possession of drugs other than alcohol without a prescription is illegal while alcohol is legally sold to anyone over 18 or 21 years of age (age restriction varies from state to state).
12. Both types of addiction cause severe medical complications.	
13. It is often necessary in planning treatment to include family members.	
14. Difficult for people in medical field to accept drug abuse as an illness; therefore, they are reluctant to treat abusers and sometimes feel that they are wasting their time.	
15. Both addictions are curable but not arrestable.	
16. After initial addiction, both may become more of a physical problem than a mental one.	

and "the jitters." Alcoholics also tend to have a spasmodic work record or show decreased work proficiency. Of the approximately 5 to 10 million alcoholics in the United States today, only 5 per cent are of the stereotyped Skid Row bum type. Most do not fit the description just presented. Instead, they are our neighbors, relatives, and friends. They go to work every day wearing neatly pressed clothes, they have families, go to church on Sunday, live in suburbia, and generally keep up a good front. With seemingly so much going for them, one might wonder why these people become alcoholics.

Factors Influencing Alcoholism

Some authorities report that the alcoholic has ambivalent feelings about living and dying and that chronic alcoholism represents a slow form of suicide. Alcoholics often have a long established pattern of self-medication using alcohol. They "medicate" themselves for promotions, weddings, new babys, job changes, and so forth, until finally they find themselves "medicating" in order to just make it through the day at the office. Many authorities see alcoholism as a lifestyle, a means of adjusting to a particular combination of circumstances and personality types. One frequently finds in the history of an alcoholic a very poor mother-child relationship and significantly poor self-esteem. Many alcoholics have passive and dependent personality traits and thus have difficulty facing up to life's daily problems. They often lack the confidence to make choices and feel inadequate to face the basic tasks of life. The alcoholic may be very angry about being so dependent and thus becomes frustrated and hostile. Since hostility often creates more hostility in relationships, alcoholics are likely to be rejected by others and may indeed begin to experience difficulty in meeting their basic needs because of such rejection. Alcoholics typically have difficulty tolerating tension and appear to always be "wrapped up" in their own problems. Personality tests given to alcoholics frequently reflect a cylic pattern in their personalities. Alcoholics feel tense and depressed and try to relieve these feelings by drinking. When they are rejected for becoming drunk, they become even more depressed and guilt-ridden. They then drink more to reduce their new feelings of guilt and depression and a vicious cycle has begun.

Besides these psychologic factors, a constitutional or genetic factor has also been suggested as a possible reason for why some people who drink become alcoholic while others do not. Although there is not a great deal of research data to substantiate this belief, many people believe strongly that there is an inborn metabolic vulnerability which causes people to become alcoholics. Some individuals cannot tolerate alcohol and may become drunk after only one drink.

Social factors may also contribute to alcoholism. The ads for alcoholic beverages stress the "good life" and society in general is very accepting of the use of alcohol. An individual drinks with others and feels accepted. Cocktail parties abound and alcohol is served at practically every social function. Alcohol is generally considered to be a social facilitator and three out of four American adults drink to some extent.

While many authorities believe that all drinkers begin to drink for the same reason, most do not believe that an individual chooses to become an alcoholic. Rather, alcoholics begin to drink in order to sedate themselves so that they do not have to face the pain that they feel from the happenings of their daily lives. The drinking temporarily makes it easier for them to face their problems. As these individuals begin to drink more and more, their self-esteem problems are severely compounded. When they do go for treatment, they often speak of themselves as a "drinking problem" and somehow divorce themselves as people from the "drinking problem." If one did not know better, one might think that the alcoholic was talking about someone other than himself. Alcoholics use massive denial as a defense mechanism and have much difficulty accepting personal responsibilities for their drinking problem. The process of being able to accept the fact that one is an alcoholic seems to be a major key in the treatment of alcoholism. Most treatment programs stress that once a person becomes addicted to alcohol, that person will always be addicted and can never regain the ability to tolerate alcohol. Alcoholics Anonymous and other such groups stress the fact that a "recovered alcoholic" must never drink.

While there are many theories about what causes alcoholism, there is very little disagreement over the fact that there is both a psychologic and a physical addiction to the drug. In fact, psychologic dependence usually occurs before physical dependence. An individual drinks, feels relief, drinks more, feels more relief, and so on, and eventually becomes physically addicted. At that point, the alcoholism often becomes as much of a physical problem as a mental problem.

Physiologic Effects

It is important to remember that alcohol is a poison and, therefore, is highly toxic to the body. It may sedate one to the extent that the problems of daily life are more tolerable but it irritates practically every organ system in the body. It inflames the gastrointestinal tract (including the pancreas and the liver), it depresses the production of bone marrow and thus the production of red blood cells and the individual's susceptibility to infection and bruises is increased. Alcohol causes both brain tissue changes and scar tissue formations in the liver (cirrhosis). Alcohol may also cause significant damage to the heart. Alcohol decreases metabolic efficiency and reduces the individual's ability to absorb vitamins. The liver may become increasingly enlarged, less functional and, therefore, less able to rid the body of toxic substances. Since alcohol sedates the cerebral cortex, an individual who is drinking is less able to think discriminately which results in impaired judgment and motor function. Therefore, when individuals are intoxicated, they are much more likely to fall and hurt themselves. Alcoholics who are seen in the emergency room setting should be carefully checked for subdural hematomas and other signs of trauma such as bruises, contusions, and fractures. Sexual impotence may also be a complication of alcoholism and further increases marital discord which is prominent when one or both marriage partners are alcoholic.

Recognizing Alcoholic Tendencies

Because alcoholics tend to use denial as a defense against having to face their alcoholism, they are likely to go for a long time without treatment. Since the alcoholic is not likely to identify himself as such, it is helpful if one can recognize a person who may be alcoholic. The following questions are provided as a means of assessing whether or not an individual may be an alcoholic. Of course, when asking these questions, it is important to keep in mind that the denial mechanism may cause the person being questioned to lie or to stretch the truth.

1. Have you ever lost work or been late for work because you were drinking?
2. Do you and your spouse ever argue about whether you drink too much?
3. Do your friends consider you to be a heavy drinker?
4. Are you quiet and withdrawn but become the "life of the party" after a few drinks?
5. Have you ever felt sorry about your drinking behavior?
6. Do you need a drink at certain times during the day or do you usually drink along throughout the day?
7. Do you often want a drink soon after waking in the morning?
8. Does drinking make it easier for you to get through the day?
9. Do you drink by yourself a good deal of the time?
10. Do you ever have difficulty recalling activities which occurred while you were drinking?
11. Do you feel better about yourself as a person when you are drinking?

A "yes" answer to any one of the preceding questions suggests the strong likelihood that an individual is alcoholic and a "yes" answer to two or more questions increases the probability significantly.

198

The Alcoholic Process

The process of becoming an alcoholic has been broken down into four stages by Jellinek (see Bibliography).

1. Prealcoholic Symptomatic Phase. In this phase, alcohol is first used to avoid problems or to bolster confidence during moments of stress or crisis. The drinking behavior takes the place of the development of adequate coping mechanisms and, as stress occurs more often, the individual's drinking becomes more frequent. There is also an increase in the individual's ability to tolerate alcohol.

2. Prodromal Phase. In this phase, the individual drinks heavily and the heavy drinking frequently leads to unconsciousness and memory blackouts. The individual cannot wait to get a few drinks but then feels guilty about drinking. There is usually no one to talk to about the problem.

3. Crucial Phase. During this phase, there is a loss of control and the individual is unable to abstain from drinking. The individual is likely to drink continuously until nausea or unconsciousness results. The individual may exhibit grandiose or aggressive behavior while drinking along with remorse, self-pity and resentment toward anyone who tries to prevent his drinking. Withdrawal symptoms will occur if the individual stops drinking.

4. Chronic Phase. The behavior in this stage is marked by frequent "benders" and prolonged periods of intoxication. There is usually daily intake of alcohol in response to the physical "craving" which occurs as a result of metabolic changes. Nutritional deficiencies occur as well as organ system difficulties and behavior problems. Individuals in this stage frequently lose their jobs because they are unable to work effectively. They are also likely to experience severe marital disruption and lose their family through divorce. If individuals in this stage are not treated, death may occur within a relatively short period as a result of malnutrition, infection, or acute problems that occur when the person is unable to obtain alcohol. At this point, alcoholic hallucinosis and acute delerium tremens (D.T.'s) are likely.

Jellinek stresses the point that not all of the phases and symptoms are experienced by every alcoholic and they do not always occur in the same sequence.

Treatment

Although we have already said that society tends to tolerate and even accept the individual who is drunk, the patient who is diagnosed an alcoholic is often rejected not only by his family and friends but also by the medical personnel who are assigned to care for him. Although medical personnel tend to view alcoholism as a disease and are usually able to view it more objectively than the alcoholic's family and friends, many are still ambivalent toward the alcoholic. The professional person may feel frustrated by alcoholics and unconsciously reject them. Some authorities believe that the longer one works with alcoholics, the more negative one becomes toward them. Alcoholics tend to have frequent relapses and resume drinking. It is difficult for staff members to determine if they are making progress. Medical personnel like to see their patients "get well" and do not like to see patients return. When alcoholic patients return time after time for detoxification, the treatment team has a tendency to become discouraged. The frequent return rate has been suggested as one of the main reasons alcoholics have difficulty finding acceptance among treatment team members. This is particularly true if patients do not appear to be trying to help themselves or if their "will power" is so poor that the very afternoon they are discharged, they are returned to the unit unconscious from an alcohol overdose. One must remember, however, that alcoholism is a chronic illness and as in all chronic illnesses, the patient is subject to relapses.

Since alcoholics are not well received by treatment teams, family members and friends, it is no wonder that a great many people have difficulty admitting their alcoholism. Perhaps for this reason, among others, the denial mechanism mentioned earlier is brought into play by the individual as a defense against admitting their alcoholism. The alcoholic's massive use of denial is a major obstacle throughout the treatment process. Because of the denial, alcoholics often feel obligated to refuse treatment and detoxification since to allow treatment would be to admit their alcoholic condition. The alcoholics use of denial, abusive language, beligerence, and manipulative behavior are severely detrimental to good patient-staff relationships. At first it may be difficult to understand why alcoholics behave as they do but if one examines the way alcoholics enter treatment, it is somewhat easier to see the reasons behind their behavior.

Ways of Entering Treatment. Alcoholics usually enter treatment in one of four ways. The most frequent way an alcoholic begins to receive treatment is through recognition of the alcoholic status by someone in the general hospital when the alcoholic has been admitted for some other reason. The patient may have sought medical attention for stomach ulcers, "nerves", urinary problems, liver disease, gastrointestinal problems or other physical complaints. Most often the physical illness is secondary to the primary problem of alcoholism. A second way alcoholics may enter treatment is that they are brought by the police after being picked up for public drunkenness. In the past, public drunks were thrown into jail to "dry out" and research indicates that many of these people died from D.T.'s (delerium tremens). Today, however, many states have legislation requiring that persons who are picked up for public drunkenness be taken to a hospital or to a treatment center for alcoholics. The third way an alcoholic may begin treatment is when a family member, concerned friend, employer, or health care worker becomes aware of an individual's drinking problem and is able to convince the person to seek treatment. The fourth, and perhaps the least likely, way for an alcoholic to begin treatment is through self-referral. There is, however, one diagnostic category of alcoholics who usually do seek treatment on their own initiative because they realize something is really wrong and want help. This category is pathologic intoxication. In *pathologic intoxication,* the individual becomes extremely intoxicated after one or two drinks. Such individuals may be hostile, belligerent, and suicidal or may become severely depressed. For either type, symptoms usually last from a few hours to a whole day.

Recognizing Signs and Symptoms. Because alcoholic patients are not likely to tell treatment team members that they are alcoholics, it is important for all team members to be aware of the signs and symptoms which indicate the possibility of a patient being alcoholic. Of course, if the patient smells of alcohol when admitted, many people are immediately alerted to the problem. However, if there is no reason to suspect that a patient is drinking, one must become attuned to other symptoms. Alcoholics may not go into active D.T.'s for a period of one to eight days after their last drink. However, many other symptoms do appear 12 to 48 hours after the patient's last drink. Anxiety and irritability are often the first symptoms to appear as the alcohol begins to be processed out of the patient's system. The patient may then develop shakiness or tremors, begin to make unreasonable demands or have temper tantrums. They may become so nauseated that they vomit or show evidence of dehydration. The patient may be extremely restless, agitated, and aggressively confused. The alcoholic can become disoriented and may sometimes begin to hallucinate. To keep environmental factors from increasing the hallucinating behavior of alcoholic patients, staff members need to maintain an attitude of caring concern and frequently reorient patients to reality and to their environment. Explain to them who you are and restrict all visitors unless otherwise ordered. Place the patient in a quiet room with no shadows so that they will not be subjected to unnecessary stimulation from TV, radio, other patients, or shadows on the wall.

At any point during withdrawal, the alcoholic patient may begin to convulse and will die if not carefully managed. As a matter of fact, a significant number of patients in active D.T.'s die due to inadequate treatment. Some patients continue to deny their alcoholism despite the presence of such significant and dangerous symptoms.

One point which is of considerable interest to people working in general hospitals and outpatient clinics is the way in which one can tell the difference between drug overdosage and an alcohol withdrawal reaction. Although there may be some individual differences, a general rule is that while both drug and alcohol withdrawal cause slowed motor responses, drowsiness and confusion, in the toxic alcohol state, the patient's vital signs are usually elevated. The patient has rapid respirations, a rapid pulse (over 100) and a normal blood pressure. In drug overdose, all vital signs are usually depressed. It is important to keep in mind, however, that alcoholics can become so acutely ill and have such poor circulation that they show a drastically lowered blood pressure. If this occurs, they must receive immediate emergency medical treatment in order to survive.

Methods of Treatment. Medical treatment of alcoholics in the pre-alcoholic and prodromal stages usually consists of some type of group therapy or, in some cases, individual psychotherapy. Treatment of alcoholics who are in the crucial or chronic phase not only requires psychotherapy on an individual or group basis but often requires hospitalization or at least treatment in a special outpatient detoxification unit. Treatment of acute withdrawal from alcoholism is accomplished primarily through the use of medication. These patients are given intravenous fluids to combat dehydration and tranquilizers to help reduce anxiety and guilt.

Librium is the tranquilizer most commonly used in the treatment of alcoholics. By the time alcoholics are in the crucial or chronic phase of alcoholism, they usually have decreased liver function due to cirrhosis or scarring of the liver and Librium is not as difficult for the liver to metabolize as many of the other tranquilizers. Another reason why physicians treat alcoholics with Librium is that while this drug is chemically similar to alcohol, it does not depress the brain centers. Anticonvulsants may be needed to reduce convulsive activity in these patients and multivitamin therapy is utilized to replace the vitamins lost due to poor nutrition. Antacids are given for gastric distress and antiemetics are given for severe nausea and vomiting. Again, it is important to realize that these patients are severely ill and may die without adequate care.

A great deal more than the appropriate use of medications is involved in the successful treatment of alcoholics. Most treatment programs make sure the alcoholic learns about the effects of alcohol on the body. Treatment teams try to provide the alcoholic with psychologic support while at the same time teaching them how to become more independent as they gradually learn to cope with the stress and problems involved in daily living. It is necessary to accept these patients without moralizing or blaming them for their behavior. On the other hand, it is necessary to help these patients begin to realize that they are responsible for their own

202

behavior. Staff members need to be consistent and should not let the alcoholic patient manipulate one staff member against another as they often try to do. It is important to carefully evaluate physical complaints. If there are valid problems, they should be treated but staff members should not let patients manipulate them into giving extra medications for nonexistent ills. At times, alcoholics going through detoxification become so desperate for alcohol that they will drink anything that they think might have some alcohol content, including mouthwash and hair tonic.

It is important to point out realities to alcoholic patients and to try to keep them functioning in the "here and now." If they are expressing remorse about what has happened in their lives or are expressing unrealistic plans for their future, they may be doing so in order to avoid coping with current problems. Activities which increase the alcoholic patient's interaction with staff members and others help to build the patient's self-esteem. It is important to reward or reinforce appropriate behaviors exhibited by alcoholics and to be sure that they receive recognition for all accomplishments.

Insofar as outpatient or follow-up care is concerned, inpatient hospital staffs and outpatient clinic staffs are rather limited in their effectiveness. Maintenance of sobriety depends primarily on the alcoholic. Most treatment centers try to work with the families of alcoholics while the patient is in treatment. Their acceptance of the patient and willingness to help are vital links in the recovery process.

After their discharge, many alcoholics take a drug called Antabuse to discourage them from drinking. If they take even one drink while on Antabuse, they experience severe nausea and vomiting, redness of the face and trunk, headaches, heart palpitations, a drastic lowering of their blood pressure and sometimes even death. Patients who have tried to drink while taking Antabuse indicate that the reaction is so severe that they will never drink alcohol again . . . at least while they are on Antabuse.

One-to-one psychotherapy on an outpatient basis has not been successful in treating alcoholics. Group therapy programs such as those offered by Alcoholics Anonymous seem to be considerably more effective. Group such as A.A. have a structured program with built-in rewards and reinforcements as well as built-in restrictions. A.A. gives the alcoholic someone or something more powerful than themselves to lean on. Alcoholics know that if their resistance to taking a drink begins to slip, they can simply call their A.A. partner and they will receive help immediately. Perhaps Alcoholics Anonymous groups are more successful in treating alcoholics because their members were once alcoholics themselves. Not only do these people have greater empathy for the alcoholic, but they also have a better understanding of the problems faced by the alcoholic.

A.A. also has a group called Al-Anon which meets to help the families of alcoholics learn to deal effectively with their alcoholic family member.

Regardless of the method, treating the alcoholic is a difficult task.

ABUSE OF OTHER DRUGS

Patients who abuse drugs other than alcohol also come from all socioeconomic levels. Male addicts, however, outnumber female addicts three to one. Most of these addicts show basic similarities in personality structure and could be described as rather unstable, immature, passive, dependent type individuals. Their self-esteem is usually poor and they seem to lack a purpose in life. They tend not to become involved in social activities and have strong self-destructive tendencies. Many are self-centered and seem to relish playing the role of a martyr. Such individuals have difficulty tolerating stress, anxiety, or pain and many have poor interpersonal relationships. Drug addicts have significant feelings of futility and have either real or imagined deprivations. Such psychologic maladjustments, along with a ready access to drugs, very often sets the stage for such individuals to become addicts.

Before becoming addicted to a narcotic, an individual has usually experimented with other types of drugs. Sometimes the addicted patient was exposed to drugs "accidentally." For example, when hospitalized, a patient may routinely receive medication for pain. Not only is the pain relieved but the medication causes the patient to feel good and to forget all problems. After being released from the hospital, the individual may then start looking for some drug to take in order to feel as he did when he got the pain medication in the hospital. An individual may become psychologically addicted after the very first dose. Physical addiction may occur after a short period of time if the drug is used on a regular basis. When a drug abuser begins to have difficulty obtaining the high he once did, he will begin to experiment with new drugs and combinations of drugs. This is, of course, related to the fact that after regular use of a drug, an individual's body develops a tolerance for that drug and it takes a larger and larger dose to produce the same "high." Many drug abusers say that the first "high" from a drug is the ultimate. After a while the drug abuser begins to take the drug not to feel good but primarily to keep from feeling bad and to prevent withdrawal symptoms. At this stage, many drug abusers begin to feel "sick" a great deal of the time. They have aches and pains, gastrointestinal problems, and stomach cramps. The symptoms of these problems are similar to the symptoms reported when an individual has the flu. In addition to these problems, the addict often has to stop working because he is either too high or too sick to function. As the addict's tolerance increases and larger and larger doses of the drug are required to get high, an overdose is likely to occur. This happens when the individual exceeds his personal tolerance level or threshold for that particular drug.

Sometimes accidental overdoses occur because the strength of drugs such as heroin and cocaine is not carefully controlled from bag to bag. For example, most heroin is only 5 per cent pure but someone might accidentally get a bag of heroin which is 50 per cent pure and consequently overdose. Individuals also sometimes get into difficulty because of the additives such as strychnine which are sometimes used to dilute the drug. Occasionally, suspected informers are intentionally overdosed by their suppliers.

When an individual develops a tolerance to a particular drug, he also develops a *cross tolerance* for other drugs in the same generic family. For example, an addict who has built up a tolerance for Demerol will not be able to obtain a high using heroine and vice versa.

Because of the cost of many of these drugs, addicts are often forced to steal to support their habit. Women frequently become prostitutes. One bag of heroin costs between $10 and $15 and since some addicted people take as many as 10 to 15 bags a day, it is easy to see that one can develop a $200 to $300 per day habit rather easily.

Although many people believe that it is the "doped up" individual who commits crime, the actual truth of the matter is almost the reverse. An individual who has had a "fix" is highly unlikely to commit any type of crime. While under the influence of the drug, the addict's needs are at least temporarily satiated and he is not interested in anything including food, sex, or more drugs. It is only when the addict is faced with the possibility of being without drugs that he turns to crime as a means of insuring his supply. Because addicts spend their money supporting their habit, they do not eat well and consequently develop significant malnutrition problems.

Adults may develop other serious problems due to the side effects that often occur as a result of taking drugs. For example, the heroin addict who takes his drug IV may develop infectious hepatitis from using contaminated needles, or the cocaine sniffer may experience deterioration or necrosis of the tissues in the nasal area. Other possible complications include overdose, local infection, respiratory infection, severe constipation, and severe malnutrition which generally weakens the body's defense system. The "rush" which the addict gets immediately after taking a drug has been compared to a sexual orgasm and for most addicts seems to erase any fear or consideration of possible side effects. After a "fix," the addict may appear to be in a state somewhere between sleep and wakefulness. Life has no problems. He is relaxed, content, and experiencing feelings of extreme well being.

While Demerol is the drug most abused by physicians and nurses, other types of drugs are abused by the general population. Narcotics and analgesics are frequently abused as are central nervous system stimulants such as the amphetamines, hallucinogenic drugs such as LSD, barbiturates such as Seconal and phenobarbital, and some of the minor tranquilizers such as Valium and Librium. Marijuana is also a commonly abused drug.

When using alcohol, individuals have a pretty good idea of what to expect when they drink. Unfortunately, the same is not true for people who abuse other drugs. The individual on speed or hallucinogens may have a good trip but he is just as likely to have a bad trip. Even when they have a good trip, they may become quite depressed afterwards and many have strong suicidal impulses.

Treatment

The drug abuser enters treatment in much the same manner as the alcoholic. They may be seen by a physician because of an overdose or other medical complications or because they are brought to the treatment center by friends. Occasionally, the addict will seek help on his own. In general, the prognosis for any drug addict is not good and the prognosis for heroin addicts is very poor. The cure rate for heroin addiction is said to be about 1 per cent.

Recognizing Signs and Symptoms. Hospitalized patients who are suspected drug abusers should be observed carefully for the signs and symptoms of withdrawal. These may begin approximately 12 to 16 hours after the patient's last "fix." These signs and symptoms include red or teary eyes, yawning, a runny nose, restlessness and, within about 48 hours, flu symptoms which may include abdominal cramps. In some cases, the patient is quite hostile and paranoid and will refuse treatment if possible. Any time one observes a large number of needle marks (tracks) on a patient's arms and hands, the possibility of drug abuse should be considered, especially if the patient has other characteristics associated with drug abuse.

Overdoses. In treating the drug addict who has overdosed, the so-called ABC's of an overdose should be observed. *A* is to establish an open airway, *B* is to breathe the patient, giving mouth-to-mouth resuscitation if other equipment is not available, and *C* is to provide cardiopulmonary resuscitation, often known as pumping. Some authorities add a *D*, the administration of an antagonistic drug which for narcotic overdoses is usually Nalline. In cases of barbiturate overdoses, the doctor will administer an anticonvulsant drug.

After the immediate medical crisis has passed, the treatment of the drug overdosed individual is very similar to that of the alcoholic. It is important to remember that the addict is a psychologically immature individual who is probably not accustomed to making decisions and who is fairly dependent. Be candid with the addict, but not judgmental. The addict needs patience and understanding. He also needs structure and consistency. The addict can also be quite manipulative and may resort to trickery in order to get the medication he needs. He may prick his finger and place a drop of blood in his urine test in order to fake a urinary tract infection. Since urinary tract infections are quite painful, that trick could be good for several analgesic pills. Both alcoholic and other drug addicts like to make others responsible for their behavior. It is necessary, therefore, to be sure that a staff member does not accept responsibility for the addict's behavior.

Methods of Treatment. In recent years, a methadone program has been started to help heroin addicts. Methadone is a drug which is similar to heroin but which does not produce euphoria. The addict does not stay high and is, therefore, better able to function. Essentially, the methadone maintenance programs allow the addict to function by substituting one addictive agent for another which has less incapacitating properties. Methadone is legal and over a long period of time, the physician may be able to decrease the amount of the drug used by the patient. Hopefully, the addict would eventually not need heroin or methadone. Methadone is fairly inexpensive and can also be used to entice patients into therapy groups by insisting that the patient go to group therapy in order to obtain the methadone. The goal of most therapy groups is to help the person develop a different perspective of the world in which he lives and help him learn how to establish positive interpersonal relationships and develop more positive feelings of self-esteem. "Therapeutic communities" and many "Halfway Houses" have been established which try to help the addict make the transition from a drug dependent individual to a productive member of society.

In summary, drug and alcohol dependent individuals are generally difficult to treat. They usually lack motivation and tend to use a great deal of denial. Treatment activities often must be carried out against the patient's will and even if the patient "recovers," relapse is more the rule than the exception. Still, some addicts are rehabilitated and it is probably the success of those few and the hope of being able to do more which keep treatment teams involved in rehabilitation efforts.

ANNOTATED BIBLIOGRAPHY

Brodsley, L.: *Avoiding the crisis: The assessment.* American Journal of Nursing, 1982, 82(1):1863–1873.

> *Outlines a technique to identify covert alcoholics and obtain specific data regarding alcohol history. An extensive table correlating the symptoms and pathology of alcoholism is provided. The National Council on Alcoholism criteria for establishing diagnosis is also provided.*

Carruth, G.R., and Pugh, J.B.: *Grieving the loss of alcohol: A crisis in recovery.* Journal of Psychosocial Nursing and Mental Health Services, 1982, 20(3):18–21.

This very interesting article postulates that the alcoholic under treatment actually grieves the loss of alcohol and must be permitted to work through this grief. Alcoholics must have assistance in determining what needs the alcohol was meeting for them and resolve this feeling of loss.

Finley, B.: *Counseling the alcoholic client.* Journal of Psychosocial Nursing and Mental Health Services, 1981, 19(6):32–34.

Concise description of effective counseling techniques in alcoholism.

Jaffe, S.: *First-hand views of recovery.* American Journal of Nursing, 1982, 82(4):578–579.

The personal feelings of sixteen alcoholic nurses undergoing treatment are related.

Jefferson, L.V., and Ensor, B.E.: *Confronting a chemically-impaired colleague.* American Journal of Nursing, 1982, 82(4):574–577.

Describes the frequency and the effects of the drug- or alcohol-dependent nurse. Points are illustrated through several case histories. Means of recognition are described. A program of treatment and rehabilitation is related in detail.

Lange, C.J.: *What Martha wanted.* Nursing '82, 1982, 12(4):192.

This realistic personal situation describes the helplessness felt by one nurse in caring for a chronically alcoholic woman.

Leporati, N.C., and Chycula, L.H.: *How you can really help the drug-abusing patient.* Nursing '82, 1982, 12(6):46–49.

Provides practical guidelines in dealing with hospitalized patients who are known or suspected drug abusers. Also contains a table of commonly abused drugs and their effects.

McCoy, S., Rice, M.J., and McFadden, K.: *PCP intoxication: Psychiatric issues of nursing care.* Journal of Psychosocial Nursing and Mental Health Services, 1981, 19(7):17–23.

Explanation of the phases and neurologic symptoms of PCP abuse. Extensive recommendations for nursing care.

Scherwerts, P.: *An alcoholic treatment team.* American Journal of Nursing, 1982, 82(1):1878–1879.

Describes the treatment program implemented at Valley Regional Hospital in New Hampshire.

POST-TEST

Chapter 16

Patients Who Abuse
Alcohol or Other Drugs

True or False. Circle your choice.

T F 1. Alcohol abuse has been said to be the third largest health problem in the United States.

T F 2. Some authorities report that an alcoholic has ambivalent feelings about living and dying and that chronic alcoholism represents a slow form of suicide.

T F 3. Most alcoholics have aggressive and independent personality traits.

T F 4. Three out of four American adults drink to some extent.

T F 5. Alcoholics use the defense mechanism of denial most frequently and have difficulty accepting responsibilities for their drinking problem.

T F 6. In the prodromal phase of alcoholism there is a loss of control and the individual is unable to abstain from drinking.

T F 7. Alcoholics may go into active D.T.'s any time from one to eight days after their last drink.

T F 8. One-to-one psychotherapy is quite successful in treating alcoholism.

T F 9. Most authorities believe that all alcoholics begin to drink for the same reason.

T F 10. In the prealcoholic phase, drinking takes the place of the development of adequate copying mechanisms.

Short Answer. Answer as briefly and specifically as possible.

1. When is an individual diagnosed as being an alcoholic?

_____

_____

2. Describe the general physical appearance of a chronic alcoholic.

_____

_____

3. What appears to be the major key in the successful treatment of alcoholism?

_____

_____

4. List three effects that alcohol has on the body.

   1. _____

   2. _____

   3. _____

5. Describe the behaviors presented in the chronic phase of alcoholism as proposed by Jellinek.

_____

_____

6. What is the most frequent way an alcoholic receives treatment?

_____

_____

Multiple Choice. Circle the letter you think represents the best answer.
   1. The best definition of an alcoholic is:
      A. A person who consumes alcohol every day.
      B. A person who regularly goes on "benders."
      C. A person who drinks to escape his problems.
      D. A person who has developed a dependency on alcohol which causes him serious problems in living.
   2. The neurotic person uses alcohol:
      1. To build confidence.
      2. To escape responsibility.
      3. As a substitute for sex.
      4. To relieve anxiety.
      5. To consciously get mothering from others.
         A. 1, 2, and 4.
         B. 2 and 3.
         C. 1, 2, 3, and 4.
         D. 3, 4, and 5.
         E. All of these.
   3. The person with acute alcoholic hallucinosis most frequently experiences:
      A. Auditory hallucinations.
      B. Visual hallucinations.

C. Tactile hallucinations.

D. Olfactory hallucinations.

4. The defense mechanisms most commonly used by the alcoholic include all of the following *except:*

   A. Rationalization.

   B. Projection.

   C. Denial.

   D. Sublimation.

5. Alcohol is:

   A. A CNS stimulant.

   B. A CNS depressant.

   C. A fat oxidizer.

   D. A major tranquilizer.

   E. A volatile anesthetic agent.

6. When a patient is taking Antabuse and consumes alcohol in any quantity, he experiences:

   A. Nausea, palpitations, and vomiting.

   B. Elation, grandiosity, and impotence.

   C. Headaches, dermatitis, and nocturnal sweats.

   D. Hepatitis and gastritis.

7. The *primary* site for detoxification of alcohol is:

   A. The kidneys.

   B. The stomach.

   C. The intestines.

   D. The liver.

   E. The brain.

8. A patient is admitted with delerium tremens (D.T.'s). Symptoms one might observe are:

   A. Restlessness, tremors, and confusion.

   B. Depression, withdrawal, and tearfulness.

   C. Suspiciousness, depression, and unpredictability.

   D. Manipulation, stubbornness, and negativism.

9. The drug which is used specifically to help alcoholics refrain from drinking is:

   A. Morphine.

   B. Dilantin.

   C. Antabuse.

   D. Chloropromazine.

   E. Librium.

10. Which of the following behavior patterns best describes the addicted individual?

    A. Ability to tolerate anxiety.

    B. Concern for the welfare of others.

    C. Inability to tolerate frustration.

D. Inability to derive pleasure.
11. Care of a drug addict should involve observing the patient for *immediate* withdrawal symptoms which would include:
    A. Lacrimation, muscle twitching, rhinorrhea, and insomnia.
    B. Drowsiness, confusion, lability, and hallucinations.
    C. Tremors, euphoria, nausea, and palpitations.
    D. Inappropriate affect, restlessness, and impotence.
12. The most difficult problem in dealing with drug addicts is:
    A. Combating withdrawal symptoms.
    B. Keeping the patient free of his dependence on drugs.
    C. Obtaining family cooperation.
    D. Teaching him the danger of resorting to stronger drugs.

17

Suicidal Patients

OBJECTIVES: Student will be able to:
1. Describe different treatment modes for dealing with the suicidal patient.
2. List steps to create a safe environment for the suicidal patient.
3. Define SIRS.
4. List therapeutic approaches to the suicidal patient in each of the SIRS categories.

In the United States, suicide is currently the tenth leading cause of adult deaths. Suicidal deaths persist despite the advent of psychotropic drugs, open door hospitals, community mental health and suicide prevention centers, and a significant increase in the number of professionals available to treat patients.

It has been estimated that 20,000 Americans die each year by their own hand. Many experts believe that this figure is actually far below the number of suicides that occur. They reason that many suicides are made to look like accidents or that they are recorded as such in order to protect the feelings of surviving family members. It is also difficult and sometimes impossible to collect life insurance if the insured committed suicide.

For each completed suicide, records indicate that there are 10 to 20 unsuccessful attempts. Records also show that men are more likely than women to succeed in committing suicide. The difference seems to be due to the fact that men and women choose different types of suicidal weapons. By using firearms, knives, poisons, rope (hanging), or automobiles, men end their lives in painful, violent ways. Women seem to prefer drugs, often those that have been prescribed by their physician. Since it takes quite a while for drugs to be absorbed from the stomach into the circulatory system, overdoses are often discovered and medical treatment provided before death can occur. This method also provides the opportunity for a change of mind by telling someone what has happened.

The possibility of suicide is higher for certain groups of people than it is for the general population. These groups include persons who have previously attempted suicide, the terminally ill, the elderly, the alcoholic, the severely emotionally ill, and people who associate socially with persons who have made suicide attempts. Highly stressful situations and the availability of lethal weapons also increase the likelihood of a suicide attempt.

TREATMENT

ALL SUICIDAL ATTEMPTS SHOULD BE TAKEN SERIOUSLY. Members of the health team sometimes find this very hard to do, especially if a person has made what seem to be several superficial suicide attempts. One may hear someone say, "Oh, they're just trying to get attention." This statement may be true to some extent, but it is sad to think that someone is so starved for human attention as to resort to such drastic measures.

The human desire to be loved and to feel worthwhile is universal. Suicidal patients desperately wish to communicate their feelings of worthlessness, abandonment, rejection, helplessness, and hopelessness. Their inability to do so results in a sense of rage or anger which they direct toward themselves. Unfortunately, many suicidal patients do not realize that they are angry, depressed or anxious. They may not be aware of the cause of their suicidal impulses or the fact that they need help. Frequently one finds in the pre-attempt history of the suicidal patient an overinvolvement in work, career, or love objects. For example, a young wife who merges her identify with that of her husband, thus losing her own sense of being a capable person, may attempt suicide if something happens to break up that relationship. Such overidentification frequently masks underlying feelings of worthlessness, insecurity, and inadequacy. To feel worthless is to feel unloved, unlovable and unwanted. Self-esteem is reduced significantly.

Suicide attempts should be viewed as an effort on the part of the individual to communicate a need for help. They should also be taken as a signal that something is drastically wrong in the individual's life and that change and improvement are necessary if the person is to survive.

Available research indicates that the vast majority of patients who commit suicide have openly expressed their intention to kill themselves well in advance of the act. Many of these people have discussed their plight with friends and relatives. They may have been told that they should not have such thoughts or have been completely ignored and thus rejected. Any time someone reacts to a suicidal patient in a rejecting manner, their desire to commit suicide may be increased since their feelings of worthlessness have once again been reinforced. Suicidal persons need someone with whom they can talk, someone willing to listen and sincerely interested in their problems. Anyone with emotional or

214

physical problems may be suicidal. This is especially true if the individual has suffered a recent loss, such as the death of a loved one, divorce, loss of a body part, or the loss of positive feelings of self-worth due to divorce, business losses, or the loss of a job. As mentioned earlier, terminally ill patients are likely to attempt suicide. This is especially true if they believe that their impending death is likely to be painful.

Recognizing Behavioral Clues

Depressed patients are a large group of potential suicides. Since they tend to stress physical complaints rather than suicidal ideas, the staff may overlook their suicidal potential. Thus, in order to help prevent suicides among such patients, one must pay particular attention to their emotional state. For example, if a patient who has been agitated and upset suddenly becomes calm, outgoing, and happy for no apparent reason, he may be "telling" you that he has decided to commit suicide. Patients seem to actually feel relieved and happier after deciding that the solution to their problems is to end their lives.

The following are other behavioral clues which may indicate the possibility of a suicide attempt. These patients deserve your close attention:

1. Patients who have extreme difficulty sleeping and especially those who also experience early morning (3 to 6 A.M.) awakenings.
2. Patients who continually talk about committing suicide.
3. Patients who express feelings of hopelessness and helplessness.
4. Patients who are very tearful and dwell on sad thoughts.
5. Patients who show the vegetative signs of depression (loss of sleep, appetite, and interest in their appearance and usual activities).
6. Patients who show unusual interest in getting their affairs in order and who may even try to give away their belongings.
7. Patients who are hallucinating (hearing voices, seeing things, and so forth) and/or who feel persecuted.

Patients who are hallucinating may commit suicide because the voices they hear tell them to do so or in an attempt to get away from those voices or to escape from the frightening creatures that they see.

Creating a Safe Environment

The creativity shown by patients in finding weapons with which to harm themselves is truly amazing. If one considers the fact that many suicide attempts seem to occur as a result of a momentary impulse over which the patient seems to have no control, the necessity for making sure that weapons are not available becomes obvious. Patients have broken mirrors, light bulbs, and lamps and then used the glass to cut themselves.

They have been known to wet themselves all over and then try to electrocute themselves by sticking something metal in an electrical outlet. They may try to stab themselves with pens, pencils, nail files, or dull dinner knives; to hang themselves with belts, simple household string, or knotted bed sheets; to poison themselves by eating abrasive cleansers, drinking shaving lotion, mouth wash, or lighter fluid; or to drown by submerging themselves in the bathtub. They may also try to drown themselves by holding their head under water in the sink, pouring gargling solution down their nose or sticking their heads in mop buckets full of water. Others may jump out of windows, step in front of cars, or set themselves on fire. Depressed patients may simply refuse to eat in an attempt to starve. There are many other suicidal methods not listed above and it is a real challenge to stay one step ahead of patients in keeping their environment as safe as possible.

Suicidal patients often need to remain under constant supervision and alertness is the staff's best defense. If the staff maintain a warm, friendly, supportive attitude while carrying out assigned responsibilities, patients may reap a special benefit. Not only will they be prevented from ending their lives before treatment has had a chance to work, but they may feel that all the attention they are receiving means that they are truly important and that people care about what happens to them. Perhaps they may even begin to feel that life really is worth living.

Techniques for Effective Interaction

To relate effectively to suicidal patients, one should realize that these patients may feel particularly discouraged and hopeless if they do not perceive a steady improvement in their condition. Such feelings are increased if these patients are led to believe that their lack of improvement is due to poor motivation or lack of will power.

Some suicidologists believe that instead of placing the responsibility for improvement on the skills of the staff or on the patient's will power, the responsibility should be assigned to the medication the patient is receiving. This tends to neutralize the patient's sense of guilt and thus reduces symptoms. Realizing that it takes days or weeks for some of the antidepressants to reach their optimal therapeutic level in the bloodstream, the staff is more likely to approach the patient in an optimistic and hopeful way. Such knowledge may also make it easier for the patient to understand and tolerate a slower than expected rate of recovery.

Since suicide is permanent, the necessity of communicating a sense of hope to these patients is of utmost importance. Life circumstances and personal aspirations vary and change. If a patient, therefore, is prevented from committing suicide and is able to internalize a sense of hope, there is a good possibility for complete recovery.

216

In working with suicidal patients, one may expect that a great deal of time will be spent with a few patients who generate crisis after crisis by making repeated suicide attempts. Dealing with such patients is often exasperating and anxiety provoking. Perhaps one of the reasons for this anxiety is that staff members perceive the anger the patient is experiencing but are unsure of how to deal with it. Unfortunately, the most common way of reacting to anger is to respond with anger. If the staff reacts in this manner, the patient only feels more rejected and his anger is increased. Staff members must realize that the ability to react appropriately is essential. They must be interested in and understanding toward the patient but must not assume the patient's emotional burdens and attitudes. When they do so, they become ineffective in helping the patient deal with suicidal feelings.

It is important to remember that patients expect staff members to be calm and controlled even in the face of their hostility and anger. They depend on the staff to recognize the destructive elements in their behavior which they cannot see and to provide a safe, structured environment in which they can regain a sense of hope. Suicidal crises can best be handled with genuine human concern and understanding. An honest attempt on the part of a staff to reach out and help will eventually be accepted by most suicidal patients.

Suicidal Intention Rating Scale

Since treatment plans will vary with the intensity of a patient's suicidal impulses, a Suicidal Intention Rating Scale (SIRS) which has been developed and found useful by the authors is presented below. It provides a systematic procedural guide which can be used in the day-to-day management of hospitalized suicidal patients. It is the responsibility of the patient's doctor or the R.N. in charge of the unit to rate the patient and then notify the rest of the staff of the preventive measures to be instituted. Even though all hospitals do not use a tool, it is included to suggest some practical approaches to the care of the suicidal patient. A recent survey of public and private psychiatric hospitals indicates that most hospitals follow a procedure similar to the one presented here when caring for the suicidal patient.

The SIRS values and suggested therapeutic approaches are as follows:

0. A SIRS value of zero (0) is assigned to a patient when there is no evidence that the patient has (or has had in the past) suicidal ideas which have been brought to the attention of another person.

Nursing Approach: A patient with a SIRS value of 0 follows usual admission procedures and hospital routines.

1+. A SIRS value of one plus (1 +) is assigned to a patient when there is some evidence of suicidal ideas but no actual attempts. This patient does not have a history of repeatedly threatening to commit suicide.

Nursing Approach: A patient with a SIRS value of 1+ follows usual admission procedures and hospital routines. However, the patient should be quietly and unobstrusively observed and evaluated for evidence of reoccurrence of suicidal thoughts.

2+. A SIRS value of two plus (2+) is assigned to a patient when a) there is evidence that the patient has attempted suicide in the past but is now actively thinking about suicide or b) when the patient is having suicidal ideas but is not threatening suicide. For example, the patient may say, "I have thought about suicide but I don't believe it is the way out."

Nursing Approach: A patient with a SIRS value of 2+ follows usual admission procedures and hospital routines. The patient is allowed to use the following items but must return them to be locked up after use:

A. Shaving kit (including razor, blade, after shave, cologne, shaving cream).
B. Mouthwash in glass bottles.
C. Belts.
D. Fingernail files and fingernail clippers.
E. Knives of any description, including penknives. These may be used under supervision only.
F. Hair picks and hair lifts.
G. Any cosmetics in glass containers.
H. Plastic clothes coverings.
I. Hairspray.

3+. A SIRS value of three plus (3+) is assigned to a patient who has been making serious suicidal threats. For example, the patient may have said, "If they don't stop bothering me, I'm going to kill myself."

Nursing Approach: Upon admission a patient with a SIRS value of 3+ must be searched to determine if there are instruments on his person, in his clothes, or in his room which may possibly be used for self-destruction. This procedure should be performed in a professional manner with the staff being extremely careful to protect the patient's dignity. The patient will then be allowed to use the following items only under direct supervision:

A. Shaving kit (including razor, blade, after shave, cologne, shaving cream).
B. Mouthwash in glass bottles.
C. Belts.
D. Fingernail files and fingernail clippers.

E. Knives of any description, including penknives.

F. Hair lifts or hair picks.

G. Any cosmetics in glass containers.

H. Hairspray.

I. Plastic clothes coverings.

J. Medications brought in on admission.

K. Coat hangers.

L. Lamps or any breakable item from his room.

M. Eyeglasses (*Note:* These should be removed only when a patient is extremely suicidal and may use the glasses as a weapon. It must be kept in mind, however, that the removal of eyeglasses may add to confusion and depression.)

This patient should be observed at least every 30 minutes and more often if at all possible. Eating meals in the dining room is permissable but a staff member should be present at the table during the meal. Unless otherwise ordered by the physician, the patient will not be permitted to leave the unit for recreational or occupational therapy activities and visitors are restricted to immediate family.

Note: It is wise to encourage patients with a SIRS rating of 3 + or below to stay out of their rooms and in the company of other patients and staff. They can thus be watched more closely.

Usually other patients on the unit know when a patient is suicidal. They often take it upon themselves to help watch the patient and will notify staff members of behavioral changes.

4+. A SIRS value of four plus (4 +) is assigned to a patient who has been brought to the hospital because of an active suicide attempt or as a precaution against such an attempt.

Nursing Approach:

A. The patient will be admitted to a seclusion room. This is for protection, not punishment. Staff members should take care to explain why this procedure is necessary. It is much easier to observe and limit behavior in a smaller area, but the staff should spend as much time as possible with the patient interacting on a one-to-one basis. With the permission of the attending physician, a family member(s) acceptable to the patient should stay around the clock while the patient is in seclusion.

B. The nurse in charge will search the patient's clothing and body, taking care to conduct such a search in a professional manner with concern for the patient's dignity. A very thorough search should be carried out. Sometimes it is necessary to carefully check the patient's hair, ears, between toes and fingers, and any other parts of the body where harmful objects might be concealed. In females, the admitting physician may consider it necessary to examine the vaginal area to be sure that nothing has been concealed there. This may seem to be an extreme precaution; however, a loaded .22 caliber pistol has been found in a vagina. There are numerous cases of drugs being concealed in this manner.

C. The patient will be clothed in a hospital gown.

D. Any clothing, supplies, or other items which are brought to the hospital and which may be needed when suicidal precautions are removed will then be placed in the patient's locker outside the seclusion room. All unnecessary items brought to the hospital will be sent home.

E. All items brought to the hospital by the family will be thoroughly inspected by the nurse on duty and anything that might be used in a suicide attempt will not be given to the patient.

F. The door to the seclusion room should be locked at all times when the patient is alone.

G. Meals will be served in the seclusion room and only paper dishes will be used if a staff member is unavailable to supervise the meal. If at all possible, a staff member should spend time with the patient during meals.

H. It may be necessary to remove all linen from the bed and a staff member must stay with any patient trying to commit suicide by banging his head on the walls or floor of the seclusion room.

I. Any time the patient is allowed out of the security room, a member of the hospital staff must be in attendance.

J. Under no circumstances will the patient be allowed to leave the psychiatric unit without a direct order from the attending physician. In the cases where the patient has the permission of the attending physician, the patient should be accompanied by an attendant at all times (for example, to x-ray, lab, an so forth).

K Visitors will be restricted altogether. The only persons allowed to visit will be those who have specific permission from the attending physician.

Ideally, all patients assigned a $2+$, $3+$ or $4+$ suicidal rating would be closely or continually observed on a one-to-one basis (one staff member to one suicidal patient). In most hospitals such a staffing ratio is impossible. One should note that drastic intervention procedures such as placing the suicidal patient in a seclusion room or searching the patient for potential weapons may become necessary. These protective measures are used as a means of preventing suicides until treatment measures such

220

as medication and psychotherapy begin to take effect. The items taken from the patient or the fact that a patient is placed in seclusion is not as important as the manner in which these procedures are performed.

All suicidal patients should be watched closely at shift change and in the early morning hours. Patients who have been unable to sleep all night often decide that they are not going to face another such night and make a suicide attempt. Others who are waiting for their unobserved chance to commit suicide often find it during the confusion of increased activity that occurs at shift change.

After visiting hours or activity periods, it may be necessary to closely check the environment and possibly the patient for objects (potential weapons) which may have been given or unintentionally left by a visitor. When hospital workmen must make repairs on the unit, be sure that patients do not take their tools and that the workmen do not leave any of their supplies on the unit when they leave.

If one finds a patient who has attempted suicide or who is just about to do so, *do not leave the patient.* If alone, call out for help. Then, while waiting, speak to the patient in a calm, reassurring manner. If the patient wants to talk about his feelings, allow him to do so. If not, try to distract him from the suicidal intention by whatever means available.

If one finds a patient who is already unconscious, call for help and then start appropriate first aid measures.

EXERCISES

1. Although a doctor or an R.N. will usually rate the patient's suicidal potential, try rating the following patients according to the SIRS scale given in this chapter. Knowledge of this scale and the signs and symptoms that patients exhibit in each category will make one a better observer of the behavior of suicidal patients. You often will be the one that reports to the other team members behavior that indicates the need for a change in suicidal precautions. Rate the following patients according to the type of SIRS rating they should be given.

    _____ A. Mrs. Brown, a 30-year-old divorced mother of three, has been hospitalized on the psychiatric unit for two weeks due to severe depression. She has spent most of this time alone in her room crying and pacing the floor. She has been your patient during her entire hospitalization and on several occasions she has verbalized to you her belief that the only solution to her problems is to end her life. She has also expressed such feelings to other staff members. You come on duty one morning and, much to your surprise, Mrs. Brown is in the day room and cheerfully says, "Good morning" as you approach her. She then immediately states the following: "You can stop worrying about me now. I know everything's going to be all right."

———— B. Mrs. Green is admitted to the hospital due to severe depression which began three weeks after the death of her husband. She says that she guesses that she has thought about suicide but that she has never seriously considered taking her life.

———— C. Mrs. Farmer, a 23 year old female, is admitted to the unit. She immediately begins to order people around and to be generally uncooperative. She says that she wants to kill herself because nobody likes her.

———— D. A private detective, Mr. Jones, is admitted to the unit following a self-inflicted gunshot wound to the head. He says that he is tired of the world and that he no longer wishes to live. He says that as soon as he gets out of the hospital he will kill himself.

2. According to your hospitals routine, what approach would be used with each of the patients described above? (Be specific.)

A. Mrs. Brown: _____

_____

_____

_____

_____

B. Mrs. Green: _____

_____

_____

_____

_____

C. Mrs. Farmer: _____

_____

_____

_____

D. Mr. Jones: _____

_____

_____

_____

_____

_____

ANNOTATED BIBLIOGRAPHY

Carmack, B.J.: *Suspect a suicide? Don't be afraid to act.* RN, 1983, 46(4):43–45, 90.

Succinctly discusses recognition of potential suicides and nursing actions, including confrontation, protection, the therapeutic relationship, communication, activity, and hope. There are special sections on pediatric suicides and the "profile of a potential suicide."

Evans, D.L.: *Explaining suicide among the young: An analytical review of the literature.* Journal of Psychosocial Nursing and Mental Health Services, 1982, 20(8):9–16.

Comprehensive and extensive review of current literature on adolescent and pediatric suicide. Utilizes over 40 references and contains a 16 article bibliography.

Hoff, L.A., and Resing, M.: *Was this suicide preventable?* American Journal of Nursing, 1982, 82(7):1106–1111.

Relates the case of a patient who committed suicide the day following discharge from a psychiatric unit. The authors investigate alternative methods of determining suicidal intent. Examples of therapeutic communication are provided.

Leon, R.L.: *Helping suicidal adolescents.* Consultant, 1980, 20(9):115–119.

Discusses the evaluation of adolescent suicidal attempts and methods of prevention.

Loughlin, N.: *Suicide: A case for investigation.* Journal of Psychosocial Nursing and Mental Health Services, 1980, 18(2):8–12.

Helpful guide for identifying the suicidal patient and clues preceeding the suicidal act are listed. Steps for the prevention of suicide are listed.

Nursing care of a suicidal adolescent. Nursing grand rounds. Nursing '80, 1980, 10(4):56–59.

> *Case study of a 15-year-old girl with severe depression. She related feelings of worthlessness, anger, and low self-esteem. Members of the psychiatric team relate the various techniques used to care for this disturbed young girl.*

Twiname, B.G.: *No-suicide contract for nurses.* Journal of Psychosocial Nursing and Mental Health Services, 1981, 19(7):11–12.

> *Describes the use of the No-Suicide Contract as developed by Goulding, Goulding, and Dyer.*

Chapter 17

Suicidal Patients

Short Answer. Answer as briefly and specifically as possible.

1. For each successful suicidal attempt, records indicate that there are approximately how many unsuccessful attempts?

2. What specific groups in the general population are more likely to attempt suicide?

3. What is an individual who has made a suicidal attempt trying to communicate?

4. As a mental health worker in a hospital setting, what is one of the best defenses available in the prevention of suicide?

5. List three behavioral clues that would be indicative of a possibility of a suicide attempt.

    1. _____

    2. _____

    3. _____

True or False. Circle your choice.

T F   1. In the United States, suicide is at present the tenth leading cause of adult deaths.

T F 2. Women are more likely to be successful in their suicide attempts than men.

T F 3. When an individual has made several superficial suicide attempts, it is not necessary to take them seriously because they are only trying to get attention.

T F 4. Research indicates that the majority of individuals that have made successful suicide attempts have expressed their intention in some form before doing so.

T F 5. Patients often appear quite happy or relieved once they have decided that suicide is the answer to their problems.

T F 6. All suicidal attempts should be taken seriously.

T F 7. Patients who are hallucinating (e.g., hearing voices, seeing things) may commit suicide because the voices they hear tell them to do so.

T F 8. A SIRS value of one plus (1+) is assigned to a patient when there is evidence that the patient has attempted suicide in the past but is not now actively thinking about suicide.

T F 9. A patient admitted with a SIRS of 4+ is admitted to a seclusion room for punishment.

T F 10. A suicide note is a bid for attention and should not be taken seriously.

T F 11. It is usually harmful for a patient to talk about his suicidal thoughts and his attention should be diverted from such topics.

T F 12. A suicidal patient whose spirits seem to suddenly improve should be observed closely, for it is likely he has decided on a suicidal plan and intends to carry it through.

T F 13. Professionals in the field of medicine usually respond in a very positive manner toward patients who have attempted suicide.

T F 14. The more violent or painful suicide method chosen, the more serious the intent of suicide.

T F 15. Persons who abuse alcohol or drugs are prone to suicidal behavior.

Matching. Match the letter(s) of the appropriate SIRS value(s) in Column B with the statements in Column A (more than one answer may be used).

Column A	*Column B*
_____ 1. Allowed shaving kit with razor and blade.	A. SIRS 0
	B. SIRS 1+
_____ 2. No evidence that the patient is actively thinking about suicide but evidence shows has attempted suicide in the past.	C. SIRS 2+
	D. SIRS 3+
	E. SIRS 4+

_____ 3. "If I don't get some relief, I'm going to kill myself."

_____ 4. Admitted and remains in seclusion room for patient's own protection.

_____ 5. No history or evidence of suicide ideas.

_____ 6. Admitted to hospital because of an active suicidal attempt.

Multiple Choice. Circle the letter you think represents the best answer.

1. Among adults suicide is the _____ cause of death in the U.S.
   A. First.
   B. Fifth.
   C. Tenth.
   D. Fifteenth.

2. Which of the following losses might be significant enough to motivate a person to attempt suicide?
   1. Death of a loved one.
   2. Loss of health due to a chronic illness.
   3. Loss of a job.
   4. Loss of a loved one via divorce.
   5. Loss of beauty.
      A. 1 only.
      B. 1, 2, and 5.
      C. 2, 3, and 4.
      D. All of the above.

3. A person attempting suicide is likely to have recently experienced which of the following feelings?
   1. Guilt and a wish for punishment.
   2. Hopelessness.
   3. Anxiety.
   4. Worthlessness.
   5. Exuberance.
      A. 2 only.
      B. 1 and 4.
      C. 1, 2, 3, and 4.
      D. All of the above.

4. Establishing a therapeutic relationship with the suicidal patient contributes to which of the following:
   1. The patient's feelings of self-worth.
   2. The patient's desire to live.
   3. A feeling of being overprotected and dependent.
   4. The patient's belief that others want him to live.

A. 1 only.

B. 2 and 3.

C. 1, 2, and 4.

D. All of the above.

5. Which of the following behaviors might be clues preceding a suicidal act?

1. Sudden changes in behavior from depression to cheerfulness.

2. Talking directly or indirectly about suicide.

3. A history of a previous suicidal attempt.

4. Giving away items of great sentimental or monetary value.

A. 1 and 3.

B. 1, 2, and 3.

C. 1, 3, and 4.

D. All of the above.

Part 4

SPECIAL PATIENT GROUPS

18

Mentally Retarded Patients

OBJECTIVES: Student will be able to:
1. Define mental deficiency and mental retardation.
2. Identify ways of meeting the physical and emotional needs of the mentally retarded patient.
3. Describe techniques of managing aggressive behaviors sometimes exhibited by the mentally retarded patient.

Despite the fact that mental retardation is a condition which has been with mankind for the whole of his existence, there are a great number of problems surrounding the ability to diagnose and treat retarded people. This is due, in large part, to our lack of knowledge about the causes of retardation and a lack of ways to effectively treat the condition.

The categorization of persons as mentally retarded has ranged from simply labeling them as "feeble minded" to the more sophisticated definition of Doll (*The essentials of an inclusive concept of mental deficiency.* American Journal of Mental Deficiency 96:214–219 (Oct.), 1941). He defined mental deficiency as: 1) social incompetence, 2) due to mental subnormality, 3) which has been developmentally arrested, 4) which obtains at maturity, 5) is of constitutional origin, and 6) is essentially incurable. The current definition of mental retardation recognizes the clinical aspects of retardation as being distinct from the social perspective of mental retardation.

This latter concept is supported by the President's Committee on Mental Retardation and suggests that clinically, intelligence is seen as being related to genetic potential, while socially, intelligence is relative to a particular social system. In other words, clinically, general intelligence would appear to be a major definition of retardation; whereas if a social situation did not require the use of a particular kind of intelligence, then the individual would not be considered retarded within that social system. Clinically, an individual is considered to be retarded if he falls within a certain IQ range; socially, he can be retarded for some systems, such as school, and normal in other situations, such as family life. In a clinical sense, psychologists or physicians see cases of retardation which a nonprofessional would not recognize. The professional might label an individual "retarded" because of certain statistical criteria, but if the retardation is not perceived socially, the individual is not considered to be retarded by the general population.

Clinically the actual number of retarded persons in a given area can be determined scientifically without taking into consideration the social structure of the area. On the other hand, a social perspective would say that the number of people who are retarded in a given area or community is determined by what is expected of persons in that community and whether or not they are able to tolerate significant differences from what is expected (J. R. Mercer: *Labeling the Mentally Retarded.* University of California Press, Berkeley, 1973).

For most purposes, retardation must be considered to be a composite of several factors. For example, conditions of retardation may be caused by brain lesions, organic defects, or traumatic injuries. Chromosomal abnormalities also account for many cases of retardation. A great deal of mental retardation is caused by unhealthy psychologic environments where an individual is deprived of the necessary psychologic support and comfort needed for adequate development.

In most instances, psychologists are called on to decide who is retarded and who is not. They have developed intelligence tests which measure the ability of an individual to do a wide range of tasks. They compare the individual's ability to perform those tasks against a set of norms which indicates how well the "average" person is able to perform those same tasks.

The most widely used intelligence tests are the Wechsler Scales and the Stanford-Binet Intelligence Scale. In most cases, the level of retardation is estimated by the number of points scored on these IQ tests. Table 1 shows how the different levels of mental retardation correspond to IQ score ranges. Of course, when determining an individual's ability to function intellectually, the psychologist must take into account many factors other than performance on the IQ tests. He must consider the

TABLE 1. Levels of Mental Retardation According to IQ Score Ranges (DSM-III)

Diagnostic Level	IQ Score Range
Mild	50–70
Moderate	35–49
Severe	20–34
Profound	19 and below

patient's background, emotional status at the time of testing, any physical abnormalities, educational background, and genetic or biologic inheritance. Therefore, when an IQ score is stated, it is important to remember that IQ scores do not reflect just native or innate potential or intellectual development, but that the score is a composite of the interaction of all of the factors mentioned above. For that reason, it should be considered a functional IQ rather than an innate IQ. This means that the IQ score obtained from a person is an estimate of that individual's ability to perform the types of tasks measured by the items on the tests at that particular time. Again, one must remember that many factors can interfere with one's performance on a particular administration of intelligence tests and may adversely affect the individual's score. For example, if John's mother dies three days before he is tested, he is likely to do much worse than he would have under better circumstances. If a patient is sick, distracted, or has suffered an emotional trauma, the results may be lowered.

Now that we have discussed the nature of mental retardation and have learned something about how the mentally retarded are classified, we need to consider the prevalence and some of the causes of mental retardation in this country. Many authorities disagree on the exact number or the exact percentage, but the number of retarded persons in the United States is considered to be between 1 and 3 per cent of the population. This figure includes all people in Table 1 except those considered borderline (IQ 70 to 84).

A serious problem for the retarded is that they often have multiple handicaps. A study by Conroy and Derr (*Survey and Analysis of the Habilitation and Rehabilitation Status of the Mentally Retarded with Associated Handicapping Conditions.* U.S. Department of Health, Education, and Welfare, Washington, D.C., 1971) suggests that about 88 per cent of all retarded persons have at least one additional handicapping problem. They also report that at least 35 per cent have a severe additional handicap. They suggest that these conditions tend to compound each other and that the more handicaps an individual has, the less functional capability he has.

A few of the major causes of retardation will be discussed briefly here. These are presented to provide a general idea of the kinds of problems which cause retardation. If one is interested in learning more about the particular syndromes presented, the bibliography at the end of this chapter should be helpful.

Perhaps the best known syndrome related to retardation is *Down's syndrome,* a chromosomal abnormality in which there is an extra chromosome in the genetic makeup of the individual. The most common type of chromosome abnormality is trisomy 21. While there are normally two chromosomes in the number 21 pair, in the trisomy abnormality, there are three chromosomes. This extra chromosome produces the retardation and other characteristics usually associated with Down's syndrome.

A large number of features associated with Down's syndrome have been delineated. Perhaps the most common of these are the facial characteristics which include upward slanting eyes, protruding tongue, and poor muscle tone. A further characteristic is moderate to severe mental retardation. One in every 600 to 700 live births is affected by Down's syndrome. Many authorities feel that the most significant factor leading to the birth of children with Down's syndrome is the age of the mother at conception. For women over 40, there is a significant increase in the risk of having a child born with Down's syndrome.

Phenylketonuria (PKU), which is also related to a genetic abnormality, is another cause of retardation. Approximately one in every 14,000 children is born with this condition. PKU is a condition in which a person is left without the genetic potential for breaking down phenylpyruvic acid. Essentially this means that the body cannot metabolize phenylalanine which is a necessary amino acid (protein). Early diagnosis and dietary treatment of this disorder can prevent brain damage and retardation.

Tay-Sachs disease is a disorder which almost exclusively affects eastern European Jewish people and their descendants. Statistics suggest that about one Jewish couple in 900 is likely to have a child with Tay-Sachs disease. The disease is usually fatal by the third year of life and a great deal of time, effort, and money have been devoted to research in hopes of developing a means of diagnosing the disorder prior to the birth of a child. This is an inheritable disease which renders the affected individual incapable of assimilating certain body fats because of metabolic abnormalities.

A large number of other factors may also cause mental retardation. Anoxia, cyanosis, prematurity, dietary deficiencies, lead poisoning, drug abuse, incompatible RH factors, and ruebella measles (German measles) are only a few of the conditions that may lead to problems.

SPECIAL PROBLEMS

Depending upon the level of retardation, one may have a great deal of difficulty communicating with these patients. Most retarded persons operate on a concrete (elementary) level and they possess low verbal expression and verbal comprehension capabilities. Retarded individuals are often easily distracted which reduces their ability to concentrate on a particular task. Difficulties with completion of tasks may then lead to feelings of frustration and anger. Since verbal expression of feelings is difficult, they frequently resort to self-injurious behaviors such as head-banging, hand biting, and so forth.

Sarason (*Psychological Problems in Mental Deficiency,* ed. 3. Harper and Row, New York, 1959) has suggested that when children have to be institutionalized because of retardation, they experience several other major problems to which they must adjust: 1) they are separated from loved ones or familiar figures, 2) they are under a great deal of pressure to adjust to a completely new physical and interpersonal environment, 3) they experience a great deal of confusion and resentfulness about their helplessness, and 4) they experience anxiety in relation to their future. In the case of prolonged institutionalization, Sarason believes that they have to deal with difficulties related to: 1) overt conformity to the institutional culture at the expense of their personal spontaneity and expression, 2) excessive fantasizing about the outside world, 3) avoidance and fear of new problem solving situations, and 4) excessive dependence on the institutional culture. Dependence on the institution is most noticeable when retarded individuals face the reality of discharge. This reality has come suddenly for many retarded persons following recent court decisions which have established the retarded person's right to treatment. Some of these court cases have even established guidelines for treatment and some states are now requiring compliance to those guidelines. For the most part, the retarded have been guaranteed certain educational rights, certain legal rights, rights to payment for work, and a right to freedom from harm.

There is considerable evidence indicating that mental illness is fairly prevalent among mentally retarded persons. To date, there has not been any concensus of opinion with regard to the best type of psychotherapy for the emotional complications found in retardation. However, behavior modification has been quite effective in bringing about changes in overt behavior. The behavior modification approach involves identifying a particular desired behavior and then arranging the conditions of reinforcement so that the desired behavior can be elicited from the patient. For example, if the behavior of eating with a fork is the desired behavior, then one discovers something that the child would consider a reward and that can be given to the child when he responds appropriately by eating with a fork. For the most part, however, much more therapeutic time is spent eliminating undesirable behaviors than is spent trying to elicit desirable behaviors. For example, a great deal of time may be spent teaching children not to eat with their hands, not to throw food, not to grab food, not to bite themselves, not to bang their heads, and many other such behaviors. This is particularly true when working with more severely retarded patients. It should be noted, however, that teaching

235

desirable behaviors may automatically eliminate some undesirable behavior because engaging in desirable behavior leaves less time for undesirable behavior.

It is primarily in severely and profoundly retarded children, those with IQ's of 35 or less, that one finds the behaviors classically associated with retardation. When seeing these children in an institutional setting, one often feels that they are hopeless and that they will never be able to function at any other level. They typically have few, if any, language skills and often are unable to communicate in any other way than a primitive fashion such as pointing or crying. Frequently these children are seen eating with their fingers or being fed by an attendant since they will not or cannot feed themselves. On the other hand, they seem to have a persistent desire to place practically everything other than food in their mouths and will chew on anything they can get. Retarded children frequently wear no clothes, particularly if left to their own choosing. They may play in their feces and may defecate or urinate without making any attempt to control their elimination. They enjoy playing for long periods of time with any item that spins, moves, makes a noise, or provides them with stimulation. In the absence of other stimulation, these children may provide their own stimulation by rocking back and forth, clapping loudly, shaking their heads, or performing other ritualistic behaviors.

The kinds of behaviors the staff hopes to alter with behavior modification usually involve basic motor skills, eating skills, and other self-care and self-help skills. The eating skills are of primary importance. Being able to use table utensils, drink from a glass or a cup, and exercise basic table manners such as eating with a spoon or fork, not throwing food, not dropping food, not eating too fast, not playing in food, and not talking or yelling while eating are desirable social skills. Another significant area of training deals with toilet behavior. Toilet training is difficult and, in many institutions, is accomplished by using behavior modification techniques. The patient's basic personal hygiene must be constantly supervised by the staff. Once a child learns good personal hygiene habits, it is necessary to continually reinforce these or the child will forget or develop other bad habits which are not consistent with good personal hygiene. Other self-help skills involve the ability to button clothes, to zip pants, to take off clothes, to put on socks and shoes and other such activities of daily living. For many of these children, basic motor skills are also a problem since they may be bedridden or confined to a wheelchair.

Occasionally, retarded children will become violent and destructive. When such behavior occurs, it is the responsibility of the staff to prevent the children from hurting themselves or others. Such outbursts frequently take the form of threats or attacks on other children, temper tantrums, rebelliousness, profanity, or a tendency to boss other children.

236

Retarded children sometimes tease children with lesser abilities and occasionally a child may try to steal another child's food or possessions. Ambulatory children sometimes try to run away or will not cooperate by being where they are supposed to be at a particular time. These children are sometimes shy and introverted but may also show such behaviors as biting themselves, assuming peculiar postures such as walking on their tiptoes, walking with their fingers in their mouth or ears, or engaging in masturbatory activities. Unacceptable personal mannerisms such as burping, passing gas, and excessive kissing or hugging of patients and staff members can be expected. Severely and profoundly retarded children appear to have a strong need for personal contact. Upon entering a ward, one may expect to have children clamoring around, holding onto one's arms and legs and demanding one's undivided attention.

One may also expect self-abusive behavior and behavior of a sexual nature from older retarded children. Much of this is due to the simple fact that these children often have had no training or feedback concerning the inappropriateness of their behavior. They continue to repeat any behavior they find pleasurable or stimulating.

Most of the behaviors mentioned above can be treated with behavior modification techniques. Again, the major advantage of this technique over any other form of therapy is that no language skills are necessary on the part of the patient and behavior modification techniques have been shown to be effective for modifying behavior at all levels of retardation.

PRIMARY RESPONSIBILITIES

Since this book is designed to present general problems associated with certain types of patients, no attempt will be made to explain in depth all of the various aspects of treating the mentally retarded. However, a brief overview is necessary and will include the following: meeting the patient's physical needs, follow-up responsibilities, meeting the patient's emotional needs, teaching the patient self-help and basic academic skills, managing the patient's aggressive and injurious behaviors, and maintaining a safe environment.

Meeting the Patient's Physical Needs

In the case of the profoundly retarded and the severely retarded, it is important to pay close attention to the patient's basic physical needs. For the most part, these patients are unable to take care of themselves without a great deal of supervision and outright help. It is particularly important for nonambulatory patients to receive help in physically exercising their bodies and to be assisted in finding comfortable positions.

Since they have so many eliminatory function problems, check frequently to make sure that they are not soiled. Soiled patients should not be allowed to sit and suffer in their soiled clothing. Staff members need to watch for the binding of limbs which could cause circulatory problems, postural problems which might lead to muscle strain and simple hazards which might cause retarded patients to fall from wheelchairs, bed, or other such places. Of course, it is of utmost importance that good physical hygiene be maintained for the patients. One of the best times to discover things that might be wrong with a patient is during their bath. By careful observation and attention to the patient's physical condition during A.M. care, one can often prevent more serious physical problems from developing.

Perhaps one of the more important aspects of caring for the retarded is making sure that each patient receives reasonable and proper treatment at mealtimes. This means being sure that each patient gets a reasonable amount of food to eat, that they are not unduly bothered by other patients trying to steal food, and that they do not spend more time playing in their food than eating.

If, as a mental health worker, one is required to administer medications to patients, it is absolutely necessary to learn to administer them correctly. Most units have a specific procedure to be followed and a copy of this procedure should be in the hospital procedure manual. Errors in medication are serious and many retarded patients have a tendency to have a highly specific allergic reaction to certain drugs. It is also important to watch patients to be sure that they actually swallow their medication instead of simply spitting it out. When administering medications or treating patients for minor or major ailments, be sure to use good sanitary techniques.

Follow-Up Responsibilities

As we have said, keeping retarded patients comfortable and helping them with any physical need that they are unable to handle is a major function of each member of the mental health team. The treatment team, however, cannot stop at that point. Continuous follow-up is a necessity for every patient. Some mental health workers find it helpful to keep a notebook in which they record important information on each of their patients. If information is recorded at the time it occurs, the mental health worker is less likely to forget important follow-up details. The notebook can then be used for special details that need to be charted, to develop a long term plan of care for each patient and as a checklist for attention to the special needs of each patient. Of course, it is helpful for a mental health worker to establish a routine procedure for attending patients. Each patient should be checked on a regular basis and any unusal circumstances brought to the attention of the appropriate persons. Since these patients often have no means of communicating, it is important to check them for bruises, lacerations, scratches, dental problems, skin rashes, scalp problems, infections, coughs, sores, swelling, irritated mucus membranes, blocked ears, noses, vaginas, and rectums (caused by patient's sticking things in these body openings), and any other condition one would expect a normal patient to report to the treatment team.

Treatment team members must be aware of the common side effects of medications given to these patients. This will insure recognition of any signs and symptoms exhibited by the patient which indicate undesirable effects or allergic reactions to a medication. As previously mentioned, there seems to be a somewhat greater incidence of allergic reactions to certain types of medications, food, and other substances among the mentally retarded. For this reason, it is important for mental health workers to periodically review medical charts and medical histories as well as to check with the patient's family, friends, or former treatment team members regarding medications, food and other substance that may cause adverse reactions. The more information one has about a particular patient, the better one is able to meet that patient's needs.

Since mentally retarded patients have a much higher incidence of seizure activity than the general population, it is important that mental health workers have some understanding of the various types of seizures and that they respond to these activities in the manner prescribed by the ward routine. By becoming familiar with each patient's background, the mental health worker will be aware of the potential for seizures and proper precautions can be taken.

In the event that a patient has a history of attempting to run away, it is important to pay particular attention to that patient's daily routines to see if there is some event occurring which causes the patient to want to leave. Good observation and reporting can sometimes help a staff member discover and correct problems of this nature.

Meeting the Patient's Emotional Needs

When faced with the demanding responsibility of meeting the physical needs of retarded patients, emotional needs are sometimes overlooked. As with any other patient, ignoring the emotional needs of the retarded can lead to a deterioration of general physical condition.

For most noninstitutionalized people, the world offers a wide assortment of interesting and exciting activities and opportunities. However, for mentally retarded patients who are hospitalized, the highlight of their day may be having an opportunity to spend a few minutes with a staff member that they like, picking up the mail for the unit from the mailman, assisting a staff member who is making rounds, or getting a haircut. Finding ways to help institutionalized retardates develop positive self-concepts and feelings of self-respect is a challenge for the staff. It is important to reward or reinforce appropriate patient efforts toward independence and improvement of self-image. Such efforts may include patients' beginning to brush their own teeth, button their own shirts, tie their shoes or bathe themselves. If patients can be helped to develop a sense of self-respect from simple personal grooming activities, two things occur. First, they are developing skills for themselves and will thus be able to feel a sense of accomplishment. Second, if they can take care of themselves, the mental health worker will have more time to spend with less fortunate patients.

It is important to keep in mind that seemingly small things, both positive and negative, can be of utmost importance. Failing to acknowledge a patient who wishes to talk may be interpreted as a serious rebuff. Forgetting to mention new shoes, new shirt or pants, or new braces may cause the patient to feel slighted. On the positive side, however, simply taking the time to chat with the patients as one reports on duty can make them quite happy. Try to remember to make some comment about the patient's looks, hygiene, grooming, and so forth. We emphasize again the necessity for behaving in an accepting and friendly manner at all times. Of course, this is not always easy. Most of the time it will be difficult to maintain a really smooth ward routine and some days will be quite harried. Still, it is important to always make an effort not to appear upset, angry, or afraid when patients seem to be getting out of control. As a matter of fact, it is extremely important to remain calm. Patients have a way of interpreting staff members' feelings and reacting accordingly. If a staff member appears fearful or upset, the patients are likely to become fearful and upset. Maintaining a calm, level-headed attitude will reassure the patients and help them relax and feel safe.

Two other points should also be considered. First, it is important to allow choices whenever possible. The fact that the patient does not like either option usually does not matter. It is reward enough just to be allowed to make the choice. If a patient must take a bath but does not wish to, offering a choice of bathing first or last may lessen resistance. Saying, "Would you rather take your bath now or after everyone else is through?" is usually easier to accept than, "Take your bath now!" Again, poor language skills are likely to create communication problems so a great deal of creativity may be needed to get such messages across. Second, when considering any particular situation, take into account the limitations or disabilities that a patient might have. Special attention should be given to the task of finding something that each patient can do reasonably well. When the patient achieves success in that endeavor, it should be brought to the attention of the staff and other patients. This acknowledgment of accomplishments should be made in the presence of the patient. This fosters both group and personal acceptance.

Training in Basic Self-Help and Academic Skills

After a retarded patient's physical and mental needs have been met, a mental health worker's next most important responsibility is to provide training in the areas of self-help and academic skills. To teach the retarded patient these skills requires a great deal of patience. Since most retarded persons function on a rather concrete level, they need a lot of repetition and reinforcement from staff members; otherwise, any learned skill is soon forgotten and must be taught again. Therefore, follow-up care is an essential element of routine care. Fortunately, behavior modification techniques are extremely successful in helping retarded patients learn and maintain basic skills. Before attempting to do any significant amount of training with retarded patients, the mental health worker should be thoroughly familiar with behavior modification techniques and procedures. Behavior modification is not the only way to teach retarded persons skills but it is by far the most effective way yet demonstrated.

In trying to determine a patient's potential for learning a particular skill, it is helpful to know as much about the patient as possible. A consultation with a unit psychologist or a psychologic consultant would be helpful in cases where there is some question about the patient's learning potential and limitations. As previously stated, much of the training for the institutionalized retardate is in the area of toilet training, skills related to eating, and self-care skills such as tooth brushing, body washing, hair combing, and dressing procedures. After the basic self-help skills have been mastered, it is important to encourage further language development and to teach the patient how to interact with others in a socially acceptable manner.

Managing Aggressive and Injurious Behavior

As with most behavior, destructive, aggressive, and injurious behavior does not occur without cause. Particularly in this area, the inability to communicate verbally leads to a great deal of misunderstanding. A patient who is throwing things, bashing his head against his bedrails, or sitting in his wheelchair crying quietly may simply be trying to communicate the fact that he wants a drink of water. He may also be trying to communicate his need to go to the bathroom or that he has soiled himself and doesn't like being dirty. In other cases, the patient may be physically ill, in physical pain or have clothing that is binding. One must consider all of these possibilities as well as others when confronted with a patient who is acting out.

241

When dealing with this type patient, it may be possible to find a means by which the patient can make his needs known by using nonverbal signals. For example, a retarded paraplegic who could move only his head and who could not speak was taught to ring a chime suspended in front of him whenever he needed water, food, or to go to the toilet. Eventually, through a behavior modification training program, the patient was able to learn to ring once to go to the bathroom, twice for water, three times for food, and four times when he was physically uncomfortable. It has been our experience that much of the aggressive behavior exhibited by retarded patients happens because of inappropriate ward control or layout. This may be beyond the jurisdiction of the ward managers, but an effort should be made to have the physical layout of the ward as conducive to peaceful, comfortable living as possible.

Whenever possible, ignore undesirable behavior. Of course, it is often necessary to intervene immediately to prevent physical harm to others if a retarded patient begins to act out in a violent, destructive manner. Care should be taken to help such patients understand what they are doing wrong and to try to help them learn more appropriate ways of expressing their unmet needs. Keep in mind that most psychologic studies indicate that the sooner reinforcement or punishment is given following a behavior, the more effective the reinforcement or punishment becomes in terms of increasing or decreasing the occurrence of the rewarded or punished event. It follows, therefore, that immediate praise and encouragement should be given for desirable behavior and immediate discipline or punishment should be given for undesirable behavior provided that the undesirable behavior cannot be ignored or that ignoring the undesirable behavior is not in the patient's best interest.

Distraction is a good technique to use when trying to channel potentially violent or destructive behavior into some other activity. This permits the patient to save face and allows the mental health worker to avoid a possible nonproductive confrontation. Usually, retarded patients want so much to please the treatment team members that approval and attention will prevent many behaviors which would otherwise cause considerable disruption.

Perhaps the most important thing to keep in mind when working with the mentally retarded is that it is necessary that they understand exactly what is expected of them and the consequences for not behaving in the expected manner. It is essential that consistent application of the stated consequences be maintained. Patients are unable to develop a sense of trust when consistency of approach is not maintained and thus are likely to exhibit more erratic behavior than if they can rely on a consistent, structured routine.

Sometimes it is not possible to discover the cause for destructive, disruptive or injurious behavior. In such cases, it is usually helpful to remove the patient to a more secluded and quiet area. At times, it may even be necessary to restrain the patient. When restraints are needed, it is best, if not mandatory by law, to get a physician's order to use them. These patients should be checked frequently to be certain that they have not become entangled in their restraints, that they are not lacerating their wrists or legs, and that they are not unduly uncomfortable. Restraints should be used only until the patient regains control. Then they should be removed immediately.

Maintaining a Safe Environment

In maintaining a safe environment, the old addage that "an ounce of prevention is worth a pound of cure" is quite appropriate. It is of immeasurable importance to be sure that the ward is a safe place for the patients. Most mental retardation treatment facilities have specially designed safety equipment such as tables with rounded corners, chairs without sharp edges and solid floors that will not chip, flake, or break.

Keep in mind that many of these patients will put anything that they find lying loose into their mouths. The object might be a nail, a pop-top tab from a soft drink can, a cigarette butt (lit or unlit), a bug caught crawling across the floor, a screw that a careless workman may have left behind or any one of a thousand other things. Access to electric outlets must also be checked to prevent shocks and burns.

Patients should not be allowed in the nurses' station unless they are closely supervised because pencils, scissors, medicines, needles, and other such dangerous materials are readily available.

Watch carefully for spills of water, urine, feces, food, cleaning solvent, and any other items which might cause a patient to fall and hurt himself. It is also important to remind the cleaning people in the area to be careful with their cleaning solution since a patient can quickly pick up a can of floor wax or cleaning solvent and drink it. Any equipment which is broken or which does not function properly should be fixed at once.

In summary, working with mentally retarded patients is a challenge. It is a test of one's patience and it is definitely not for those who have little ability to tolerate frustration. For many people, however, it is a rewarding career and certainly one in which a mental health worker has an opportunity to give of himself.

ANNOTATED BIBLIOGRAPHY

Backus, H., Blanchard, C., and Spitz, S.: *It took ten of us—from various disciplines—to care for one troubled patient.* Nursing '81, 1981, 11(10):62–64.

A nurse relates the personal experience of dealing with a mentally retarded, psychotic pregnant 15-year-old. An interdisciplinary approach was utilized in meeting the needs of this teenager.

Bell, A.: *Venturing into the world.* Nursing Times, January 6, 1982, 78:28 30.

Relates a case history whereby a mentally retarded young man was trained to enable him to work outside his supportive living home.

Dixson, D.L.: *Manic depression: An overview.* Journal of Psychosocial Nursing and Mental Health Services, 1981, 19(6):28–31.

Includes a section on manic depression in the mentally retarded.

Felce, D., Smith, J., and Kushlick, A.: *Evaluation of the Wessex experiment.* Nursing Times, December 2, 1981, 77:2113–2116.

Reports on a study that placed mentally handicapped persons in small, local group homes. The study concluded that this method was a better social environment and was more cost effective than placement in large psychiatric hospitals.

Gray, M.: *It's O.K. to cry: Feeling outlets for mentally retarded children.* Journal of Psychosocial Nursing and Mental Health Services, 1980, 18(3):22–31.

Mentally retarded children have difficulty understanding and expressing their emotions. This article suggests methods that facilitate the expression and release of four basic emotions; happiness, unhappiness, anger, and fear.

Mansheim, P., and Cohen, C.M.: *Communicating with developmentally disabled patients.* Journal of Psychosocial Nursing and Mental Health Services, 1982, 20(10):24–26.

Describes the disappointment and guilt experienced by parents of developmentally disabled children.

244

POST-TEST

Chapter 18

Mentally Retarded Patients

True or False. Circle your choice.

T F 1. Clinically, an individual is considered to be retarded if he falls within a certain IQ range, whereas socially, he can be retarded in some situations and normal in others.

T F 2. A person with an IQ of 52 would be diagnosed as being severely retarded.

T F 3. There is considerable evidence indicating that mental illness is fairly prevalent among mentally retarded persons.

T F 4. The behavior modification approach involves identifying a particular desired behavior and then arranging the conditions of reinforcement so that the desired behavior can be obtained from the patient.

T F 5. Severely and profoundly retarded children appear to have a strong need for personal contact.

T F 6. Mentally retarded patients have a much lower incidence of seizure activity than the general population.

T F 7. It is important for staff members to make all choices for their retarded patients.

T F 8. Distraction is a good technique to use when trying to channel potentially violent or destructive behavior to a socially acceptable outlet.

T F 9. No matter what the circumstances, a mentally retarded person should never be physically restrained.

T F 10. Usually the level of retardation is estimated by the number of points scored on an IQ test.

T F 11. It is primarily the mildly or moderately retarded child that exhibits the behaviors classically associated with retardation.

Short Answer. Answer the following questions as briefly and specifically as possible.

1. List three causes of mental retardation.

1. _____

2. _____

3. _____

2. Give the names of the two most widely used intelligence tests.

   1. _____

   2. _____

3. Explain briefly Down's Syndrome.

   _____

   _____

   _____

4. List three major problems a child must adjust to when institutionalized.

   1. _____

   2. _____

   4. _____

5. What are the basic kinds of behavior associated with mental retardation that a staff might hope to alter through behavior modification
   techniques?

   _____

   _____

6. What is the major advantage of the behavior modification technique?

   _____

   _____

7. List three features that are associated with the Down's Syndrome.

   1. _____

   2. _____

   3. _____

8. Which therapy technique would be most effective in toilet training
   institutionalized children?

   _____

19

Elderly Patients

Since aging begins at the moment of conception, it seems that it should be considered a natural process of living. Unfortunately, this is not the case in our society. Americans, as well as most people in the Western world, have become so engrossed with the idea of youthfulness that to become old is often seen as a "fate worse than death itself." Billions of dollars are spent each year on beauty aids, cosmetic surgery, and other "miracle" treatments by individuals who are seeking to prevent, or at least cover up, the telltale signs of aging.

This emphasis on youthfulness is not the only factor that causes the elderly to feel that they are no longer valued members of our society, but it seems to be the major culprit. The mere presence of the elderly seems to make younger generations uncomfortable, for their existence serves as a constant reminder that aging does indeed occur. Maybe this is the reason why so many elderly are abandoned by their families and their society. One wonders what attitudes will prevail in the 1990s when it is predicted that more than half of our country's population will be over age 50 with one third being 65 years of age or older.

In addition to the normal day-to-day problems of living, the elderly must cope with special situations associated with old age and retirement. They tend to suffer a significant loss of self-esteem and therefore develop negative feelings about themselves. This loss of self-worth occurs for a variety of reasons, but retirement seems to be a major contributor. Our society values workers and often disregards nonproductive or unemployed individuals.

Retirement is viewed as the time in life when one is supposed to sit back, relax, and reap the benefits of years of hard work. Unfortunately, the mere act of reaching age 65 does not automatically change the work habits and attitudes an individual has developed over a lifetime. Many persons equate one's worth as a human being with what one contributes to society as a worker, and therefore, to retire is to become worthless.

Retirement also brings about a drastic reduction in income which in turn contributes to the loss of self-esteem. Older individuals may no longer be able to afford to live independently of their children or may be forced to live in substandard housing. Inadequate nutrition may result from poor eating habits necessitated by a lack of money. Most often there is little, if any, money left over for entertainment, recreational activities, or hobbies. Frequently, the older individual settles down into a life of drudgery and boredom.

Activities are further restricted by a loss of hearing, poor eyesight, and other physical ailments that occur with greater frequency as the individual grows older. Poor health coupled with the loss of family and friends forces one to face the inevitability of death. Some older individuals have a greatly decreased ability to tolerate emotional stress and few resources or opportunities to compensate for their losses. In such cases, interest in living begins to diminish. Perhaps this loss of interest is a contributing factor to the results of a recent survey which indicates that people live only an average of 60 months past retirement.

All people, regardless of age, need to love and be loved, to have sufficient economic resources to meet basic physical needs, to feel a sense of achievement, and to receive recognition from others. Elderly people begin to lose many of these satisfactions so that a healthy adjustment to aging requires the ability to realistically appraise circumstances, making the most of the negative aspects and capitalizing on the positive. An elderly widow may not like the fact that she can no longer afford to live alone and must now live with a married daughter. On the other hand, she can make the most of the situation by offering to help with appropriate household chores and child care. By contributing in this manner, the grandmother may feel that she is a part of the family rather than a guest.

Emotional adjustment to old age is usually a continuation of lifelong adjustment patterns. People often believe that they are going to change their ways when they get old. Instead of being cantankerous, they say they are going to become sweet and loving. There is little likelihood that such a change will occur. Basic personality traits and ways of handling stress are formed early in life and, if anything, the aging process exaggerates these traits and behaviors as the elderly person experiences the stress of losing authority, independence, and usefulness. The fact that people behave in ways that get them what they want is also not necessarily altered by age. The elderly may scream, yell, have temper

248

tantrums, or become depressed or withdrawn in much the same way as they did early in life if such behaviors helped to get what they wanted. On the other hand, they may be calm, quiet individuals who look at any new situation in an objective problem-solving manner just as they did as well adjusted young adults.

In mentally healthy individuals, the final years of life are years in which they have an opportunity to judge their contributions to themselves, their families, and their society. They recognize that whatever they have done with their lives must now be accepted since they cannot live their lives over again. For individuals who have been reasonably successful and who have developed healthy self-concepts, these tasks may be accomplished fairly easily. For individuals who have not been successful and thus do not feel reasonably fulfilled, aging is likely to bring a great deal of stress in the form of regret, guilt, and remorse. When elderly individuals cannot resolve such feelings, they often experience neurotic or psychotic disorders. Others may show significant behavioral disorganization as a result of organic brain damage.

Despite the many potential problems, most elderly people in this country are alert, competent, and functioning with reasonable independence in their communities. As Caldwell says in *Geriatrics: Study of Maturity* (Delmar Publishers, Albany, N.Y., 1975), "Advanced age is reached only by those who have proved themselves capable of survival." Available data suggests that only 5 per cent of the elderly need custodial care and that only 1 per cent are found in mental hospitals, taking up about 30 per cent of all public mental health beds. Included in that 30 per cent are patients who have 1) been in mental facilities all their lives, 2) those who have been admitted off and on throughout their lives and who cannot cope with added stresses of old age, and 3) those elderly patients who have become ill for the first time. Another 10 per cent of our elderly population seek care for physical and mental disorders on an outpatient basis from community clinics. Several million more elderly people live under economic and environmental conditions which contribute to emotional breakdown. Although the elderly now account for only 10 per cent of our total population, 25 per cent of all suicides in this country are committed by elderly individuals.

Of the elderly patients confined to mental health institutions, most suffer from senile brain atrophy or brain changes that occur due to arteriosclerosis. Cerebral arteriosclerosis is a condition marked by a thickening and hardening of the arteries of the brain. When this occurs, less blood and oxygen reach the brain and the patient experiences periods of confusion and varied levels of consciousness. The patient may also be forgetful and complain of headaches, dizziness, and weakness. They seem to have little emotional control and are often irritable and argumentative

249

with family members, other patients, and staff. They may wander about aimlessly, having a noticeable shuffling gait and a tendency to lean backward as they try to maintain their balance.

The cause of senile brain atrophy is unknown, but in the course of the disease, calcium deposits appear in brain tissues. The size and weight of the brain decreases and the amount of cerebrospinal fluid increases. The patient becomes progressively more and more confused. The patient has trouble remembering recent events, but can recall in detail experiences of the past. Emotional instability is common and tears or rage come quickly with little justification.

Elderly patients may also experience any of the other psychiatric disorders. Depression is common and neurotic and paranoid reactions occur frequently. All forms of therapy are used in treating these disorders and elderly patients respond to therapy in about the same manner as any other age group.

Staff members working with elderly patients must be careful to distinguish between individual mannerisms, temporarily stressful situations, and true psychotic or neurotic disorders. Is Mr. Jones, who walks up and down the hall talking to himself, confused because of a psychiatric disorder, disoriented because he was suddenly moved to unfamiliar surroundings in the middle of the night, still oversedated from his sleeping pill, or just a person who has always walked around mumbling to himself as he thought things over? Various physical factors such as infection, dehydration, hunger, traumatic injuries (e.g., broken bones) may cause the elderly patient to become temporarily confused. Restraining such patients often makes matters worse. Staff members must try to discover and understand the cause of behavior and help the patient to control it with as little loss of freedom and dignity as possible.

Extreme caution should be used when ordering or administering medications to elderly patients. Often a smaller amount of a given drug is indicated due to such factors as increased sensitivity to medications, decreased body weight, impaired circulation, and liver dysfunction. The likelihood of adverse drug reaction or overmedication (especially with barbiturates) is increased since kidney function is decreased and, therefore, drugs are not excreted from the system as quickly as in a younger person.

Working with elderly patients requires that certain basic principles of care be followed. Staff members should allow them to maintain as much independence as they can safely handle. Feelings of frustration which contribute to fears, anxieties, restlessness, and agitation are much like the frustration experienced by teenagers. Teenagers long for independence from adult authority, yet are afraid to give up the security of having someone on which to rely. Elderly patients, while wanting to maintain their independence, also long for the security of depending on

250

others. Elderly persons, may also be compared to toddlers in that both groups cannot quite accomplish all the functions necessary to allow complete freedom. A toddler can get his shoes on, but cannot tie the laces. An elderly person may have the same problem due to arthritic changes which make it difficult to bend over and to use the hands. Both situations cause feelings of frustration and probably angry outbursts at anyone nearby.

Despite some similarities, elderly patients should not be treated as if they were children. This mistake is often made by well meaning family members and friends. When bossed around in an authoritarian, condescending, or parent-to-child manner, their response may become obstinate and contrary.

Correct names should be used. Despite what many people believe, few of the elderly enjoy being called "Granny" or "Gramps." Names are important to people and being addressed correctly conveys respect. Most elderly patients especially dislike being given pet names by staff members. An individual struggling to maintain self-identity and respect has no wish to become a mascot.

The feeling of being accepted is needed. Personal habits such as dressing in a certain sequence or always drinking coffee from a saucer should be permitted. However, staff members should try to correct unsanitary on self-defeating habits by encouraging more appropriate behaviors and by restructuring the environment to eliminate the need for some of the inappropriate behavior. For example, if Mr. Green insists on taking a short walk despite the fact that he can hardly walk, a staff member might try to find an easily accessible place, provide him with a cane or walker, and walk with him. If he is really not able to walk very far, he might agree to a shorter walk if the staff member will get a picture book of world travels to show and discuss with him.

Loneliness is a major problem for older people, even those who are hospitalized. They greatly need someone they can trust and who will be supportive. Sometimes a simple pat on the arm, a gentle hug, or a back rub can communicate a sense of warmth and affection. Most elderly patients need this type of human closeness and should not be rejected when they reach out to a staff member for comfort.

They need to be encouraged to talk about their feelings, fears and worries. If they want to talk about old memories, they should be permitted to do so. Sometimes elderly patients have difficulty remembering recent events due to organic brain changes, but more often they dwell in the past as a means of dealing with the painfulness of the present. They may also be attempting to understand their present situation by reviewing past events in their lives. However, if an elderly patient continually "lives" in the past, staff members should attempt to focus their attention on daily events.

Patients and their families should be encouraged to maintain close communication. Fortunately, there is now a significant trend to hospitalize mentally ill patients in their own community instead of sending them to large, distant, state hospitals. This fosters a continuing relationship with family and friends and helps the rehabilitation process. Many elderly patients do not need to be hospitalized if they can participate in day care programs and return to their homes at night.

Older individuals need to be encouraged to participate in activities that bring them in contact with other people. Staff members should help patients choose activities that they not only enjoy, but that bring satisfaction and a sense of purpose while helping to fill the long hours of the day. They must practice their socialization skills in order to keep them. Socialization is also important because it helps patients to maintain satisfactory orientation to their environment. They learn names and places and make friends. A few other things can be done to help keep patients oriented. Placing a large clock in the room and a cube calendar that can have the date changed each day is helpful. Patients are more aware of the year, month, day, and time if such devices are available. To help with orientation to place, patients may be taken for walks or wheelchair rides or placed by windows so that the front, side, or back of buildings can be pointed out.

Older patients do not like to be rushed. They rise early and their days are long so they should not be pushed. They also fare much better in a calm, consistent environment that functions at a moderately slow pace and follows a well established routine.

The physical needs of the elderly are of primary importance and the staff should insure that these needs are met. Most will readily report physical problems to staff members but patients who are confused must be carefully observed. They may be unable to accurately report problems. It is imperative for elderly patients to stay active. Activity promotes good health by increasing circulation, stimulating appetite, helping regulate bowel function, and preventing the complications of inactivity such as joint immobility, bed sores, and pneumonia. Fresh air is good for the elderly and, if dressed warmly, being outside on cold winter days is not harmful.

Staff members should be constantly alert for potential hazards in the environment. Those having problems with dizziness should be assisted when walking, climbing stairs, or getting in or out of the tub. In order to minimize stumbling by those with impaired vision, furniture should not be rearranged. Floors should not be slippery and carpets and tiles should be kept in good repair. Throw rugs should never be used since they slide easily and may cause a fall. If elderly patients are confused or groggy, they should not be allowed to smoke alone. A staff member should sit with them and utilize that time to interact with the patients.

252

Staff members should be aware that patients may need help with personal hygiene, especially if they are confused or forgetful. The degree of help needed will vary. Some patients will need total care and others will need only minor assistance such as fastening a dress with buttons up the back or tying shoe laces. Patients should be allowed to do all they can for themselves even when it would be much quicker and simpler for a staff member to assist.

It is usually not necessary for elderly patients to take a complete bath every day. The face, underarms and perineum do need daily washing. Since the skin has a tendency to be dry, frequent washing will increase dryness. Soap must be thoroughly rinsed to avoid itching and skin irritation. Elderly patients may enjoy showers since it is hard to get in and out of a tub and they are often afraid of falling. If a patient tires easily or is unstable, a chair can be placed in the shower stall so that he can shower in a sitting position. Remember, elderly patients are usually very modest and their right to personal privacy and dignity should be respected whenever possible.

A well balanced diet is essential to health; however, physical changes may lead to problems in this area. Ill fitting dentures and tough, undercooked meats and foods may make chewing difficult if not impossible. Dentures must be worn consistently in order to avoid a misfit. Conversely, any time a patient consistently does not wear dentures, it usually means they hurt and are not properly fitted. Most elderly patients do not like to eat alone and appetite may decrease as activity level decreases. Constipation may cause discomfort and lead to a poor appetite. Plenty of fluids, fruits, and vegetables should be included in the diet to aid digestion. If a patient is used to taking a mild laxative on a routine basis, there is probably no harm in allowing this practice to continue. If there is a problem, the doctor should be consulted. Elderly individuals often eat slowly and need to be allowed to finish their meals at a leisurely pace. Most seem to prefer small meals served frequently rather than three big meals a day.

Staff members must be alert to behavioral changes that indicate physical problems. If Mr. Jones does not answer when his name is called, he may not be acting stubborn, but may actually have a hearing problem due to a buildup of ear wax. A patient who stumbles over objects may need glasses. A male patient who urinates frequently may have an enlarged prostrate. Bunions, corns ingrown toenails, or ill fitting shoes may be the real reason a patient refuses to go outside for a walk.

If a patient does not sleep well at night, his sleeping pattern during the day should be observed. If he has been taking a daytime nap, the length of that nap might be shortened, bedtime delayed, activities increased, and relaxation methods such as a warm bath or warm milk used just before bedtime. If sleeping pills are used, the patient may be groggy and sleepy during the day and awaken just in time to go to bed again. This pattern is not uncommon and should be considered if a patient has difficulty sleeping.

Working with the elderly is not easy and staff members who do this work need a great deal of patience. In not too many years, today's staff members may be elderly patients themselves. One should be the kind of staff member that one would like to have if he became the patient.

ANNOTATED BIBLIOGRAPHY

Armstrong-Esther, C.A., and Hawkins, L.W.: *Day for night—circadian rhythms in the elderly.* Nursing Times, 1982, 78(30):1263–1265.

Describes the physiologic changes in the elderly that affect circadian rhythm. This may explian why the elderly, disoriented adult becomes active and unruly at night.

Britnell, J.C., and Mitchell, K.E.: *Inpatient group psychotherapy for the elderly.* Journal of Psychosocial Nursing and Mental Health Services, 1981, 19(5):19–24.

Describes one model for group therapy. Also outlines the theoretical framework and provides nursing implications.

Cohen, S., and Bunke, E.: *Programmed instruction: Sensory changes in the elderly.* American Journal of Nursing, 1981, 81(10):1851–1880.

Enables the reader to understand the sensory changes that affect the functional ability of the older adult.

Fitzsimons, V.: *When the older patient's apathetic . . . A problem you can solve.* Nursing '83, 1983, 12(4):52–57.

Discusses aids in dealing with the elderly person who is depressed and has "given up."

Fuller, S.S., and Larson, S.B.: *Life events, emotional support, and health of older people.* Research in Nursing and Health, 1980, 3(2):81–89.

This research study explores the relationship between life events and physical illness. Also correlates the presence of emotional support by loved ones and physical illness in older adults.

Wysocki, M.R.: *Life review for the elderly patient.* Nursing '83, 1983, 13(2): 47–48.

Life review permits the elderly patients to reconcile the events of their lives. This process reduces anxiety and promotes a good state of mind.

254

POST-TEST

Chapter 19

Elderly Patients

True or False. Circle your choice.

T F 1. Most elderly patients hospitalized for psychiatric problems suffer from senile brain atrophy or brain changes that occur due to arteriosclerosis.

T F 2. Calling the elderly "Granny" or "Gramps" tends to make them feel more at home.

T F 3. It is necessary to encourage the elderly to hurry because they tend to be so slow.

T F 4. Many elderly people feel that they are no longer valued members of our society.

T F 5. Life situations often cause elderly individuals to suffer a significant loss of self-esteem and, therefore, to develop negative feelings about themselves.

T F 6. Emotional adjustment changes drastically with increasing age.

T F 7. The majority of elderly people are alert, competent, and functioning in their communities.

T F 8. Depression is a common psychiatric disorder seen in the elderly.

T F 9. It is important for the elderly to maintain their independence whenever possible.

T F 10. When elderly patients begin acting like children, they should be treated as children.

T F 11. Twenty-five per cent (25%) of all suicides in this country are committed by elderly individuals.

Short Answer. Answer the following questions as briefly and specifically as possible.

1. What is a major factor contributing to the elderly individual's loss of self-worth and self-esteem.

_____

2. What are some of the main factors that should be considered before administering medications to elderly patients?

_____

_____

3. What is one of the main reasons why elderly patients have difficulty remembering recent events?

_____

4. What are some basic things the mental health workers can do to keep the elderly patient well oriented?

_____

_____

5. Why is it necessary for the elderly patient to stay active?

_____

_____

_____

_____

Multiple Choice. Circle the letter that represents the best answer.
1. People become old:
   A. At the same rate.
   B. When they reach age 65.
   C. When they reach age 75.
   D. At a very individual rate.
2. The basic attitude of Western culture toward the elderly is that:
   A. They should be held in esteem.
   B. They are of lesser importance.
   C. Their opinions should be sought.
   D. Their skills are valuable.
3. Changes in self-image are brought about by:
   A. Loss of vigor and vitality.
   B. Loss of independence.
   C. Loss of physical stamina.
   D. All of the above.
4. The mental health worker can help increase a patient's self-esteem by:
   A. Calmly accepting him and his behavior.
   B. Being critical of his behavior.
   C. Firmly stating what behavior is acceptable.

D. Ignoring him until he behaves in an acceptable way.
5. If an elderly patient complains that everyone is mumbling these days, which of the following is most likely to be true?
   A. He is just being cranky.
   B. He is probably becoming emotionally disturbed.
   C. His hearing is becoming less acute.
   D. None of the above.
6. Staff members must come to an understanding of their own feelings about the aged and aging because:
   A. They can be more therapeutic.
   B. Feelings are difficult to hide.
   C. Feelings are easily transmitted.
   D. All of the above.
7. A person's identity is reinforced when he wears:
   A. His own clothes.
   B. A hospital gown.
   C. A uniform.
   D. A friend's clothing.
8. The elderly person will probably eat better if:
   A. Food servings are large.
   B. Hard rolls are included.
   C. The foods are chewy.
   D. Food servings are small.
9. A general precaution to remember when considering the safety of the elderly is:
   A. Confine the elderly individual to a small area.
   B. Keep their clothing less fitting and long.
   C. Have sufficient light.
   D. Use open heaters in the bathroom.
10. The most common accident to the elderly involves:
    A. Falls.
    B. Burns.
    C. Cuts.
    D. Bruises.

20

Crisis Intervention

OBJECTIVES: Student will be able to:
1. Define crisis.
2. Identify the goal of crisis intervention.
3. Identify ways a crisis may be precipitated.
4. Define social crisis.
5. Identify the four phases of a crisis.
6. Identify the steps in crisis intervention.

Mental health authorities define crisis as a state of psychological disequilibrium brought about by a conflict, problem, or life situation which an individual perceives as a threat to self and cannot effectively handle by using previously successful problem-solving and coping techniques. The crisis develops not because of the event itself, but because of the person's inability to cope with the event. When this situation occurs, individuals become increasingly anxious and tense and feel that their self-esteem and well-being are seriously threatened.

Without swift and effective intervention these feelings usually intensify rapidly and the individual may become behaviorally disorganized, have difficulty thinking in a rational manner and experience feelings of anger, depression, helplessness, and guilt.

Clients in crisis are likely to repeat phrases such as: "I don't know what to do," "I feel so helpless." "What's happening to me?" over and over again.

Therefore, crisis intervention is usually conducted in an outpatient setting on a short-term basis and utilizes problem solving techniques to help clients resolve stress-provoking problems. The goal of this type therapy is to help clients return to a level of functioning that is at least equal to their pre-crisis state. It is hoped that crisis therapy will also enable clients to learn new coping and adaptive behaviors, thus actually improving levels of mental health.

A crisis state may be precipitated by two types of events. Developmental or maturational crises are those that occur at foreseeable stages in the lives of most individuals. As discussed in earlier chapters, each stage of development has its developmental task. In order to carry out these tasks, certain traits and behaviors must be strengthened prominent while others must be restrained. Such changes often produce a great deal of stress, especially during the transition period between two developmental stages.

For example, many middle-aged couples become depressed when their long awaited freedom from dependent children is replaced with greater emotional and financial responsibility for elderly parents. Learning to find workable solutions to this problem is one of the predictable developmental tasks of the middle years of life. This type of crisis can often be prevented by anticipatory guidance, an education process that alerts individuals and their families to behavioral changes that they are likely to experience in current stages of development. This allows the client to foresee problem areas and to develop ways to adapt in a positive manner. Anticipatory guidance also helps individuals and their families to distinguish between normal experiences and unusual ones. The anxiety normally produced when an individual faces an unknown situation is thus reduced.

A second circumstance that may produce a crisis state is called a situational event. This kind of crisis is precipitated by an unexpected event that suddenly disrupts a person's life and threatens his or her emotional security. Some examples of events that may lead to situational crises include the loss of a loved one from death or divorce, loss of a job, a move to a new city or a new job, graduation from school, marriage, or an unwanted pregnancy.

Even a long awaited promotion or career change may cause trouble because of added stress. Such events produce new situations with increased demands and challenges that the individual must meet.

A person may experience both types of stress-producing situations at the same time. Many middle-aged women trying to adjust to an empty nest syndrome find themselves also adjusting to the loss of a mate through divorce and the economic need to return to the work force. It is understandable that persons experiencing multiple stressful events in close succession are likely to have difficulty coping in a positive manner.

Some authorities break situational crises into two subtypes: those discussed above, and the social crises. A social crisis is defined as an unanticipated crisis that involves multiple losses or extensive environmental changes or both. Those may include fires, floods, war, murder, and racial persecution. This type of crisis does not usually occur in the everyday life, but when it does, stress levels become so high that the coping mechanisms of everyone involved are seriously threatened.

Every individual reacts to a stressful event in a different way. Some seem to be able to handle an extraordinary amount of stress, while others find minor occurrences upsetting. A degree of stress resulting from routine changes and challenges is unavoidable in day to day living. This type of stress is not necessarily bad, since it motivates us to complete our daily tasks, such as working or studying, in a satisfactory manner.

The individual in crisis is rarely the only person affected by a given situation. The individual's support system of significant others (family, special friends, neighbors) is invariably involved and should be assumed in a state of crisis.

The development of a crisis seems to follow four different, overlapping phases. The first phase is denial and usually lasts only for a few hours. Denial is a mental mechanism to temporarily defuse overwhelming anxiety. In mentally healthy persons, reality is quickly recognized, leading to an understanding of what is occurring. An example of denial is a wife's refusal to believe that the husband she kissed goodbye that morning has died in a car accident on the way to work. She may insist that the police and medical personnel have mistaken his identity. As she is given more detail concerning the accident, the wife will begin to confront the reality of her situation.

In phase two anxiety increases as the individual tries to continue daily activities while also searching for ways to handle the increased tension. The new widow somehow manages to make the funeral arrangements for her late husband and to get through the formalities.

The next stage is one of disorganization, when individuals in crisis seem to "go to pieces." They are unable to think clearly and neglect many of the activities of daily living. They are also preoccupied with the event. Persons in this stage are conscious of extreme anxiety since coping mechanisms have failed and there may even be fears of insanity. In this stage individuals may seek professional help to deal with the situation. The young widow at this stage may become unable to cope with household tasks such as cooking meals, preparing the children for school, and cleaning. She may neglect her personal appearance, while dwelling on her husband's death and her inability to live without him. Decisions may become difficult or impossible for her to make.

With professional help the fourth and final stage should be one of reorganization and the development of new skills that allow individuals to function as before their crises when the challenges of day-to-day living must be faced. If there is no improvement, anxiety will continue to increase until the patient experiences a state of panic and, possibly generalized personality disorganization.

For the individual whose unusual defense mechanisms are already functioning poorly, the extreme levels of stress and anxiety experienced during crisis are strong motivators. During this period persons are more likely to change their behavior in response to new problem solving and coping techniques.

Since the acute stage of a crisis usually lasts approximately four to six weeks, clients who have not resolved the crisis, or learned to cope completely in that length of time may be referred to other professionals or to mental health agencies that are equipped to provide long-term therapies.

Aguilera and Messick[1] state that effective resolution of a crisis situation is more likely to occur if the individual's perception of the precipitating event is realistic, if there are significant others in the client's environment who are available and willing to help, and if positive coping mechanisms to deal with the stressful events in life have previously been developed and can be called upon. Resolution is also affected in a positive way by the therapist who is able to establish rapport quickly and who conveys to the client a warm and caring attitude.

The first step in crisis intervention is to collect information about the nature of the crisis and the effect it is having on the client and his family and friends. In the initial interview the mental health professional should identify the precipitating event and the client's perception of that event, learn the client's positive characteristics and coping mechanisms, and determine the strength of support the client can expect from family and friends.

People usually seek help within two weeks of the precipitating event. Often the event may have occurred as recently as a day before the client asks for help. In this stage of intervention, questions such as the following will help the mental health professional to obtain useful information:

> What has happened that brought you here for help at this time?
> When did it happen?
> Tell me how you feel.
> How is this situation affecting your life?
> How is it affecting those around you?
> Have you ever faced a problem like this before?
> When you are anxious or tense, what do you do to feel better?
> Have you tried that this time?
> What do you think might help you feel better?
> Do you live with someone? Who?
> Do you have a friend that you trust?
> Do you have someone that you feel understands you?

Questions such as these may help the client and his family to put their thoughts and feelings in order at a time when they are likely to be disorganized. It may also be helpful to have the client give an account of his activities for the weeks preceding the intervention if he has difficulty identifying the event that precipitated the crisis. Talking about the situation should help lower the client's state of tension, helping them to see the situation more clearly. At this point the therapist may find it helpful to reassure the patient that seeking help is both a sign of strength and a step toward resolution of the problem. False reassurance should never be given. Instead, the therapist should express belief in the patient's ability to learn to cope, while encouraging the patient to help himself in every way possible.

Planning is the second stage of the intervention process. All available data from the client, his family, and any other professional sources should be reviewed and evaluated. A solution or solutions should be outlined and alternatives provided. The skills the client will need to work through the problem should be identified and supportive community resources pointed out.

The third stage of crisis intervention is to implement the plan developed in stage two. First, the mental health professional should discuss his or her perception of the problem with the patient to see if their perceptions correspond, making corrections as needed. As both explore the precipitating event and the resulting crisis, the client should be encouraged to verbalize his feelings about the situation.

Next, possible solutions to the problem may be discussed, identifying the client's coping skills that will be useful, and the availability of supportive individuals in the person's environment. The mental health worker and client may even role play the new problem solving techniques to allow the client to become more comfortable with them in a controlled environment.

Sometimes the best approach to alleviating a crisis situation is to change the client's physical or interpersonal environment. A middle-aged woman who faces the prospect of serious surgery and who also is responsible for her healthy but sometimes slightly confused elderly mother, may have to make other living arrangements for the mother, despite the latter's strenuous objections. The mother may have to live temporarily with another son or daughter, or if this is not a feasible solution, the client may need help in finding a home for senior citizens that provides the level of care her mother needs. If this type of care is too expensive for the daughter to finance alone, she will need to be referred to social agencies that can help her apply for funds to defray the additional cost.

Anticipatory guidance is also an effective way of dealing with many situational crises. Stages of grief have been identified for those who are seriously ill or dying, and these stages also apply to the feelings associated with the loss of a spouse through death or divorce, or diminished feelings of self-worth due to the loss of a job.

Education concerning these stages may be a very effective way of helping the client deal with the situations and the emotions involved. In all crisis counseling it is extremely important to establish a rapport with clients and to provide a therapeutic climate in which clients feel comfortable in voicing their feelings and concerns.

The final stage of crisis intervention process is evaluation. In this stage the mental health worker and the client have the opportunity to compare the goals they set in the planning stage with the actual behavioral changes in the patient's life style. In the evaluation process, other unmet needs may be identified and appropriate patient actions or referrals to other helping agencies can be initiated.

It should be kept in mind that the goal of successful crisis intervention is at least to return clients to their pre-crisis level of function, hopefully with improved adaptive capabilities, within a relatively short time. Such short-term therapy in an outpatient setting allows community mental health workers to reach a greater number of clients more quickly and in this manner to prevent more severe mental problems that might require long-term hospitalizations.

ANNOTATED BIBLIOGRAPHY

Brennan, P.J.: *A family close to crisis.* Nursing Times, August 5, 1981, 77: 1390–1392.

> *Case history of how a nurse dealt with depression and the multiple stressors in one family.*

Creson, D.L.: *Ways to help patients get off the emotional roller coaster.* Consultant, 1982, 22(10):163–176.

> *Discusses the role of health care workers in crisis intervention. Includes suggestions for counseling and drug therapy.*

Harrison, D.R.: *Nurses and disaster.* Journal of Psychosocial Nursing and Mental Health Services, 1981, 19:(12):34–36.

> *Describes the role of the nurse in disasters. Recommends early recognition and intervention in disaster related emotional trauma.*

Pattison, E.M.: *Managing agitated persons in a crisis.* Consultant, 1980, 20(11): 143–149.

> *Discusses 12 specific techniques to intervene in crisis situations. Includes information on dealing with suicidal threats.*

Schmidt, A.M.: *Adolescent female rape victims: Special considerations.* Journal of Psychosocial Nursing and Mental Health Services, 1981, 19(8):17–19.

> *Explores the considerations of crisis intervention in young female rape victims. Includes the threats to the victim's developmental issues.*

Twiname, B.G.: *No-suicide contract for nurses.* Journal of Psychosocial Nursing and Mental Health Services, 1981, 19(7):11–12.

Advocates the use of contracting when intervening with threatened suicides.

Walker, P., and Brook, B.D.: *Community homes as hospital alternatives for youth in crisis.* Journal of Psychosocial Nursing and Mental Health Services, 1981, 19(3):17–19.

Recommends the use of "sponsor homes" to avoid institutionalization of adolescents and children in home crisis situations.

REFERENCE

1.　Aquilera, D.C., and Messick, M.: *Crisis Intervention: Theory and Methodology,* ed. 3, C.V. Mosby, St. Louis, 1978.

POST-TEST

Chapter 20

Crisis Intervention

Short Answer: Answer the following as briefly and specifically as possible.
1. State the goal of crisis intervention therapy.

2. List and describe the four overlapping phases in the development of a crisis.

3. Define crisis.

4. Define social crisis.

5. List the four steps in crisis intervention.

Multiple Choice: Circle the best answer.
1. A crisis state may be precipitated by which of the following events?
   A. developmental and maturational stages
   B. transition period between two developmental stages
   C. unanticipated external event
   D. B and C
   E. A, B, and C

2. Which of the following situations could precipitate a crisis?
   1. Marriage
   2. Career change
   3. Pregnancy
   4. Job promotion
      A. 1 and 2
      B. 2 and 3
      C. 1, 2, and 3
      D. All of the above
3. Which of the following are manifestations of a person in crisis?
   1. anxious and tense
   2. increased feelings of self-esteem
   3. feelings of anger and depression
   4. behaviorally disorganized
      A. 1 and 2
      B. 2 only
      C. 1, 3, and 4
      D. all of the above
4. Which of the following is not a recognized phase in the development of a crisis?
   A. disorganization
   B. reorganization
   C. denial
   D. anger
5. The acute stage of a crisis usually lasts approximately:
   A. four to six weeks
   B. six to eight hours
   C. three to four days
   D. four to six days
6. The initial step in crisis intervention is to:
   A. try to resolve the problem
   B. collect information
   C. identify the strength of support
   D. identify the patient's positive characteristics
7. The final stage of the crisis intervention process is:
   A. evaluation
   B. anticipatory guidance
   C. implementing the plan of action
   D. exploring possible solutions
8. Which of the following would not be considered a social crisis?
   A. flood
   B. war
   C. racial persecution
   D. loss of job

True or False: Circle your choice.

T ☐ F ☐ 1. Sometimes the best approach to alleviating a crisis situation is to actually change the client's physical or interpersonal environment.

T ☐ F ☐ 2. It is all right to give false assurance to the patient if it helps them get through the crisis.

T ☐ F ☐ 3. It is necessary to hospitalize a person in a crisis situation most of the time.

T ☐ F ☐ 4. The first phase in the development of a crisis is denial.

T ☐ F ☐ 5. Anticipatory guidance is an effective way of dealing with many situational crises.

T ☐ F ☐ 6. A certain amount of stress in life is unavoidable.

APPENDIX A
Answer Keys

CHAPTER 1

Attitude Inventory.

1. F	22. F
2. F	23. F
3. T	24. F
4. F	25. T
5. T	26. T
6. F	27. F
7. T	28. T
8. F	29. T
9. F	30. F
10. F	31. F
11. T	32. F
12. F	33. T
13. F	34. F
14. F	35. F
15. F	36. F
16. F	37. F
17. F	38. F
18. T	39. F
19. T	40. F
20. F	41. T
21. F	

True-False

1. T
2. T
3. F
4. T
5. F

6. T
7. F
8. F
9. F
10. F

Fill in the Blanks

1. F, D
2. E
3. C
4. A
5. G

Multiple Choice

1. C
2. B
3. D
4. D
5. C

CHAPTER 2

Fill in the Blanks

1. B
2. A
3. D
4. C
5. E

True-False

1. F
2. T
3. T
4. F
5. F

Multiple Choice

1. B
2. C
3. B
4. D
5. A
6. B
7. A
8. D
9. C
10. D

11. B
12. E
13. B
14. C
15. E
16. D
17. C
18. D
19. C

CHAPTER 3

Matching
1. G
2. C
3. E
4. A
5. I
6. D
7. B
8. F

True-False
1. T
2. F
3. T
4. F
5. F
6. T

Fill in the Blank
1. C
2. A
3. B, F
4. E
5. G

Multiple Choice
1. D
2. C
3. D
4. C
5. A
6. C
7. C
8. E
9. E
10. E
11. C
12. D
13. A
14. C
15. C
16. B
17. D
18. D

CHAPTER 4

Matching
1. D
2. A
3. E
4. F
5. B
6. C
7. F

True-False
1. F
2. F
3. T
4. T
5. F
6. F
7. F
8. T
9. F
10. F

Multiple Choice
1. A
2. B
3. D
4. D
5. B
6. C
7. D
8. A
9. A
10. C
11. D
12. D
13. D
14. E
15. C
16. C
17. B
18. B

Short Answer
1. Persistent and irrational fear of some object, place, or condition.
2. Rigid; perfectionistic; often obstinate.
3. Tendency to be self-indulging; poor self-concept; exaggerated dependency needs.
4. Accept the patient.
5. In organic psychosis, pathology can be demonstrated, while functional psychosis is caused by psychologic stress.

CHAPTER 5

True-False
1. F
2. T
3. F
4. F
5. T
6. T
7. T
8. F
9. T
10. T
11. T
12. F
13. F
14. T

Matching
1. D
2. C
3. A
4. F
5. E

Short Answer
1. Willful neglect, abuse, harassment, or failure to attend adequately to a patient.
2. In a voluntary admission the patient admits himself. Involuntary admission involves legal action in which it is determined by a judge or a doctor (depending on state law) that a person is to be admitted.
3. Tell the patient you do not know the answer but will attempt to find out and tell him.
4. To protect the patient from harming himself or others.
5. A negligent act.

CHAPTER 6

True-False
1. T
2. T
3. T
4. F
5. T
6. T
7. F
8. T
9. F
10. T

Multiple Choice
1. D
2. D
3. D
4. D
5. C
6. B
7. D
8. E
9. B
10. C
11. D
12. D
13. D

CHAPTER 7

Matching—I
1. C
2. A
3. E
4. B
5. F

Matching—II

1. E
2. D
3. F
4. E
5. B

6. A
7. C
8. D
9. A

True-False

1. F
2. T
3. F

4. T
5. F
6. F

Short Answer

1. Help calm the patient, control severe agitation, and decrease hallucinations.
2. Increase fluid intake to help prevent dry mouth, caution them to decrease fatty foods and increase intake of salads because of excessive weight gain and constipation problems.
3. Tricyclic compounds and MAO inhibitors.
4. Dry mouth, fatigue, weakness, blurring vision, constipation, parkinsonian syndrome, and increased perspiration.

Multiple Choice

1. D
2. E
3. D
4. B

5. C
6. E
7. C

CHAPTER 8

True-False

1. F
2. F
3. T
4. F
5. T
6. F

Multiple Choice

1. A
2. D
3. B
4. A
5. C

Short Answer

1. Helps the patient to forget.
   Perceived by the patient as a form of punishment.
2. ECT may place a great deal of strain on the patient's heart.

3. Depressed patients.
4. To prevent the patient from aspirating during the treatment.

CHAPTER 9

True-False
1. T
2. T
3. F
4. T
5. F
6. T

Multiple Choice
1. C
2. A
3. D
4. B
5. C
6. C
7. C

Short Answer
1. 1. A patient must want to get better.
    2. Must come to a better understanding of what is causing the problems and learn methods of dealing with them more effectively.
    3. Have an environment which is possible for change.
2. An environment in which it is possible for change to take place.
3. Help the patient gain insight and/or understanding into his problems so he can learn to deal with them more effectively.

CHAPTER 10

True-False
1. T
2. F
3. T
4. T
5. T
6. F
7. T
8. F
9. T

Matching
1. C
2. C
3. B
4. D
5. D

Short Answer
1. Confront him with the behavior.
2. Plan a program of activities which will not permit the patients so much free time that they become bored.
3. Feels threatened and unable to do anything else.
4. Patients are usually calmer when they don't have an audience.

CHAPTER 11

True-False
1. T
2. F
3. F
4. T
5. F
6. F
7. F
8. T
9. T
10. F

Multiple Choice
1. D
2. A
3. C
4. C
5. B
6. A
7. C
8. B
9. B
10. C
11. E

CHAPTER 12

True-False
1. T
2. F
3. T
4. T
5. T
6. F
7. T

Multiple Choice
1. C
2. C
3. C
4. C
5. D
6. E

CHAPTER 13

True-False
1. T
2. T
3. F
4. F
5. T
6. F
7. F
8. T
9. T
10. F

Multiple Choice
1. D
2. A
3. B
4. D
5. C
6. C

CHAPTER 14

True-False

1. F
2. F
3. T
4. F
5. T
6. T

Multiple Choice

1. B
2. B
3. B

Short Answer

1. Two of the following: schizophrenia, senile dementia, manic-depressive psychosis.
2. May first exhibit loud talk, rapid pacing, grandiose ideas.
3. Delusions, illusions, and hallucinations.
4. An illusion is a false or misinterpretation of a real sensory impression.
5. A hallucination is an idea or perception which does not exist in reality.

CHAPTER 15

Multiple Choice

1. E
2. B
3. E
4. E
5. A
6. B
7. B
8. B

True-False

1. F
2. T
3. T
4. F
5. F

Short Answer

1. J = Judgment
   O = Orientation
   C = Confabulation
   A = Affect
   M = Memory
2. Be as brief as possible.
3. Five of the following:
   1. Wear large name tags.
   2. Put patients' names on their room doors.
   3. Put up large calendars with big numbers.
   4. Use big clocks and place several around patient areas.

5. Show patients around the unit and help them only as much as they need it; don't be overly helpful as this increases dependency.
6. Let patients bring favorite and familiar things from home; this will help their new room to become "theirs."
4. The patient may not remember what he said or did and thus feels that he is being unfairly punished.
5. Routine and structure.

CHAPTER 16

True-False	Multiple Choice
1. T	1. D
2. T	2. A
3. F	3. B
4. T	4. D
5. T	5. B
6. F	6. A
7. T	7. D
8. F	8. A
9. T	9. C
10. T	10. C
	11. A
	12. B

Short Answer
1. When they have lost control of their drinking to the extent that interpersonal, family and community relationships have become seriously threatened or disturbed.
2. Tend to be pale, skinny and poorly nourished, may have dilated blood vessels in their faces and a bulb-like, fleshy nose.
3. The process of being able to accept the fact that one is an alcoholic.
4. 1. Depresses bone marrow and thus the production of RBCs.
   2. Causes brain tissue changes.
   3. Scar tissue formations in the liver (cirrhosis).
5. Marked by frequent "benders," usually daily intake of alcohol in response to the physical "craving."
6. Through recognition of the alcoholic status by someone in the general hospital when admitted for some other reason.

CHAPTER 17

Short Answer
1. 10 to 20.
2. Persons who have previously attempted suicide, the terminally ill, the elderly, the alcoholic, the severely emotionally ill, and people who associate with persons who have made suicide attempts.
3. The need for help and the recognition that something is wrong and a change is necessary for survival.
4. One's acute awareness and alertness.
5. Any three of the following:
   1. Persons who continuously talk about suicide.
   2. Persons who show the vegetative signs of depression.
   3. Persons who have extreme difficulty sleeping.
   4. Persons who dwell on sad thoughts.

True-False

1. T	9. F
2. F	10. F
3. F	11. F
4. T	12. T
5. T	13. F
6. T	14. T
7. T	15. T
8. F	

Matching   **Multiple Choice**

1. A, B	1. C
2. C	2. D
3. D	3. C
4. E	4. C
5. A	5. D
6. E	

CHAPTER 18

True-False

1. T	7. F
2. F	8. T
3. T	9. F
4. T	10. T
5. T	11. F
6. F	

Short Answer
1. Any three of the following: brain lesions, organic defects, traumatic injuries and chromosomal abnormalities.
2. Wechsler Scales and Stanford-Binet Intelligence Scale.
3. A chromosomal abnormality in which there is an extra chromosome in the genetic makeup of the individual.
4. 1. They are separated from loved ones or familiar figures.
   2. They are under a great deal of pressure to adjust to a completely new physical and interpersonal environment.
   3. They experience anxiety in relation to their future.
5. Basic motor skills, eating skills, and other self-care and self-help skills.
6. No language skills are necessary on the part of the patient.
7. Slanting eyes, protruding tongue, and poor muscle tone.
8. Behavior modification.

CHAPTER 19

True-False	Multiple Choice
1. T	1. D
2. F	2. B
3. F	3. D
4. T	4. A
5. T	5. C
6. F	6. D
7. T	7. A
8. T	8. D
9. T	9. C
10. F	10. A
11. T	

Short Answer
1. Retirement.
2. Factors such as increased sensitivity to medications, decreased body weight, impaired circulation, and liver dysfunction.
3. Organic brain damage.
4. Placing a large clock in the room and a cube calendar.
5. Activity promotes good health by increasing circulation, stimulating appetite, helping regulate bowel function, and preventing the complications of inactivity such as joint immobility, bed sores, and pneumonia.

CHAPTER 20

Short Answer:
1. The goal of crisis intervention therapy is to help the client return to a level of functioning that is at least equal to their pre-crisis state.
2. The first phase is denial and usually lasts for only a few hours. Denial is a mental mechanism used by the mind to temporarily defuse overwhelming anxiety. In phase two, anxiety increases and the individual tries to continue his daily activities while attempting to find a way to handle the increased tension. The third state is one of disorganization, where the individual in crisis just seems to "go to pieces". The fourth stage is one of reorganization and the development of new skills that will allow the individual to function at a pre-crisis level.
3. Mental health authorities define crisis as a state of psychological disequilibrium brought about by conflict, problems, or life situations which an individual perceives as a threat to self and cannot effectively handle by using previously successful problem-solving and coping techniques.
4. A social crisis is defined as an unanticipated crisis that involves multiple loses and/or extensive environmental changes, such as fires, floods, war, murder and racial persecution.
5. Collecting information, planning, intervention, evaluation

Multiple Choice
1. E
2. D
3. C
4. D
5. A
6. B
7. A
8. D

True-False
1. T
2. F
3. F
4. T
5. T
6. T

APPENDIX B
Patient's Bill of Rights*

1. The patient has the right to considerate and respectful care.
2. The patient has the right to obtain from his physician complete current information concerning his diagnosis, treatment, and prognosis in terms the patient can be reasonably expected to understand. When it is not medically advisable to give such information to the patient, the information should be made available to an appropriate person in his behalf. He has the right to know, by name, the physician responsible for coordinating his care.
3. The patient has the right to receive from his physician information necessary to give informed consent prior to the start of any procedure and/or treatment. Except in emergencies, such information for informed consent should include but not necessarily be limited to the specific procedure and/or treatment, the medically significant risks involved, and the probable duration of incapacitation. Where medically significant alternatives for care or treatment exist, or when the patient requests information concerning medical alternatives, the patient has the right to such information. The patient also has the right to know the name of the person responsible for the procedures and/or treatment.
4. The patient has the right to refuse treatment to the extent permitted by law and to be informed of the medical consequences of his action.
5. The patient has the right to every consideration of his privacy concerning his own medical care program. Case discussion, consultation, examination, and treatment are confidential and should be conducted

---

*Reprinted with permission of the American Hospital Association, copyright 1972.

discreetly. Those not directly involved in his care must have the permission of the patient to be present.

6. The patient has the right to expect that all communications and records pertaining to his care should be treated as confidential.

7. The patient has the right to expect that within its capacity a hospital must make reasonable response to the request of a patient for services. The hospital must provide evaluation, service, and/or referral as indicated by the urgency of the case. When medically permissible, a patient may be transferred to another facility only after he has received complete information to such a transfer. The institution to which the patient is to be transferred must first have accepted the patient for transfer.

8. The patient has the right to obtain information as to any relationship of his hospital to other health care and educational institutions insofar as his care is concerned. The patient has the right to obtain information as to the existence of any professional relationships among individuals, by name, who are treating him.

9. The patient has the right to be advised if the hospital proposes to engage in or perform human experimentation affecting his care or treatment. The patient has the right to refuse to participate in such research projects.

10. The patient has the right to expect reasonable continuity of care. He has the right to know in advance what appointment times and physicians are available and where. The patient has the right to expect that the hospital will provide a mechanism whereby he is informed by his physician or a delegate of the physician of the patient's continuing health care requirements following discharge.

11. The patient has the right to examine and receive an explanation of his bill regardless of source of payment.

12. The patient has the right to know what hospital rules and regulations apply to his conduct as a patient.

Index

Injurious behavior of mentally re-
tarded patients, 241–243
Institutionalization of mentally re-
tarded patients, 235
Intelligence quotient tests, 232–233
Intimidating behavior, 143–144
Introjection, 36
Involuntary admission, 72
discharge and, 73
Involutional melancholia, 60
Involutional psychotic reactions, 60
IQ tests. See Intelligence quotient
tests.

JOCAM, 183
Judgment, impairment of, due to neurological deficits, 183–186

LEGAL considerations, 71–72
confidentiality of patient information
and, 74
consent and, 74, 119–120
electroconvulsive therapy and,
119–120
incompetency, legal declaration of
and, 72
involuntary admission and, 72
patients in seclusion and, 74
patients' rights and, 72–73
visitors and, 73–74
voluntary admission and, 72
Librium, 105
in treatment of alcoholics, 202
Lithium carbonate, 109
Lying, 142–143

MANIC-DEPRESSIVE phases, 59
MAO inhibitors, 105–106
Masochism, 63
Masturbation
in adolescents, 19
in preschool children, 18–19
Medications
allergic reactions to, in mentally
retarded patients, 239
anticonvulsants, 108
antidepressants, 105
MAO inhibitors, 105–106
tricyclic, 106
antiparkinsons, 108
barbiturates, 107
charting of, 90
hoarding of, prevention of, 74
hypnotics, 107
in treatment of alcoholics, 202
overmedication, elderly patients
and, 250

phenothiazines, 101–102
sedatives, 107
tranquilizers, 101
major, 101–104
minor, 104–105
Melancholia, involutional, 60
Memory, impairment of
due to organic brain damage, 183–184
in elderly patients, 250
Mental health, guidelines for evaluation of, 28–29
Mental Health Attitude Inventory, 3–5
Mental illness
aggressive patients and, 137–151
alcohol abuse and, 193–204
anxious patients and, 153–161
auxiliary therpies and, 127–129
basic concepts of the mind and,
27–48
behavior modification therapy
and, 126–127
communication when working with
patients with, 81–100
depressed patients and, 169–176
determination of, 6–7
drug abuse and, 193–194, 204–207
drug therapy and, 101–116
elderly patients and, 247–257
electroconvulsive therapy and,
117–124
factors which influence, 5–6
introduction to working with patients with, 3–11
legal considerations of working with
patients with, 71–78
mental retardation and, 231–246
organic brain damage and, 183–191
patients who have lost reality contact and, 177–182
personality development and, 13–26
psychotherapy and, 125–126
suicidal patients and, 213–228
suspicious patients and, 163–168
understanding diagnoses of, 49–69
Mentally retarded patients
behaviors of, 236–237, 241–243
classifications of, 232–233
concepts of retardation and, 231–232
Down's syndrome and, 233–234
emotional needs of, 239–241
follow-up care of, 238–239
intelligence tests and, 232–233
phenylketonuria and, 234
physical needs of, 237–238
special problems of, 234–237
Tay-Sachs disease and, 234
training of, 241

291